PROTESTANT CHURCH COLLEGES
IN CANADA

Etudes sur l'Histoire d'Enseignement Supérieur au Canada
Studies in the History of Higher Education in Canada

SPONSORED BY THE ASSOCIATION OF UNIVERSITIES AND
COLLEGES OF CANADA, WITH FINANCIAL SUPPORT FROM
THE CARNEGIE CORPORATION OF NEW YORK

VOLUMES IN THIS SERIES

1. Robin S. Harris and Arthur Tremblay. *A Bibliography of Higher Education in Canada* (1960). $6.50

2. W. P. Thompson. *Graduate Education in the Sciences in Canadian Universities* (1963). $5.00

3. Robin S. Harris. *A Bibliography of Higher Education in Canada: Supplement* (1965). $6.50

4. D. C. Masters. *Protestant Church Colleges in Canada: A History* (1966). $7.50

PROTESTANT CHURCH COLLEGES IN CANADA

A History

D. C. MASTERS

UNIVERSITY OF TORONTO PRESS

© UNIVERSITY OF TORONTO PRESS 1966
PRINTED IN CANADA
Reprinted in 2018
ISBN 978-1-4875-8141-1 (paper)

Foreword

IN 1958 THE CARNEGIE CORPORATION of New York made a grant of $25,000 to the National Conference of Canadian Universities to make possible a series of studies in the history of higher education in Canada. About a dozen monographs are planned.

This work by Professor Masters is one of three on church colleges. The second will be a history of English Catholic colleges and the third will describe the development of French Catholic colleges.

Here we see a panorama of Protestant religious thought and controversy as reflected in the creation, the development, and sometimes the demise of church-related liberal arts colleges and denominational theological seminaries. As Professor Masters tells the story, it is clear that a century ago it was extremely important to active members of the churches that their children should receive higher education in a Christian atmosphere. Each denomination had its own concept of the true Christian atmosphere, so each denomination established its own colleges. But theology changed, church-related liberal arts colleges were subjected to increasingly strong secular influences, and the churches were unable to provide the necessary financial support. One after another, the church colleges became non-denominational universities or affiliates of non-denominational universities. There are now but four completely independent Protestant universities in Canada.

As Professor Masters so ably demonstrates, the church college has made a significant contribution to higher education. All but a dozen of the universities of Canada had their origins as church-sponsored institutions. And the pluralistic university which resulted from the grouping of church and state colleges over the century and a half covered by this history is a unique Canadian compromise.

EDWARD F. SHEFFIELD

Association of Universities and Colleges of Canada

Acknowledgments

I WISH TO THANK Dr. Edward F. Sheffield, the Director of Research, Association of Universities and Colleges of Canada, for encouragement and wise advice in the preparation of my manuscript and Dr. Frank Stiling, the Chairman of the N.C.C.U.C. Committee on the History of Higher Education, for helpful co-operation. I am grateful to Mr. A. D. Longman, of United College, Winnipeg; Dr. Neil Smith, Librarian, Presbyterian College, Montreal; Mr. H. P. Gundy, Librarian, Queen's University, Kingston; Miss Marget H. C. Meikleham, Librarian, McMaster University; and Mr. A. D. Banfill, Librarian, Bishop's University, for extensive and invaluable aid in the acquisition of material.

For valuable aid in providing information and material I am indebted to: Principal Elias Andrews, Queen's Theological College, Kingston; the Rev. T. C. B. Boon, Archivist, Diocese of Rupert's Land; the Right Rev. W. R. Coleman, Bishop of Kootenay; Principal F. H. W. Crabb, Emmanuel College, Saskatoon; Professor Pieter de Jong, St. Andrew's College, Saskatoon; Professor W. O. Fennell, Emmanuel College, Toronto; Professor Kenneth Hamilton, United College, Winnipeg; Professor and Mrs. T. A. Judson, Bishop's University, Lennoxville; Dean D. G. G. Kerr, Talbot College, University of Western Ontario; Dean R. S. Longley, Acadia University, Wolfville; Professor D. M. Mathers, Queen's Theological College, Kingston; the Right Rev. J. A. Meaden, Bishop of Newfoundland; Mr. Ralph D. Mitchener, Dominion Bureau of Statistics; Professor G. H. Parke-Taylor, Huron College, London, formerly of the Anglican Theological College of British Columbia; the Ven. W. F. Payton, Prince Albert, Saskatchewan; Dr. Arthur G. Reynolds, United Church Archives, Toronto; Miss Patricia Reid, United Church Archives, Toronto; Principal R. F. Schnell, St. Andrew's College, Saskatoon.

I wish to thank Dr. James J. Talman, Librarian, University of Western Ontario, for permission to use a quotation from his *Huron College 1863–1963* (London, 1963) on page 147 of this volume. The quotation from T. R. Glover and D. D. Calvin, *A Corner of Empire:*

The Old Ontario Strand on page 148 is published by permission of The Cambridge University Press and The Macmillan Company of Canada Limited. I am indebted to Mrs. Donald Gammon, formerly Miss Francis Firth, and to Professor A. G. Bailey for permission to use the quotation on page 73 from *The University of New Brunswick Memorial Volume* (Fredericton, 1950). I am grateful to the Rev. Thomas Saunders of Winnipeg for permission to quote on page 181 from his unpublished manuscript "Doctrine," and Dr. Arthur C. Hill of Sherbrooke gave me an excellent memorandum on the early history of the Inter-Varsity Christian Fellowship in Canada. I also wish to thank the Carnegie Corporation of New York for financing the preparation and publication of this volume. Finally, I wish to extend my sincere thanks for help and encouragement to my colleagues at Bishop's University where I was Professor of History during the preparation of this book.

D. C. MASTERS

Wellington College, University of Guelph

Contents

FOREWORD   v

ACKNOWLEDGMENTS   viii

1. Introduction: The Ideological Background   3

2. Early Origins (1785–1829)   17

3. The Golden Age (1829–1867)   29

4. Changing Ideas (1867–1890)   89

5. The Onset of Liberalism (1890–1920)   133

6. The Modern Adjustment (1920 and after)   173

7. Conclusion   207

BIBLIOGRAPHY   213

INDEX   219

PROTESTANT CHURCH COLLEGES
IN CANADA

1. Introduction
The Ideological Background

THE TERM "CHURCH COLLEGE," as considered in this volume, requires description. Often the nucleus of a church college in Canada has been a liberal arts college. Sometimes, it had other appendages: a department of education, a law school, a medical school; but the essential nucleus, that which gave the institution its character, was the arts college under religious auspices. The greater part of this volume is concerned with those church colleges which included a liberal arts college.

The motives which inspired the founders of these church colleges were mixed. One was simply the desire to provide institutions of higher education for people who would otherwise be deprived of such facilities. The founders of Victoria regarded their institution as a college for the common people of Upper Canada. A report of the College, published in 1842 declared that "the operations of Victoria College are not less important to the agricultural and commercial community of Western Canada, than those of Upper Canada College have heretofore been to the Professions."[1] In 1843, a correspondent writing in the *Christian Guardian*, Egerton Ryerson's paper, described Victoria as "the college of the people . . . a college adapted to the wants of the mass, affording that kind of education, and in that manner, best adapted to make sound, practical men, in every department of life."[2]

The founders of church colleges usually proposed that instruction in the field of secular education should be accompanied by "moral and religious instruction." This was not invariably the case. Acadia[3] was quite late in providing courses in religious knowledge for its students. It did not establish compulsory courses in Biblical Studies for freshmen and sophomores until about 1890. Usually, however, the founders of church colleges proposed to provide training for the whole man, in his spiritual, as well as in his intellectual capacity. This was notably

---

[1]Nathanael Burwash, *The History of Victoria College* (Toronto, 1927), 106.
[2]*Ibid.*, 88.   [3]Incorporated in 1841.

true of Trinity and of Bishop's, whose founders showed an intense desire to have secular study pursued in a religious environment. The *Christian Guardian* sounded the same note in reference to Victoria College, on May 24, 1843, when it declared that the College endeavoured to send out mature graduates "by inducing habits of industry, order and diligence, and imbuing their minds with true religion and sound morality."[4] Egerton Ryerson, the first president of Victoria, believed that it was possible to teach general Christian truth and morality without sectarian dogma.[5] When the Methodist Episcopal Church was contemplating the establishment of Albert College, the Bay of Quinte Conference issued a circular in 1852 enlisting support for the institution. It concluded, "We shall then enjoy facilities for imparting a sound mental and moral as well as religious education to the children of our numerous friends, and especially to those young men who are desirous of qualifying themselves more fully for the ministry of our church."[6]

Jasper Nicolls, the principal of Bishop's College, in a lecture at Quebec in 1857, stressed the importance of developing character by moral and religious instruction. He asked:

Where else will you find the man you require, but among those whose powers of mind have been carefully nurtured under a system which took pains with the formation of character, which stamped that character with a form and lasting outline, by giving to it an abiding sense of the fear of God and desire of His favour.[7]

The founders of church colleges not only believed in the value of moral and religious instruction as such, but they felt that secular learning could only be really understood when taught in a Christian setting.

The charter of Upper Canada Academy (1836), the forerunner of Victoria College, indicated this intention to illuminate secular instruction by Christian thought in mentioning the determination of its founders to establish an academy "for the general education of youth in the various branches of literature and science on Christian principles."[8] In a great convocation address at Bishop's College in 1860, Jasper Nicolls argued that it was unsound to divide secular from religious knowledge, for they were simply two aspects of a magnificent whole. He continued:

[4]Burwash, *History of Victoria*, 88.   [5]See p. 32 of this volume.
[6]See Waldo Smith, *Albert College 1857–1957*, 1. Originally what became Albert College was called the Belleville Seminary.
[7]Jasper H. Nicolls, *The End and Object of Education, lecture delivered before the Quebec Young Men's Protestant Education Union* (Montreal, 1857), 6–7.
[8]Quoted in Burwash, *History of Victoria*, 489.

For it is the business of an University to gather into itself all the branches of learning, to adopt and interweave with the old and well-tried, what is new and modern; to assist in its measure, and according to its capability in the work of scientific discovery, but far more to sanctify scientific discovery. When man searches and investigates, argues and proves, pronounces at his study-table, that this or that field or rock, produces or does not produce a certain precious metal, or indicates by calculations the existence of some hitherto undiscovered heavenly body, and points out the very spot it occupies at the moment; when the human mind thus strides onwards, let it be the University's privilege to demonstrate that the excellency of all this, is not of man, but of God; that while man discovers, he discovers what God has made, what *God gives* him to understand. Universities let us remember are Christian Institutions.[9]

To some extent the efforts by the Anglicans to establish and control church colleges stimulated the other churches into similar activity. King's College, York had already been chartered for fourteen years as a purely Anglican institution when Victoria was chartered in 1841. The Methodists in Canada West were determined that their young people would not be trained in a college controlled by Anglicans. F. H. Wallace, in his preface to Burwash's *History of Victoria*, says that the University was founded "as a protest against the sectarian exclusiveness which would have confined the benefits of higher education to one church."[10] That Methodist fears of proselytization by Anglicans were not entirely groundless is suggested by a letter from Bishop G. J. Mountain to Jasper Nicolls, on January 17, 1845, in reference to the admission of "dissenters" from the Eastern Townships into Bishop's. The Bishop argued:

> The youth of all that tract of country may be won once for all to the bosom of the Church by her opening her arms to afford them education under her auspices: if she repell them, they are driven to the nurseries of the neighbouring republic which are very readily accessible to them.[11]

In many cases the founders of church colleges were anxious to provide their denomination with an educated clergy. At Bishop's this was the primary motive in establishing the institution. Bishop Machray, the bishop of Rupert's Land who reorganized St. John's College, Winnipeg in the eighteen-sixties, said later, "when we look to the future a further question is pressed upon us—namely, Education. I feel increasingly the importance of our being able to raise up a Ministry of our

---

[9] J. H. Nicolls, *An Address delivered before the Convocation of Bishop's College, Lennoxville,* June 27, 1860 (Sherbrooke, 1860), 12.
[10] Burwash, *History of Victoria*, v.
[11] Bishop's University, Nicolls Papers.

own."[12] In some institutions the theological students were given a general arts training and also a specialized course in divinity. This was the system at Bishop's from the beginning of its history. In other colleges, including Victoria, in its early career, prospective candidates for the ministry were given the same course as all the arts students.

Among the more Evangelical church colleges there were some religious revivals. Burwash reports the existence in the eighteen-fifties at Victoria of a deeply religious group of men who held weekly prayer meetings. He reports:

They were not men satisfied to be merely harmless in the midst of a "crooked and perverse generation," they aimed at a spiritual victory, and for this purpose banded themselves together for daily private prayer for their unconverted fellow students, for faithful, kindly, personal dealing with them whenever possible, and for weekly meetings for prayer and mutual encouragement.[13]

This influence within Victoria was reinforced by a prolonged religious revival which began in the local church at Cobourg where the Rev. G. R. Sanderson was pastor and which spread with great power to the College. Burwash's account continued:

In the College, especially, deep seriousness began to prevail and before long, scores of students began to decide for a better life. The work spread with great power. The ordinary work of the students was almost completely suspended. Instead of the usual lectures, the professors were holding meetings for deeply distressed inquirers. . . . At the end of six weeks not half a dozen students had resisted the influence of this college revival.[14]

In 1858, there was a similar revival at Albert College, a Methodist institution. It began with a preaching mission in the town of Belleville and spread to the College. The historian of Albert College writes:

It brought students and teachers together for prayer each evening, meeting in the Principal's study. The numbers increased so that they moved to the chapel and teachers took turns to give an address. All this was in addition to the prayer meetings that had regularly been held on Thursday.[15]

These early Methodist revivals were perhaps exceptional in the history of Canadian Protestant church colleges. There were probably not many formal attempts to utilize the colleges for purposes of religious revival. Yet the fact that many of their supporters and most of their staffs in the early period had orthodox religious opinions was a factor of great importance in shaping the minds of students.

While this study is largely concerned with those institutions which

[12]Quoted in T. C. B. Boon, *The Anglican Church from the Bay to the Rockies* (Toronto, 1962), 96.   [13]Burwash, *History of Victoria*, 179.
[14]*Ibid.*, 180–181.   [15]Smith, *Albert College*, 7–8.

included a liberal arts college, attention will also be devoted to those theological schools, like Knox and Wycliffe, which developed independent of any association with a church-related arts college. These theological schools were just as much "church colleges" as were the more comprehensive church-related institutions.

In order to understand the climate of opinion in the church colleges, the historian must have some grasp of the basic religious beliefs which they held. The clergy of all the principal non-Roman Catholic churches in Canada agreed on a certain body of belief in this period. All believed that man was a sinner, bound for hell, unable to rescue himself, in need of a redeemer, but capable of salvation if he would avail himself of the divine sacrifice. All accepted the authority of the Bible which all believed to be divinely inspired. All regarded the achievement of everlasting life as the dominant aim of the Christian. Material, earthly comfort, while pleasant, was considered as of secondary importance.

While there was, therefore, a substantial area of agreement among the founders of church colleges in Canada, there were important differences in theology also. These must now be explained. They represented the projection into the field of higher education of the basic differences between the various non-Roman Catholic denominations in Canada. The principal schools of thought among the non-Roman Catholic churches may be classified into two groups. It is difficult to conceive precise terms which will be free of associations not intended by the author, but, for the purposes of this discussion, I use the terms "High Anglican" and "Protestant." The term High Anglican is self-explanatory; but the term Protestant must be understood to include the low church or Evangelical Anglicans as well as the Presbyterians, Methodists, and Baptists. The two schools of thought, High Anglican and Protestant, represented very different conceptions of the nature of Christianity and of the Christian church.

The Protestant was chiefly concerned with the relationship of the individual Christian to God. The Christian, he believed, was saved from the consequences of sin by a personal acceptance of God the Son as his Saviour. The church for the Protestant was an invisible body, composed of all those individuals who had established this vital connection with the Deity. The High Anglican, too, was concerned with salvation, but, in the effort to secure it, he stressed the importance of membership in God's corporate church, rather than the establishment of an individual or personal relationship with the Deity. The church to the High Anglican was the visible church, especially the clergy, a body of priests in direct succession, if not from St. Peter himself, at least from the original group of apostles.

Out of this initial difference came other differences. For the Protestant, salvation was secured by faith. Good works were a part of the Christian life and were an inevitable result of faith, but they were not a means of salvation. The High Anglican by no means disregarded faith, but he thought primarily in terms of salvation as a result of good works. He regarded faithful participation in the sacraments of the church as both a source of refreshment and a species of good work. The Protestant stressed the need of some process of conversion by which the individual became fundamentally transformed in a new relationship with God the Son. The High Anglican thought less of conversion than of a continuous association with the church through participation in its offices: baptism, confirmation, and holy communion. He tended to assume that all who were in close communion with the visible church were converted. Differences in attitude toward the church and the nature of salvation involved a difference in attitude toward the clergy. To the Protestant, the clergyman was essentially a minister in the literal sense; to the High Anglican, he was a priest, not perhaps a mediator, but at least an essential agent between the individual Christian and God. The authority of the Protestant was essentially the Bible; that of the High Anglican, the Bible and the church, which interpreted it. In short, the Protestant was in the tradition of the Reformers of the sixteenth century, the High Anglican was in the tradition of the mediaeval church.

There were some significant differences within the two broad classifications mentioned above. Among the High Anglicans, the old-fashioned high churchmen, while in agreement on basic doctrine with those influenced by the Tractarians, were alienated by their emotionalism, which they called "unction." Thus when Bishop G. J. Mountain, an old fashioned high churchman, was consulted about the engagement between his daughter, Harriet and Jasper Nicolls, the principal of Bishop's College, he confessed to Mrs. Mountain, "he may have some *leanings* in Religion upon particular points, acquired at Oxford, which are not in *perfect* accordance with my own views upon those points"[16] but he added that Nicolls was "a sound believer—and an uncompromising Churchman." Nicolls had been at Oriel College, Oxford in Newman's time.[17]

[16]Nicolls Papers, Bishop G. J. Mountain to Mrs. Mountain, Jan. 22, 1847.
[17]While Mountain would be classified as a high churchman, his views on doctrine occupied a middle position between that of the high church and Protestant

Within the Protestant group, there were two principal issues in dispute: election or predestination versus free will in the process of salvation and adult baptism versus infant baptism. The Calvinist Presbyterians believed in election, the Methodists in free will, while the Evangelical Anglicans attempted a position midway between them. In this question the views of Charles Simeon, the great English Evangelical, may be regarded as typical of Anglican Evangelicalism. Simeon argued that the roles of human free will and divine intervention in the process of salvation were not irreconcilable. He pointed out that the Bible contained other concepts difficult to reconcile such as the holiness of God and the existence of sin; but that this was no reason to doubt either truth.[18]

On the question of baptism, the Baptists, of course, believed in adult baptism; the Evangelical Anglicans, the Presbyterians, and the Methodists in infant baptism. The Evangelical Anglicans were distinguished from other Protestant groups by their affection for the Anglican liturgy and by their loyalty to the Church of England. They were able to preserve this loyalty despite serious differences with the High Anglicans.

Such was the theological and ecclesiastical background to the establishment of church colleges. The sponsors of three of the Church of England arts colleges, King's Nova Scotia, King's York, and Bishop's, were High Anglicans. St. John's College, Winnipeg was a low church foundation, having been established by representatives of the Church Missionary Society (C.M.S.). The low church Anglicans established theological colleges such as Wycliffe and Huron, and schools such as Havergal and Ridley. Western University, which developed out of Huron in 1878, and which remained Anglican until 1908, was a low church foundation. Protestant thinking, as above described, provided the background for the establishment of these low church institutions

---

traditions in the Church of England. In his stress on the importance of achieving personal salvation he sounded like an Evangelical; but as a high churchman he stressed the role of the visible church in its achievement. See D. C. Masters, "G. J. Mountain: Frontier Bishop," Canadian Historical Association, *Report*, 1963.

[18]*Memoirs of the Life of the Rev. Charles Simeon, M.A.* (London, 1847), 178–9. Simeon argued (p. 181): "It is supposed by many, that the doctrines of grace are incompatible with the doctrine of man's free will; and that therefore the one or the other must be false. But why so? Can any man doubt one moment whether he be a free agent or not? He may as well doubt his own existence. On the other hand, will any man who has the smallest spark of humility affirm, that he has 'made himself to differ; and that he has something which he has not received' from a superior power? Will anyone refuse to say with the Apostle, 'By the grace of God I am what I am?'"

and for Acadia, Victoria, Queen's, Mount Allison, and other non-Anglican church colleges.

So far, the background of religious thought in the founding of church colleges has been considered. The connection between religious and political thought in Canada was also reflected in the establishment of church colleges. Because of the close association between Anglicanism and Toryism, it was inevitable that the Anglicans who sought to establish colleges should have political as well as religious motives. At its worst this coupling of politics and education could mean a not very edifying desire to secure the dominance of one particular party. At its best it reflected a Burkian concept of society in which political order and religion were felt to rely upon each other. The leading exponent of this view was John Strachan, the great champion of Tory Anglicanism. A sermon which Strachan preached, probably in 1838, illustrates this view:

A love of order is not only essential to the tranquillity but to the very being of any State. It becomes the foundation of mutual faith and confidence and security. When we behold an indifference to the observation of the laws and a restless diligence to evade them, a want of reverence to Magistrates & Superiors, a disrespect to stations, offices, ranks, and orders of persons, a contempt for the experience of the wise grow upon the minds of the generality of men and appear through all their actions, when we perceive absolute independence in public and private conduct affected and encouraged; a general forwardness, self sufficiency, presumption and licentiousness cultivated, commended and propagated through the different classes of the people we may consider these as symptoms fatal to the true liberty of that Country. . . . To prevent these evils a love of Order becomes necessary, by which we are induced to conform to the laws and to promote the welfare of the community. To give steadiness and effect to this love of order we must call in the aid of religion, which is the only firm and lasting foundation upon which the tranquillity and security of a people can be strengthened. . . . Wherever an irreligious spirit goes through the land it overturns all liberty, civil and religious, and gradually leads to anarchy and tyranny. Free government and true liberty are the natural consequences of pure religion (which secures) a modest deference to superior wisdom and virtue, a willing submission to just authority, a sense of due subordination, a reverence for the laws, a lover of order and good Government.[19]

In Strachan's thinking, order, that is British order, and the Anglican religion, were closely linked; while dissent and disorder, in the form of American republicanism, were also linked.

In March, 1826, Strachan wrote to the Lieutenant-Governor, Sir

---

[19]Quoted in S. F. Wise, "The Origins of Anti-Americanism in Canada," *Fourth Seminar on Canadian-American Relations at Assumption University of Windsor*, 1962, 304–5.

Peregrine Maitland, arguing that unless a university was established in Upper Canada, young men proceeding to the professions of law, medicine, and divinity would go to the United States for training. There they would be lured away by the wiles of American republican sentiment and would cease to have any regard and affection for British institutions. He insisted:

> It is, indeed, easy to perceive the danger of sending our most prominent youth to a country to finish their education where they hear nothing in praise of their native land, and where everything bespeaks hatred and defiance, where her merits are considered defects, and all her noblest virtues and glories soiled by the poison of calumny; nor can it be expected that any of them, on their return, will give up their hearts and affections to their parent state with the same cordiality that they would have done had they been carefully nurtured within the British Dominions.[20]

Strachan went on to argue that it was particularly necessary to produce a locally educated Anglican clergy in order to cope with the republicanism so prevalent among the dissenting clergy.

> When it is further considered that the religious leaders of all other Protestant denominations, a very few respectable ministers of the church of Scotland excepted, come, almost universally, from the Republican States of America, where they gather their knowledge and form their sentiments. It is evident that, if the Imperial Government does not step forward with efficient help, the mass of the population will be nurtured and instructed in hostility to all our institutions, both civil and religious.[21]

For Strachan the lesson was plain. For political, as well as for religious reasons, the university must be established under Anglican control. The Bishop of the diocese would be appointed Visitor and "the Principal and Professors, except those of Medicine and Law, should be Clergymen of the Established Church; and no tutor, teacher or officer, who is not a member of that Church, should ever be employed in the institution."[22] In short, it was politically necessary that the university should be under Anglican, and therefore under Tory, control.

The connection between non-Anglican colleges and political parties was less obvious. There was certainly an ideological connection between Reform opposition to the Family Compact in Upper Canada and the establishment of Victoria in 1836–41. Ryerson, the moving spirit, was prominently identified with Reform. Acadia, while it represented Baptist opposition to Anglicanism was not identified with

[20]J. George Hodgins, *Documentary History of Education in Upper Canada* (Toronto, 1894), I, 211–13.
[21]*Ibid.*, 213.   [22]*Ibid.*, 214.

Reform, since the Nova Scotia Baptists became one of the mainstays of Nova Scotia Conservatism.

While the church colleges reflected the influence of the Christian theology, they were also heirs to several educational traditions, British, American, and continental. The Church of England colleges were largely dominated by the influence of Oxford and Cambridge from which they derived most of their early faculty members. The first Principal of Bishop's College was an Oxford graduate. Trinity began teaching with a faculty of three: two Cambridge graduates and one from Oxford.

The preoccupation of these English universities with classics and mathematics was reflected in the curricula of those Anglican colleges such as King's Nova Scotia, Bishop's, and Trinity. King's Toronto and King's Fredericton developed broader programmes of study in the years when they were moving toward secularization but were still under Anglican control.

Since only Anglicans could secure Oxford and Cambridge degrees prior to passage of the University Acts of 1854 and 1856, the influence of Oxford and Cambridge on the Canadian colleges established by other denominations was not so pronounced. To some extent it was passed on to them through the influence of the Anglican colleges in Canada. The non-Anglican colleges were influenced by other university traditions. The Scottish universities, particularly Edinburgh, were dominant in the Presbyterian colleges. Most of the early professors at Queen's were Scots and established much the same pattern as at Edinburgh, Glasgow, and Aberdeen. This explains the early emphasis at Queen's upon the teaching of moral philosophy.

The early Methodist and Baptist colleges, Acadia, Albert, and Victoria, were more professedly Canadian than were the Anglican and Presbyterian institutions. Nathanael Burwash who knew the men who founded Victoria wrote of Ontario church colleges, "In Queen's, King's, and Trinity the type in each case came from the Old World. Victoria alone was purely Canadian and of this western continent in its early development."[23]

Although the native strain was more predominant in the case of these Methodist and Baptist colleges, this did not mean that they were completely cut off from outside influences. The varied nature of the Acadia curriculum was partly a result of the influence of New England colleges. Acadia established an early connection by sending prospective faculty members to Harvard for further study. Silas MacVane

[23]Burwash, *History of Victoria*, 134.

graduated from Acadia in 1865, entered Harvard in 1871, and returned to Acadia in 1875 as instructor in history and political economy. John Freeman Tufts, an Acadia graduate of 1868, after study at Harvard was appointed to the staff at Acadia in 1874 as professor of history. A. W. Sawyer, the professor of classics (1855–60) and president (1869–96) at Acadia, was born in Vermont and educated at Dartmouth College and the Newton Theological Seminary. Victoria and Albert Colleges in Ontario were both influenced by the New England tradition. Victoria in the eighteen-sixties began the practice of appointing to its staff Victoria graduates who had had further training abroad, particularly in German universities. A. H. Reynar, a graduate of 1862, was appointed in 1866 to teach French and German and, after two years post-graduate study in France and Germany, began work at Victoria. A. R. Bain, also a Victoria graduate was appointed professor of mathematics in 1868, but was given the same period for preparation at Harvard and Paris before commencing his duties at Victoria. Eugene Haanel, a Ph.D. of Breslau University, was professor of natural history at Victoria from 1872 to 1890. Other appointments of men with European or American training were made at Victoria. German scholarship exercised a direct influence over the Victoria faculty for at least fifty years.

The native Canadian influence on the curriculum and educational philosophy of church colleges is more difficult to trace. Probably the inclusion of navigation and surveying and levelling in the curriculum of Victoria in 1845 and of Acadia in 1851 was in response to a local demand. It should be noted that Canadians at least developed their college curricula within an academic organization which was distinctively Canadian. The small denominational arts college was a Canadian as well as an American phenomenon. The development of pluralistic universities which included denominational and secular colleges, a process which began at Manitoba in the eighteen-seventies and at Toronto in the eighteen-eighties, was a unique Canadian achievement.

Differences in the approach of the church colleges were partly the result of their basic philosophies and partly a result of the constituencies which they served. The Anglican colleges proposed to train a social *élite*: clergy, lawyers, and doctors. Because of this they tended to attract the sons of the local aristocracy in so far as there could be an aristocracy in a frontier society. To a considerable extent the Presbyterians thought in terms of producing a professional class—the clergy. The Methodists and Baptists thought much more in terms of training the whole people: the farmers, the business men and the housewives, as well as the professional people. Thus they attracted a varied clientele, one which demanded a broader curriculum than one largely restricted to classics, mathematics, and moral philosophy.

Contemporary evidence of the democratic nature of the Victoria constituency may be cited. Egerton Ryerson, its first president, wrote to the Provincial Secretary of Canada West on December 20, 1842, inviting inspection of the institution by various provincial authorities who were members of the college Board and added:

> The performance of this part of their duty, by the officers of the Government and Legislature concerned (while it will confer important benefits upon the institution), will, I am persuaded, satisfy them that the operations of Victoria College are not less important to the agricultural and commercial community of Western Canada, than those of the Upper Canada College have heretofore been to the Professions.[24]

There is evidence to suggest that the Anglican colleges catered to a more narrowly professional constituency than did the Methodist and Baptist institutions. When Bishop Strachan was enlisting official support to establish King's College, York, he stressed the function of the proposed institution in providing instruction in law, medicine, and divinity.[25] In the period from 1802 to 1855, King's College, Nova Scotia produced one hundred and fifty-eight graduates, including fifty-three clergy, fifty-six members of the legal profession, thirty-nine in the army or navy or some other walk of life, and ten members of the medical profession.[26] Dr. William Cochran, the first principal of King's, in a memorandum presented at the end of his career in 1832, said that he reckoned among his pupils now living in British North America one bishop, one archdeacon, very many missionaries and other preachers, one chief-justice, six judges, one attorney-general, two solicitors-general, and very many eminent barristers, besides many of great worth in other professions.[27]

An examination of the financing of early church colleges helps to explain the character of these institutions. The English influence on the Anglican colleges was partly a result of the fact that they received support from the great missionary societies: the Society for the Propa-

---

[24]*Ibid.*, 106.

[25]See letter from Bishop Strachan to the Lieutenant-Governor, Sir Peregrine Maitland, March, 1826 published in Hodgins *Documentary History of Education in Upper Canada* (Toronto, 1894), I, 212.

[26]Henry Youle Hind, *The University of King's College, Windsor, Nova Scotia 1790–1890* (New York, 1890), 82.

[27]*Ibid.*, 83.

gation of the Gospel (S.P.G.), the Society for the Promotion of Christian Knowledge (S.P.C.K.), and the Church Missionary Society (C.M.S.). Specific examples of the assistance follow later in this volume. King's College, Nova Scotia also received grants directly from the British government.[28] The Methodist and Presbyterian colleges received some British support. For instance, in 1836–37, Egerton Ryerson was in Great Britain where he experienced some success in raising money for Upper Canada Academy, the forerunner of Victoria College.[29] However, the non-Anglican colleges depended more completely for support on Canadian sources, most of them voluntary.

Two characteristics of voluntary contributions to Canadian church colleges in the nineteenth century appear. Some contributions were comparatively large. Among these were Thomas Harrold's gift of six-thousand pounds to be used for the founding of Bishop's College, C. F. Allison's offer to purchase land and erect buildings, which made possible the establishment of Mount Allison Academy, and William McMaster's donations to McMaster University including a legacy of nine hundred thousand dollars.

For the most part the colleges depended on numerous small contributions. Many of these donations came from people who were far from wealthy. In 1835, when Upper Canada Academy was being organized, Egerton Ryerson reported that the Methodists of Upper Canada had subscribed seven thousand or eight thousand pounds and that three thousand pounds had been collected. The number of subscribers probably numbered over two thousand and the average subscription was less than four pounds in Halifax currency.[30] At the first public meeting to promote Queen's College, held at Toronto on December 10, 1839, a subscription list was opened and six hundred pounds was subscribed.[31] When Bishop's College was in difficulties in 1849–50, Jasper Nicolls, the principal, made a trip to Quebec City and raised two hundred and forty-five pounds. This sum was contributed by some thirty-one subscribers. The subscriptions ranged from twenty-five pounds, contributed by Bishop Mountain, down to one of sixteen shillings. There were eight subscriptions of five pounds each and six of two pounds ten shillings each.[32]

Some subscriptions could be described as sacrificial. In 1834 or

[28]*Ibid.*, 74.
[29]Burwash, *History of Victoria*, 45.
[30]*Ibid.*, 17–18, 23.
[31]*Queen's University Domesday Book 1831–1924*, 30–7.
[32]Nicolls Papers, Armine Mountain to Jasper Nicolls, Jan. 9, 1850, enclosing list of subscribers to Bishop's College.

1835 the Treasurer of Upper Canada Academy, Ebenezer Perry, appeared before the Methodist Conference which consisted of seventy or eighty ministers with salaries averaging not much over two hundred dollars a year. He informed them that members of the Building Committee of the Academy were in danger of imprisonment for debt and that the building of the Academy was likely to be sold for debt. Some fifty of the ministers each gave Perry a note for one hundred dollars in order to prevent the collapse of the work.[33]

During the winter of 1860–61, when Albert College was having a struggle for survival, Philip Carman, the father of the Principal, Albert Carman, was one of those who came to its assistance. In spite of difficulties in farming he sent along supplies of food regularly. In November, 1860, he sent ninety-four pounds of beef, twenty-four pounds of pork, and fifty-eight pounds of butter. For several years he came to the rescue by backing notes for the College and meeting those which came due. On one occasion Philip Carman and his friend, James Sisk, were joint guarantors of a note on behalf of the College. Owing to misfortune Sisk was unable to meet his part when the note fell due, but Carman sent an additional two hundred dollars to meet Sisk's share. Later Sisk paid it back.[34]

[33]Burwash, *History of Victoria*, 18.
[34]Waldo Smith, *Albert College*, 10–12.

2. Early Origins (1785-1829)

IT WAS AGAINST THE BACKGROUND OF THOUGHT described in the previous chapter that church colleges were established in British North America.

The first period (1785-1829) was one of tentative beginnings. King's College, Fredericton, King's College, Nova Scotia, McGill (in a sense a "church college" during its first stage), and King's College, York were all chartered; but King's College, York did not begin teaching during the period; McGill gave instruction only in medicine, and the other two colleges made only modest progress. Pictou Academy, a Presbyterian institution, began its career as a grammar school, made progress into the field of college work, only to be reduced once more to the level of a school. King's College, Nova Scotia was the first institution in Canada to begin teaching at the college level; although its counterpart in Fredericton, the forerunner of the University of New Brunswick, appears to have been the first to open as a school. King's College, Nova Scotia stood for two basic ideas: (1) that university training should be a monopoly of the Church of England, (2) that the curriculum should be the old classical one derived from the English universities of the eighteenth century.

King's College owed its inception largely to the efforts of Bishop Charles Inglis. It began with the establishment of an academy (i.e. a school) at Windsor, Nova Scotia on November 1, 1788. In the following year, the Nova Scotia legislature made a special grant of five hundred pounds and an appropriation of four hundred pounds a year to found a "college" in connection with the school. The College was incorporated in 1789 by the Nova Scotia legislature which passed "An Act for Founding, Establishing, and Maintaining a College in this Province." (29 Geo. III, cap iv.)[1] The Governors of the College were described in the act as a body politic and corporate under the name "The Governors of King's College of Nova Scotia."

In a sense King's was the heir to the tradition established by King's College, New York which had been founded in 1754 and which ended

[1]Henry Youle Hind, *The University of King's College Windsor, Nova Scotia, 1790-1890* (New York, 1890), 21.

its career 1776 on the eve of the American Revolution. King's College, New York had been founded by a Yale group, including President Cutler, all of whom had renounced Congregationalism and embraced Anglicanism. According to Dr. Dix, the group "acknowledged the claim of the ancient catholic and apostolic Church from which dissent had cut itself off."[2] Bishop Charles Inglis, founder of King's Nova Scotia, was an M.A. of King's College, New York. His prayer at the laying of the corner stone of the College at Windsor on August 4, 1791, indicated the spirit of the institution, the familiar combination of Anglicanism and Toryism. After asking God to bless the College, Inglis continued:

May it be a permanent source of sound religion, useful learning and science, virtue, order and loyalty. May these and other blessings, spiritual and temporal, flow from hence, and be widely diffused through all the American dominions, and particularly in the Province of Nova Scotia. Amen.[3]

The College received its royal charter on May 12, 1802, under the title, "The Governors, President, and Fellows of King's College at Windsor in the Province of Nova Scotia."

King's College, Nova Scotia was for a time even more exclusively Anglican than King's College, Fredericton, and King's College, Toronto. After the grant of the royal charter, a committee consisting of Bishop Inglis, Chief Justice Blowers, and Judge Alexander Croke was appointed to draft the statutes for the College. The two laymen were more Anglican than the Bishop. Despite his protests, they insisted on taking the Oxford statutes as a model, including the one requiring all matriculants to sign the Thirty-nine Articles. The other two King's Colleges were under Anglican control but the student body was not limited to Anglicans as at King's Nova Scotia.

This exclusiveness continued to annoy the clergy. The Archbishop of Canterbury, in 1806, annulled the statutes, including the one requiring the signing of the Thirty-nine Articles but this did not end the matter. Mr. Croke protested at a meeting of the Board of Governors in 1807 that

a Public Establishment for the education of youth in the Principles of true Religion, of which the Archbishop of Canterbury is the Patron, & which is supported by a revenue from the English government, ought to be confined to the members of the Church of England, the Religion which by law is established in this Province.[4]

---

[2]F. W. Vroom, *King's College: A Chronicle 1789–1939* (Halifax, 1941), 5.
[3]*Ibid.*, 31.
[4]Hind, *The University of King's College*, 45.

The Governors adopted the statutes as amended by the Archbishop of Canterbury on May 2, 1807; but, incredible as it may seem, the new statutes were not printed or made known. The old statutes continued to circulate until 1820.

During this early period, students at King's were forbidden to enter any other places of worship than those of the Church of England. The statutes declared:

No member of the University shall frequent the Romish Mass or the Meeting Houses of Presbyterians, Baptists, or Methodists, or the Conventicles or places of Worship of any other dissenters from the Church of England, or where Divine Service shall not be performed according to the Liturgy of the Church of England, or shall be present at seditious or rebellious meetings.[5]

Even after matriculants were relieved of the necessity of signing the Thirty-nine Articles, those desiring to take degrees at King's were still required to do so. It was not until 1827–30 that Bishop John Inglis and the Board removed this requirement as a qualification for degrees in arts; but the signing was still required of the president, professors, and fellows.

By 1830, therefore, all the clauses offensive to non-Anglicans had been removed from the statutes, with the exception of the test for the president, the professors, and the fellows. The removal of all tests on admission and of all tests on taking degrees in arts opened the College to non-Anglicans of all denominations, with freedom to attend their own places of worship as indicated by their parents or guardians.[6]

The movement which culminated in the establishment of King's College, Fredericton began in 1785. On December 13, a group of loyalists, including William Paine, Ward Chipman, and General Coffin, presented a petition to the Governor in Council of New Brunswick representing the necessity and expediency of an early attention to the establishment in this infant province of an "academy of liberal arts and sciences." Lieutenant-Governor Thomas Carleton and his advisers drew up a constitution and set aside six thousand acres of land to support the proposed institution. Instruction began almost at once. By 1787, the Fredericton Academy was functioning in temporary quarters and by March of 1793, it had seventeen scholars.[7] Carleton's list of principal books in the library indicates that the curriculum was classical. The list was headed by "Lilly's Accidence Enlarged or a

[5]*Ibid.*, 50–1.   [6]*Ibid.*, 71.
[7]Alfred G. Bailey, ed., *The University of New Brunswick Memorial Volume* (Fredericton, 1950), 15–21.

complete Introduction in English prose to the several parts of Latin Grammar" and included also

the Colloquies of Corderius; Excerpta ex Nove Testamento Historia; Clark's Introduction; Exempla Moralia, English examples to be rendered into Latin; Electra ex Ovidio et Tibullo; Salustii Opera, in Usum Delphini; Ciceronis Orationum Selectorium; Caesaris Commentarii; Ciceronis Opuscula; and Opera Virgilli in Usum Delphinii.[8]

Although the first draft of the charter of the Fredericton Academy had been drawn in 1785, it was not finally granted until 1800. The delay was due in part to the differences of opinion concerning the nature of the proposed incorporation and, in part, to the opposition of the Bishop of Nova Scotia, Charles Inglis, to the establishment of an institution in Fredericton which might prove to be a rival of the college which was at the same time being founded in that province.

The Charter of February 12, 1800, vested legal powers in "The Governors and Trustees of the College of New Brunswick." The list of governors included Lieutenant-Governor Carleton; Jonathon Odell, the Provincial Secretary; Chief Justice George Duncan Ludlow, late of the Supreme Court of New York; Ward Chipman, the Solicitor-General; Edward Winslow, a member of the Executive Council; and the Rev. George Pigeon, the rector of the parish of Fredericton. They were empowered to grant degrees and all honours "as are usually granted and conferred by any or either of our Universities or Colleges in that part of our Kingdom of Great Britain called England. . . ."

The "College of New Brunswick" was narrowly Anglican in personnel. Earlier drafts of the charter had envisaged opening the doors of the College to students of all denominations, but in the Charter of 1800 its privileges were to be restricted to Anglicans. The President was to be in the Holy Orders of the Church of England and the professors were to be Anglicans.

At first the College was merely a school. It was mainly through the influence of James Somerville, who became preceptor in 1811, and president in 1820, that more advanced work was undertaken. He has been described as "a man . . . who, through his broad learning, his strength of character, and his long persevering service, was to make a contribution of the first importance to the development of higher education in New Brunswick."[9] Under Somerville's presidency, the College of New Brunswick undertook instruction of a university character and conferred degrees on February 21, 1828, upon Daniel Hailes Smith, Samuel Denny Lee Street, and Timothy Robert Wetmore.

[8] *Ibid.*, 16.   [9] Bailey, ed., *New Brunswick Memorial*, 19.

In March, 1823, the college Council decided to seek a royal charter. The plan was taken up with enthusiasm by the new Lieutenant-Governor, Sir Howard Douglas. Douglas secured the introduction of liberal features in to the draft charter. Students not pursuing studies in divinity were not required to subscribe to the Thirty-nine Articles. At the same time, Anglican control was to be maintained through the provision that all members of the college council must be Anglicans, although non-Anglican members of the faculty might be permitted in practice. The draft charter drawn up in New Brunswick was eventually set aside in favour of another similar in form to the charter given to King's College, Toronto. However, both charters embodied the same provisions in regard to the position of the Anglican church.

The charter for King's College, New Brunswick was dated December 15, 1828, and the reconstituted College opened under its new name on New Year's Day, 1829.

The first Presbyterian venture into higher education in the Maritimes began in 1816 when Pictou Academy was chartered. It was established by Thomas McCulloch, the famous Nova Scotian divine, and a group of associates representing the Secession Presbyterian Church. Pictou began instruction in 1818. Although chartered as an academy, it was really a college teaching the classics, Hebrew, history, philosophy, mathematics, and natural philosophy (science). Candidates for the Presbyterian ministry took some theology during their arts course and then completed their studies in theology. Pictou had a notable, but comparatively brief career. The connection with the Secession Church involved the Academy in controversy with the adherents of the Church of Scotland. The latter were obviously anxious to curtail the ability of Pictou to train clergy for service in a rival church. Adherents of the Church of Scotland were eventually able to reduce Pictou to the status of a grammar school by insisting on the letter of its charter which entitled it to be merely an "Academy" not a "College." The Nova Scotia government which had supported Pictou, turned to support Dalhousie and left Pictou as little better than a grammar school on a small annual grant. McCulloch went to Dalhousie in 1838 and the life at Pictou as a significant element in higher education was over. Yet the Academy had begun a tradition of higher education among Nova Scotia Presbyterians which was destined to continue.[10]

The removal of religious tests at King's came too late to prevent

[10]Harold L. Scammell, "The Rise and Fall of a College," *Dalhousie Review*, XXXII (1), spring, 1952.

the establishment of Dalhousie at Halifax, a reaction to Anglican exclusiveness. Lord Dalhousie, who was lieutenant-governor of Nova Scotia 1816–19, favoured a less exclusive college than King's, particularly after the Archbishop of Canterbury refused in 1819 to abandon the signing of the Thirty-nine Articles for those receiving degrees at King's. Dalhousie was founded by George Ramsay, the ninth Earl of Dalhousie "for the education of youth in the higher branches of science and literature." The Earl decided to found the College "on the same plan and principle of that at Edinburgh;" classes were to be open to all sects of religion.

Dalhousie College was established in 1818 when royal assent was given for the use of money earned through customs duties to purchase land. In the same year a board of governors was chosen. In 1819 a grant was made by the provincial legislature and in 1820 the cornerstone of the college building was laid at Halifax. The bill to incorporate the Governors was passed in 1821. A proposal to unite King's and Dalhousie was rejected in 1823–24 by the King's Board of Governors. The two institutions went their several ways.[11]

The establishment of Dalhousie in 1818–21 represented the first formal step in the development of non-sectarian colleges in British North America. It should be noted, however, that the College was dominantly Presbyterian for much of the nineteenth century. When teaching at the college level began in 1838, the first professors were all Presbyterians. The close association of Dalhousie and the Presbyterian Church in the eighteen-sixties will be noted below.

McGill University owed its inception to the Hon. James McGill who died in 1813 leaving land and ten thousand pounds for the establishment of a university or college. This bequest was conveyed to the Royal Institution for the Advancement of Learning, a corporation which had been established in 1801 to supervise the schools of Lower Canada. In 1821 the Royal Institute secured a royal charter "for the more perfect erection and establishment of the said College." So the university began its career; but instruction in arts was delayed until 1843 by quarrels between the Board of the Royal Institute and the Governors of the College.[12]

The only teaching at McGill in the eighteen-twenties was given by

[11]Hind, *The University of King's College*, 50–62. Ralph D. Mitchener, "On Determining the Seniority of Canadian Universities," *Dalhousie Review*, XL (2).
[12]*The Universities of Canada Their History and Organization*, Appendix to the Report of the Ontario Minister of Education, 1896 (Toronto, 1896), 147–9. Henceforth this volume will be referred to as *The Universities of Canada*; Cyrus MacMillan, *McGill and Its Story 1821–1921* (London, Toronto, 1921), 67–153.

the Medical Faculty which the University had secured ready-made. James McGill had stipulated that if the University or College were not established within ten years, his bequests were to be reclaimed from the Institute. In the dispassionate language of a history published by the Ontario Department of Education:

> To aid in securing their [the bequest's] permanent application to the development of higher education, the "Montreal Medical Institute," which had been organized in 1824 in connection with the Montreal Hospital, was in 1828 invited to become the medical faculty of the McGill University. The invitation was accepted.[13]

In this way the Governors were able to comply with the terms of Mr. McGill's bequest. There was no teaching at McGill until 1843 except in the Medical Faculty.

McGill was, to a considerable extent, under Anglican control in this early period. In the Charter of 1821, the Anglican Bishop of Quebec was named a governor of the University. G. J. Mountain, the archdeacon of Quebec, was principal and honorary professor of divinity from 1823 to 1835. One of the avowed objects of the institution was the "education of youth in the principles of true religion." In current political parlance "true religion" meant Anglicanism. However, at the opening, on June 29, 1829, Mountain said that there would be no religious tests for students or professors. McGill was less of a "church college" than the three other "church colleges" mentioned in this chapter, the three King's Colleges.

The charter of King's College, York was the culmination of a dialogue between Upper Canadian and British political authorities which began in 1792. Having arrived in Canada to become Lieutenant-Governor of Upper Canada, John Graves Simcoe wrote from Quebec to the British Secretary of State for the Colonies pointing out that while "lower education" might be provided for out of the resources of the Province, "The higher must be indebted to the liberality of the British Government."[14] In 1796 Simcoe suggested to the Secretary of State that part of the Clergy Reserves be appropriated for the erection and endowment of a university.[15] On July 3, 1797, the Upper Canadian legislature petitioned the Crown to appropriate "a certain portion of the waste lands of the crown" as a fund for the establishment of a respectable grammar school in each district and of a college or

[13] *The Universities of Canada*, 148.
[14] Hodgins, *Documentary History of Education*, I, 11; *The Universities of Canada*, 8–9ff.
[15] Hodgins, *Documentary History of Education*, 14.

university.[16] The British government answered, before the end of 1797, that the petition would be granted after consultation with the Executive Council, the judges, and the law officers of the Crown.

So the discussion continued. In its later stages an active participant was Dr. John Strachan, the Anglican rector of York, who had been appointed to the Executive Council in 1818. In March 1826, in a statement prepared at the request of the Lieutenant-Governor, Sir Peregrine Maitland, Strachan indicated the reasons which made the establishment of a university a matter of urgency. He also gave a sketch of the curriculum of studies which he deemed advisable and described the procedure which should be adopted in order to procure the necessary ways and means.[17] In order to press upon the British government the expediency of his plan and the advisability of granting a royal charter as the constitution of the university, Strachan was despatched to England where he remained for nearly twelve months. He returned to York in March, 1827, bringing with him the charter of the projected University of King's College.

Strachan's charter was one of the most hotly contested documents in Canadian educational history.[18] Like the charters of the college of New Brunswick and King's College, Nova Scotia, it was calculated to establish Anglican control of the University. The President of the University was to be an Anglican and Strachan was to be the first President. The college Council, consisting of the Chancellor, the President, and seven professors must all be Anglicans. The Council was the regulatory body of the College, vested with the power to make statutes and rules concerning the college government, the performance of divine service, studies, lectures, and degrees in "arts and faculties." In one important respect the charter was more liberal than the rules of King's, Nova Scotia. No religious test was to be required of students except those proceeding to degrees in divinity. The latter were to make the same declarations as those required of divinity students at Oxford.

Strachan felt that in some respects the charter was needlessly stringent. He was in favour of himself being President, but not in his capacity as archdeacon of York. He wanted the seven professors on the college Council to be Anglican but did not want them required to subscribe to the Thirty-nine Articles. He wanted divinity students to be

[16]*The Universities of Canada*, 10.
[17]This letter has already been described in Chapter I. Quoted in Hodgins, I, 211–13.
[18]Quoted in *The Universities of Canada*, 363–71.

guided by regulations made by the college Council rather than having to "make such and the same declarations and subscriptions, and take such and the same oaths, as are required of persons admitted to any Degree of Divinity in Our University of Oxford." In all of these points Strachan appears to have been over-ruled by the British government and the more restrictive clauses were retained.[19]

Strachan's action in promoting Anglican dominance of the University was part of the long struggle which he conducted against Methodism. In the same year that he went to England to secure the charter he had a famous exchange with Ryerson. He made a bitter attack on Methodism in his memorial sermon on Bishop Jacob Mountain, and Ryerson made an equally vigorous reply. Strachan's return to York with the charter was the occasion of an acrimonious and protracted controversy with the Methodists and the Reformers which paralyzed the attempt to establish King's College for sixteen years. A number of petitions were sent to the Legislative Assembly at York during the Session of 1828. These petitions, together with the charter and other information obtained from the Lieutenant-Governor, were referred to a special committee. The committee was under the chairmanship of Marshall Spring Bidwell, a prominent Reformer who was strongly supported by another great Reformer, John Rolph. It reflected the views of the anti-Anglican element in Upper Canadian politics and its report was a vigorous denunciation of the charter.[20] After describing the charter, the report declared that "the sectarian character and tendency of the Institution will be manifest." The report asserted that Strachan had described the projected college as essentially a missionary college "for the education of Missionaries of the Church of England" and had argued that the ultimate effect of the university would be to make the greater part of the population of Upper Canada members of the Church of England. The report continued:

That such must be the natural tendency of putting into the hands of that Church the only seminary in the country where a liberal education can be obtained is obvious. . . . An University adapted to the character and circumstances of the people, would be the means of inestimable benefits to this Province. But to be of real service, the principles upon which it is established, must be in unison with the general sentiments of the people. It should not be a school of politics, or of sectarian views. . . . It should be a source of intellectual and moral light and animation, from which the

---

[19]The draft of the charter with changes suggested in Strachan's hand-writing. Quoted in Hodgins, *Documentary History of Education*, I, 221–25.

[20]Hodgins, *Documentary History of Education*, I, 240–42; *The Universities of Canada*, 19–20.

glorious irradiations of literature and science may descend upon all with equal lustre and power. Such an institution would be a blessing to a country, its pride and glory. Most deeply, therefore is it to be lamented, that the principles of the Charter are calculated to defeat its usefulness, and to confine to a favoured few all its advantages.[21]

Denunciations of the charter followed first from a Committee of the British House of Commons and from the Colonial Secretary, Sir George Murray, in a despatch to the new Lieutenant-Governor, Sir John Colborne, dated September 29, 1828, in which it was asserted that,

"It would be deservedly a subject of regret to His Majesty's Government, if the university, recently established at York should prove to have been founded upon principles which cannot be made to accord with the general feelings and opinions of those for whose advantage it was intended."[22]

As a result Colborne, in his capacity as chancellor, suspended the charter almost immediately after his accession to office. According to Strachan, Colborne "convened King's College Council, and acting, it is supposed, under special instructions, stated that no further steps should be taken towards bringing the University into operation."[23] Colborne appeared to assume that Murray's despatch of September 29, 1828, authorized the legislature of Upper Canada to amend the royal charter. There was further discussion of the matter in the eighteen-thirties, but the controversy effectively blocked the opening of the College until 1843.

The other important academic reaction against Anglicanism came in Nova Scotia in 1829 with the establishment of a Baptist institution, Horton Academy, the forerunner of Acadia College.

Horton was formed from a group of Anglicans who had seceded from St. Paul's Church, Halifax. The parishioners had petitioned the S.P.G. for the appointment as rector of an Evangelical, the Rev. John Thomas Twining, who stressed "a personal religious experience." The denial of their petition and the appointment of a high churchman precipitated the departure from the church of a large group. Some later returned to St. Paul's, but about twenty, including James and Lewis Johnston, L. W. Nutting, John Ferguson, and E. A. Crawley refused to return. Eventually they purchased the Granville Street Chapel and established a Baptist meeting house.[24]

[21]Hodgins, I, 240–41.
[22]*The Universities of Canada*, 21–23.
[23]*Ibid.*, 23.
[24]R. S. Longley, *Acadia University, 1838–1938* (Wolfville, N.S., 1939).

This group was largely responsible for the opening of the Academy at Horton (later Wolfville) in 1829. The school was supported by the Baptist Education Society. At least ten members of its Board of Directors were to be Baptist ministers. The curriculum was to include instruction in English literature, science, classics and other studies "which usually comprise the course of education at an Academy and College." Theological instruction, if it was given, was to be under the direction of the Baptist members of the Board. Moral and religious instruction was to be provided, but as the school was to be open to students regardless of religious denomination, instruction was to be non-sectarian. The first Principal was Ashael Chapin.

During the period before 1829, three Anglican institutions and one in which Anglicans were influential had been founded. Table I indicates their comparative exclusiveness.

TABLE I
ANGLICAN CHARACTER OF COLLEGES FOUNDED BEFORE 1829

College	Administration	Professors	Students
King's N.B.	Anglican	Non-Anglicans permitted in practice	All Anglicans by Charter of 1800; others admitted by Charter of 1828
King's N.S.	Mainly Anglican[25]	Anglican	Anglicans only, until 1827–1829
McGill	Mainly Anglican	Open to all	Open to all
King's York	Anglican	Open to all	Open to all

The achievements of the period, while appreciable, were not too impressive. McGill and King's College, York had been chartered but had not begun teaching, except for the Medical School at McGill. King's Fredericton and King's Nova Scotia had begun instruction soon after their establishment, but were still small. Annual student entries to King's Nova Scotia averaged 3.5 in 1802–10, 4.1 in 1810–20, and 6.9 in 1820–30.[25] The College of New Brunswick, the forerunner of King's Fredericton, conferred only three degrees, all in 1828, during its career.[26] The Baptists and the Presbyterians in the Maritimes had each established an "academy" or school.

[25]The Board of Governors of King's Nova Scotia included holders of political office. It was mainly, but not entirely, Anglican. By the new act of incorporation of 1853, the Board became exclusively Anglican. Hind, *The University of King's College*, 99–101.

[26]*Ibid.*, 49; Bailey, ed., *New Brunswick Memorial*, 19.

Several factors retarded the development of the church colleges. The efforts of Archdeacon Strachan to secure monopoly control at York had produced bitter resistance from non-Anglicans and had thus delayed the organization of the College. Quarrels between the Royal Institute and the college governors, as well as within the College itself, had retarded the development of McGill. At Fredericton and in Nova Scotia, the comparative poverty of the colonies and the exclusiveness of the colleges themselves, had prevented more rapid and extensive development. In the case of King's Nova Scotia, Anglican exclusiveness had been a factor in producing a rival, the avowedly non-sectarian, although dominantly Presbyterian, Dalhousie. The tendency of British North Americans to rely on the British for support in the initiation of desirable ventures, often produced results but probably tended to discourage local initiative.

Already the principle had been established that in the development of higher education the churches and the government were both to participate. The fact that Dalhousie was avowedly non-sectarian also helped to establish the principle that church colleges and non-sectarian institutions were to hold the field side by side.

3. The Golden Age (1829-1867)

THE YEARS BETWEEN 1829 AND 1867 may be called the Golden Age in the history of church colleges. Those already established became more active and twelve more were established: Acadia, Victoria, Queen's, Bishop's, Mount Allison, Knox, St. John's, Trinity, Albert, Huron, Morrin, and Queen's Newfoundland.

The curriculum was still largely confined to the classics and mathematics, but other subjects were taught at the beginning and they gradually increased in numbers and influence. The non-Anglican institutions such as Victoria and Acadia presented a wider range of courses in their early stages than the Anglicans, although the latter made some attempt to broaden their curricula, even in the early period.

One gets some notion of the vigour with which some Anglicans adhered to the restricted course of classics and mathematics from an editorial in the Quebec *Mercury* in 1856 which discussed Sir William Dawson's inaugural address at McGill. Dawson, although a devout Christian, was a leading exponent of secular universities. The Quebec *Mercury* served as a spokesman for the church colleges. Its publisher and editor, G. T. Cary, was a friend of Bishop G. J. Mountain, the founder of Bishop's College. The *Mercury* was scornful of Dawson and of McGill because of their secular character. It particularly objected to Dawson's desire to broaden the McGill curriculum by adding the study of natural history, geology and minerology. It asserted that these subjects should be studied as post-graduate work. The undergraduate curriculum should be restricted to classics and mathematics,

for classics and mathematics embrace a very wide range of subjects, when properly taught, and experience has shown that diffuseness of study tends to weaken not strengthen the powers of the mind. The result produced by a correct and accurate study of these two great branches of education is well known. It produces that healthy robustness of mind, that equally diffused intellectual vigour which characterizes for the most part the people of England and Scotland; and pre-eminently distinguishes them in the senate, in literature, and in the various transactions of life.[1]

---

[1]Quebec *Mercury*, Jan. 8, 1856.

The establishment of King's College, York (Toronto in 1834) was held up by a lengthy controversy over revision of the charter, in which the Council of the University, the legislature of Upper Canada, the lieutenant-governors, and the British government, all engaged. The charter was finally modified by an act of the Upper Canadian legislature passed in 1837 (7 William IV, cap. 16) which partially secularized the University. However, Strachan remained as president, and members of the Council, while not required to be Anglicans, were required to make a declaration of belief in the authority and divine inspiration of the Old and New Testaments. The outbreak of the Rebellion of 1837 and the period of political reorganization which followed, postponed the opening of King's until 1843. Before its opening, the Methodists and Presbyterians in Canada West and the Baptists in Nova Scotia had all established colleges.

According to Lord Elgin, it was the unsatisfactory nature of the King's College question which induced the authorities to give the degree-granting power to Victoria and Queen's. Lord Elgin later asserted to Earl Grey:

The authority in question would not, it is believed, have been granted to the denominational Colleges of Queen's & Victoria . . . if the charter of King's College had been originally framed on a comprehensive principle, or if the provisions of the Provl. Act 7 Wm. 4 Ch. 18 under which that institution came into operation had been carried out according to its true intent and meaning.[2]

Upper Canada Academy, the forerunner of Victoria College, was opened by the Methodists at Cobourg in Upper Canada, on June 18, 1836, and a royal charter was secured on October 12, 1836.[3] The Academy offered a wide range of subjects. Some attention was devoted to Latin, Greek and Hebrew; but the curriculum also included geography, English grammar, French, rhetoric, navigation, surveying and levelling, and book-keeping. The founders and the staff of the Academy were sensitive to the needs of the frontier society and felt that the classics must be supplemented by "practical" and "modern" subjects. The Academy did not give courses in Scripture, but the Christian character of the institution was indicated by the fact that students were required to attend church and were enjoined to practise daily Bible reading and prayer.[4]

[2]Public Record Office, G, vol. 461, p. 481 Elgin to Grey, Feb. 4, 1851, No. 20, quoted in Elgin-Grey Papers (Toronto, 1937), p. 1547.
[3]Nathanael Burwash, *The History of Victoria College* (Toronto, 1927), 44; C. B. Sissons, *A History of Victoria University* (Toronto, 1952), 19–20.
[4]*Acta Victoriana*, January, 1905.

A unique feature of the Academy was the fact that it was co-educational. Nathanael Burwash commented,

> the young women of that day were not slow to avail themselves of the opportunity to prepare for high ideals and strong work in the future. The Upper Canada Academy was the first institution of provincial rank and influence to offer such an opportunity.[5]

Upper Canada Academy, although nominally a school, did some work almost at university level, particularly, according to Burwash, in moral philosophy, orientals, mathematics and science.[6] Several of its teachers subsequently became professors at Victoria College.

The first Principal of Upper Canada Academy was a Methodist minister, the Rev. Matthew Richey, who had "won a high reputation by his splendid command of a chaste and beautiful English style and the ability of his pulpit ministrations."[7] Other members of the staff were W. Kingston, who was English master at the Academy and later professor of mathematics at Victoria (an indication of the versatility of teachers in a frontier society); J. B. Hurlburt who succeeded Richey as principal in 1839, and who was the first professor of natural science at Victoria, and the Rev. D. C. Van Norman who was mathematics master at the Academy and later professor of classics at Victoria.

In 1841, the Canadian legislature extended the charter of Upper Canada Academy under the name Victoria College and formal university work began in May 1842.[8] Work was continued also at the secondary school level throughout the period covered in this chapter.

Victoria represented the tradition of independence from Anglican control referred to in Chapter I. The founding of both Upper Canada Academy and Victoria were part of the long struggle against Anglicanism which had made the Methodists allies of Mackenzie and the radical Reformers prior to 1833. It was a struggle which continued to inspire suspicion of Anglicanism even after the Methodists had broken with Mackenzie.

The Methodists did not propose to force their religion on reluctant students. Teaching at Victoria was to be non-denominational although

[5]Burwash, *History of Victoria*, 55.
[6]*Ibid.*, 64.
[7]*Ibid.*, 43.
[8]Dr. W. E. McNeill argues that the session which followed the granting of the Victoria charter on August 27, 1841, was merely the usual session of Upper Canada Academy "with possibly a slight reorganization to segregate a matriculation class" and that the opening of the college proper was postponed until May 26, 1842. See W. E. McNeill, "Queen's or Victoria, Which Was First?" *Queen's Review*, December, 1943, 1–15.

the intellectual atmosphere was to be Christian. The College was to be open to all.

The philosophy of Victoria, in regard to religious instruction, was clearly indicated by the ideas of Egerton Ryerson, its first president. Ryerson believed it possible to teach general Christian truth and morality without sectarian dogma. In November, 1831, when the establishment of Upper Canada Academy was being considered, he wrote:

No peculiar system of theological opinions is to be taught in it; every pupil is to be left at liberty to attend such places of religious worship as may be directed by his parents or guardians. At the same time, those principles and precepts of morality will be carefully inculcated and enforced which will guard the pupil from the contagion of vicious practice and example and will lead him to the love and practice of virtue.[9]

In his report as superintendent of education to the Provincial Secretary in 1846, Ryerson explained that religious instruction did not involve teaching the doctrines of any particular church, but rather the "truth and morals" contained in the Bible.

By religion and morality I do not mean sectarianism in any form, but the general system of truth and morals taught in the Holy Scriptures. . . . To be zealous for a sect and to be conscientious in morals are widely different. To inculcate the peculiarities of a sect, and to teach the fundamental principles of religion and morality, are equally different. To teach a child the dogmas and spirit of a sect, before he is taught the essential principles of religion and morality, is to invert the pyramid . . . to reverse the order of nature . . . to feed with the bones of controversy instead of with the nourishing milk of truth and charity.[10]

In Ryerson's Special Report of 1847, the idea of non-sectarian religious instruction was further developed.

While the several religious denominations possess equal facilities for the special instruction of their own youth, there is a wide common ground of principles and morals, held equally sacred, and equally taught by all, and the spirit which ought to pervade the whole system of Public Instruction, and which comprehend the essential requisites of social happiness and good citizenship.[11]

---

[9]J. George Hodgins, *Documentary History of Education in Upper Canada*, 2 volumes (Toronto, 1894), II, 9–10.

[10]Report on a System of Public and Elementary Instruction for Upper Canada (March 26, 1846) Montreal, 1847, 22–23; See also Franklin A. Walker, *Catholic Education and Politics in Upper Canada* (Toronto, 1955), 59 ff.

[11]Special Report of the Measures Which Have Been Adopted for the Establishment of a Normal School, and for Carrying Into Effect Generally, the Common School Act, Montreal, 1847, 25–6; Walker, 64.

THE GOLDEN AGE

Ryerson further elaborated the spirit of his system in the *Journal of Education* which he began to publish in 1848. He wrote in the *Journal* in January, 1849.

In the columns of this *Journal* we have nothing to do with parties, sects or personal controversy, but with what equally concerns persons of all persuasions and parties upon the basis of our Common Christianity and in harmony with our civil institutions.

Ryerson's reports of 1846 and 1847 and his writings in the *Journal* were in reference to the public school system in Canada West; but the views which he expressed are characteristic of his thinking in regard to religious instruction at the college level.

Continuing in the tradition already established in Upper Canada Academy, Victoria developed a curriculum which was more diversified and more practical than the curricula of the Anglican colleges. In his induction as president on June 21, 1842, Ryerson defined the scope of education to be offered at Victoria. He laid great stress on the place of science and English in the curriculum, while not disparaging the classics unless they "be so taught and studied as to render the English language and the active industry of common life contemptible in the estimation and feelings of the student."[12]

Ryerson wished to develop a well-educated clergy. He hoped that four years of comprehensive study, presumably at Victoria, would be required of candidates for the Methodist ministry. He did not want the ministers to be unduly academic and insisted that he would not "make the House of God a philosophical Lecture-Room, or the Christian Minister a literary teacher or metaphysical disputant."[13] He did not regard Victoria as primarily a theological seminary and informed President Liddell of Queen's, when the latter was exploring the possibility of college union, that Victoria was primarily an arts college.[14]

After the public examination in 1843 at the close of the session, a letter in the *Christian Guardian* of May 24, indicated the nature of the course at Victoria. The writer, "A Spectator," praised the work in the Classics, Mathematics, and Science Departments. He described Ryerson's classes in history as well attended and deeply interesting. Of the class in Paley's *Evidences of Christianity*, the writer asserted that it "excited the admiration of all present, from the completeness of information and strength and vigour of intellect displayed by the young

[12]Sissons, *Victoria University*, 47.   [13]*Ibid.*, 47.
[14]*Ibid.*, 53.

gentlemen who composed it." "A Spectator" closed by stressing the practical nature of the work at Victoria:

> This institution is emphatically the college of the people . . . a college adapted to the wants of the mass, affording that kind of education, and in that manner, best adapted to make sound, practical men, in every department of life—sound lawyers, sound divines, sound physicians, merchants, mechanics, agriculturists, and to qualify them for filling the various offices in society with honour to themselves and benefit to the community. . . . It cannot send them forth professional characters, but it labours to send them forth men, and that not only by cultivating the intellect and refining and elevating the tastes and feelings, but by inducing habits of industry, order and diligence, and imbuing their minds with true religion and sound morality.[15]

A list of the subjects taught in 1845, provides more specific evidence of the work of Victoria. It included mathematics, classics, science (physiology, natural philosophy, chemistry, astronomy), history (England, the British Constitution), and a considerable number of other subjects: French, navigation, surveying and levelling, rhetoric, evidences of Christianity, Hebrew, intellectual philosophy, logic, moral and political philosophy, natural theology, and history and philosophy of the Bible.

A serious problem at Victoria was the attempt to secure an effective head, who would remain at Victoria for a considerable period of time. Ryerson was president (really principal) for only three years and retired in 1844 to become chief superintendent of education for Upper Canada. His successor, the Rev. Alexander Macnab became acting principal in 1844, and principal in 1845. Under Macnab, Victoria encountered serious difficulties which all but ruined the institution. Macnab began his career with serious losses in staff. His period in office was characterized by frequent changes in staff and by weaknesses in discipline. It remained for Samuel Sobieski Nelles, one of the great presidents of Victoria, to pull the College together in the face of threatened disintegration. Nelles became acting principal in 1850–51 and then president. According to Sissons he may justly be called the "saviour of Victoria." He strengthened discipline and, by a series of wise appointments, built up a tradition of continuous and strong university work.

Of the early staff at Victoria, the one who had the most lasting influence upon the college tradition, apart from Ryerson himself, was D. C. Van Norman, who began as mathematics master in Upper Canada

[15]Burwash, *History of Victoria*, 85–8; Sissons, *Victoria University*, 59.

Academy and eventually became professor of classics at the College. Nathanael Burwash, who came to Victoria in 1856 as a student, eleven years after Van Norman's departure, said that in his earlier days at the College, the tradition of Van Norman's work and of his critical accuracy still survived at Victoria as well as among Van Norman's former students. Burwash wrote glowingly:

> Van Norman was essentially a literary man both by genius and training.... But he was practical as well as classical, and his practical genius took the educational form of perfection in the use of English. Under his guidance, the students were inspired with the desire for excellence in public speaking, a desire already kindled by the brilliant example of Dr. Richey, and also stimulated to exercise and accuracy in English composition, and both these subjects were provided in their curriculum of study and in their literary society.[16]

It was a distinct loss to Victoria when Van Norman resigned in 1845 in order to found the Burlington Ladies Academy in Hamilton.

Another key figure in the early Victoria was John Wilson, a graduate of Trinity College, Dublin, who was appointed professor of classical literature in succession to Hurlburt in 1847. In addition to the teaching of Latin and Greek, Wilson also gave courses in Hebrew, to candidates for the ministry. Important early teachers in science were John Beatty, who was appointed professor of natural philosophy and chemistry in 1845, and G. C. Whitlock, who was added to the staff in science in 1856.

Whitlock was an important addition. An ardent enthusiast in every branch of science, "He belonged to the period, then just beginning to disappear, when men did not limit their studies to one field, but sought the wider outlook."[17] He had studied in his earlier days in Paris and was completely at home in the French language. He had kept himself in touch with French scientific literature during a period in which France disputed with England and Germany the leadership in scientific work.

Elijah P. Harris succeeded Beatty as professor of natural sciences in 1857. Harris, a Ph.D. of Goettingen University, was probably the first Ph.D. from a German university, appointed to a Canadian university.[18] He took charge of chemistry, mineralogy, and electricity and magnetism, leaving biology and geology to Whitlock.

Under Nelles' principalship the curriculum at Victoria was revised. The classical subjects were, on the whole, abridged. The unit of

[16]Burwash, *History of Victoria*, 58.   [17]*Ibid.*, 183.
[18]*Ibid.*, 184.

measure was one hour a day for five days throughout the year and sixteen such units after matriculation were required for the Bachelor of Arts degree. Five of these were assigned to classics; three to mathematics; three to science; two to philosophy; one to rhetoric and logic; and two to an option of Hebrew, French, German or mathematics. The course in mathematics included three scientific subjects, treated mathematically: mechanics, optics, and astronomy.

The important change was the lessening of the reading in classics and the enlargement of the work in science. The course in physics was expanded to include electricity and magnetism. Mineralogy was added to chemistry. Physiology was expanded to include general biology and botany, leading to classification of the animal and vegetable kingdoms. The first year in science included chemistry and physics; the second, physiology, biology and botany, and the third, mineralogy and geology. An option of political economy or the history of English literature was offered in the fourth year. Burwash commented on the character of this programme of study:

The course was one not to make a specialist, but to gain a broad outlook over the varied fields of human thought, and to give a sound mental training in the use of language, in exact reasoning, in the observation of nature, in the development of the intuitive convictions, especially in morals, and in the deduction of general truth from observed facts in the physical world and in history.[19]

In 1863, an important advance was made by the introduction of honours work in the arts course. It was different from modern honours courses in requiring additional work not merely in one or two subjects, but in the whole course. Burwash explained that the new departure was a result of the wide variations in the previous preparation, as well as in the natural ability of students admitted to Victoria. About a third of each matriculating class consisted of students whose preparation for the examination was "excellent beyond the average, owing to superior talents or to better instruction." "Such students," wrote Burwash, "can do more work than the average student and, if not given such work, they will lose in time or in dissipation of mental energy."[20]

The faculty of Victoria met this problem by requiring "additional and more advanced work in each of the departments of study." This the faculty regarded as preferable "to merely pass work in all but one special department." The additional requirement for honours included work in classics and mathematics for two years, in science for two

[19]*Ibid.*, 188-9.   [20]*Ibid.*, 231.

terms, in metaphysics for one year, and in a modern language or Hebrew for two years. Burwash estimated that this added about twenty-five per cent to the extent of the course.[21]

Like other church colleges, Victoria attempted to broaden the base of its activities and presumably to increase its income by the establishment of new faculties. In 1854, negotiations were opened for the affiliation of the Toronto Medical School, and in 1855, the first class graduated with an M.D. degree from Victoria. The Faculty of Law was established in 1860–63.

In its appointments to the faculty, Victoria began to develop a native tradition far earlier than the Anglican colleges which continued to demonstrate their colonialism by restricting appointments to recent arrivals from Great Britain. Victoria, in the eighteen-sixties, began the practice of appointing to its staff Victoria graduates with postgraduate training abroad. Most of these appointments came after 1867 and will be dealt with in the next chapter; but the first important Canadian appointment occurred in 1866, when Nathanael Burwash was appointed to the Chair of Natural Science. Burwash had graduated from Victoria in 1859 and had served as a Methodist pastor in Hamilton. He spent a brief period in preparation at Yale University, 1866–67, and entered the work at Victoria in 1867.

Presbyterianism in Canada had two mutually contradictory theories as to the appropriate relation between the Presbyterian Church and universities. One theory was that the church should leave secular education to the state or to private individuals and should merely establish a theological college in conjunction with a purely secular university. Theological students and other Presbyterians could secure training in arts at the secular university. The other theory was that the church should establish and maintain a university in which training in arts and theology were to be carried on in conjunction with each other. Knox College, Toronto, established in 1844, was in accordance with the first of these two theories. Queen's University was in accordance with the second.

Queen's was founded by members of "The Presbyterian Church of Canada in Connection with the Church of Scotland." The establishment of the College was the result of the desire of its founders to provide the means of secular education in a religious environment. At a meeting held in Toronto, on December 10, 1839, to promote the cause of a Presbyterian university, it was resolved: "That the circumstances of the Presbyterians in these Provinces require that means be

[21]*Ibid.*, 230–1.

adopted to afford them the benefit of a literary and scientific education, based on scriptural principles."[22] At a similar meeting held in Kingston a week later, John A. Macdonald, then a young lawyer of 24, seconded the first resolution, "deeply regretting the limited means afforded to the youth of the country of acquiring a liberal education, founded on religious principles."[23] To the founders of Queen's, education "based on religious principles" meant education free of Anglican control. In describing the establishment of Queen's, Dr. W. E. McNeill has written, "It was considered highly dangerous for a boy to be taught any subject save by a member of his own Church."[24] To Presbyterians in Upper Canada the danger appeared to lie in what they regarded as the machinations of the Church of England. In the fields of primary and higher education, they felt that existent facilities were woefully inadequate and objected to those which did exist being under Anglican control.

In the field of primary education, members of the Church of Scotland in Canada were most concerned with the inadequacy of the system. Under the Act of 1807 (47 Geo. III, cap. 6), eight district grammar schools had been established in Upper Canada; but their fees were high and they were only available to "the sons of the more opulent classes."[25] Little had been done to support common schools in the Province. In 1816, the legislature voted twenty-four thousand dollars to support common schools but the amount was reduced in 1820, and for thirteen years no addition was made to "this miserable pittance." In 1839, the situation was still deplorable. According to the Queen's University *Domesday Book*,

One half of the population of those of school age were left to grow up in a state of semi-barbarism. The annual attendance at school of the other half was for only seven months, generally in log houses with accommodation of the rudest kind, where they were initiated in the mysteries of reading, writing, and some simple rules in arithmetic by teachers hired by the year, wretchedly paid, and as might be expected little qualified for their office.[26]

The Presbyterians felt that the dominant party in the Legislative Council (the Family Compact) was satisfied with extending aid, scanty as it was, to the grammar schools for the benefit of the wealthy classes and as feeders for a university, King's College, which was to

[22]*Queen's University Domesday Book, 1831–1924*, 32.
[23]*Ibid.*, 38.
[24]W. E. McNeill, "The Story of Queen's," in *Queen's University, A Centenary Volume 1841–1941* (Toronto, 1941), 9.
[25]*Domesday Book*, 43.
[26]*Ibid.*, 46.

be under Anglican control. The grammar schools, too, were under Anglican control, since the trustees of the schools were appointed by the Lieutenant-Governor in Council. In 1830, the Presbytery of Upper Canada, in a memorial to the Legislative Assembly, complained of the appointment of the trustees from "one Communion alone" and petitioned the legislature to afford to the petitioners "provision for other schools to be placed under their superintendence."

Members of the Presbytery in 1830 were equally concerned in reference to the Anglican character of King's College. They contemplated action to meet their problem both in regard to the schools and a college. Pending consideration by the legislature of the allegations and the prayer in the memorial on the district grammar schools, the Presbytery appointed a committee to report on the feasibility of establishing a "Literary and Theological Seminary." In 1831, the Presbytery of Upper Canada resolved to apply to Lieutenant-Governor Colborne "requesting him to procure for the United Presbytery of Upper Canada the privilege of choosing a professor of Divinity in King's College, to sit in the Council, and in every respect to be on an equal footing with the other professors in the said College."[27] This two-fold action of establishing a Presbyterian College and of securing a Presbyterian divinity professor at King's was endorsed in 1832 at a meeting of the "United Synod of Upper Canada." "Pleasant Bay, Hillier" in Prince Edward County was selected as the location of the proposed "Seminary" and an unsuccessful attempt was made to procure the necessary financial assistance from Presbyterians in Great Britain and in the United States.

After passage of the King's College Act of 1837, the Presbyterians hoped that their position in the institution would be improved. When it became clear that King's was still dominantly Anglican, efforts were made, under the authority of the United Synod of Upper Canada, to secure the disallowance of the Act of 1837, but Lord Glenelg, the Colonial Secretary, declined to interfere.

While these unavailing negotiations on behalf of the Church of Scotland proceeded, the scarcity of ministers to fill vacancies in the pastorate of the church made it imperative that the education of young Canadians for this work should be undertaken.

In 1838, the Synod appointed a committee to report on the best means of securing this objective. The committee prepared a draft bill for the incorporation of a college and submitted it to the Synod which met in St. Andrew's Church, Kingston, on July 4–9, 1839. The

[27]*The Universities of Canada*, 109.

Synod accordingly decided to have the bill introduced in the legislature of Upper Canada. The site of the College was to be Kingston and the name "Scottish Presbyterian College."

Public meetings were held in order to promote the cause. The first was held in St. Andrew's Church, Toronto, under the chairmanship of the Hon. William Morris, a Brockville merchant and member of the Legislative Council. On the platform were a number of political figures and clergy including the Hon. James Crooks, a Niagara merchant and Legislative Councillor, and the Rev. Robert McGill, the moderator of the Synod. The meeting passed resolutions to provide for collections for the College. A similar meeting at St. Andrew's Church, Kingston, on December 18, 1839, was notable because of the presence of three young men who later had distinguished political careers, John A. Macdonald, Alexander Campbell and Oliver Mowat.[28]

Action by the legislature of Upper Canada followed quickly. The act which was passed and which secured the royal signature on February 10, 1840, incorporated the College under the title, "The University of Kingston."

The Act of 1840 (3 Vict., cap. 35) fixed the Presbyterian character of the institution. The trustees were to consist of twelve Presbyterian clergy and fifteen Presbyterian laymen who must be communicants. The trustees, the principal and the professors in Theology, must all subscribe to the Westminster Confession and indicate their adherence to the standards of the church in government, discipline, and worship. The professors not in the theological department must also subscribe to the doctrines of the Westminster Confession. No religious tests were required of undergraduates except the divinity students.

The original list of trustees was named in the act and included such prominent Presbyterian laymen as the Hon. John Hamilton of Kingston, the Hon. James Crooks, and the Hon. William Morris, all of whom were merchants and members of the Legislative Council. The Hon. Peter McGill, of the famous Montreal family and President of the Bank of Montreal, and John A. Macdonald were also named as trustees.

At the first meeting of the trustees, held on May 20, 1840, it was resolved to send a petition to the Queen asking for the grant of a Royal Charter. The petition encountered difficulty owing to the opinion of the law officers of the Crown that the incorporation or establishment of a university was part of the prerogative of the Crown and that the original act of incorporation was therefore objectionable,

[28]*Domesday Book*, 30–8.

even though it had become law in virtue of the royal assent given to it. The law officers maintained that the only way to meet the wishes of the applicants was to disallow the act and "grant a new charter framed as the original incorporation and foundation of the institution." The Act of 1840 was accordingly disallowed by proclamation, and the royal charter, creating "Queen's College" at Kingston "with the style and privileges of an university, for the education and instruction of youth and students in Arts and Faculties" was issued on October 16, 1841. There were few important differences between the act and the charter. The latter made the corporation consist of all the "Ministers" and "Members" of the "Presbyterian Church of Canada, in connection with the Church of Scotland," while under the act the Board of Trustees was the corporation.

In accordance with the provisions of the charter, the Colonial Committee of the Church of Scotland appointed as the first principal the Rev. Thomas Liddell, a Scottish clergyman who had been educated at Glasgow and Edinburgh Universities.

On March 7, 1842, the first session of the University was begun in a small two-storied frame building on the north side of Colborne Street.[29] At the first meeting of the university Senate, ten students passed the matriculation examinations and were admitted to the University.

The second college session began in October, 1842, with a staff of three: Principal Liddell, who taught theology and moral philosophy; Professor Campbell (classics, rhetoric and belles lettres), and James Williamson (mathematics and natural philosophy).

During the first seven years of its history there was a distinct possibility that Queen's would move to Toronto and become affiliated with King's.[30] In 1842 the Board of Trustees passed a resolution declaring that they had "no wish to appear to stand in an attitude of rivalry" to King's and that they were ready "to concur in any enactment that would empower them to limit Queen's College to the department of theological instruction" and to authorize its removal to Toronto provided the professors of Queen's were allowed a fair influence in the

---

[29]During the first year of its operation, the finances of Queen's were in a position of great difficulty. One of the Board members, the Rev. Robert MacGill, wrote a series of letters to the chairman, arguing that Queen's should confine itself to the teaching of theology, and depend upon King's to provide teaching in arts for Queen's students. See the Rev. Robert MacGill, *Letters on the Condition and Prospects of Queen's College, Kingston addressed to the Hon. William Morris, Chairman of the Board of Trustees* (Montreal, 1842).

[30]*The Universities of Canada*, 113–14.

administration of King's College. In 1843, the Queen's Board of Trustees attempted to lay their views before the Council of King's College but were thwarted in the attempt by Bishop Strachan.

The secession of the Free Church group from the Church of Scotland, which occurred in 1843 in Scotland, and on July 9, 1844, in Canada, deprived Queen's of a great deal of support and increased the reluctance of many of its supporters to maintain an arts college at Kingston. Queen's considered the abandonment of teaching in arts and continuance merely as a theological college. The Board made renewed efforts in 1845 to bring about affiliation with King's College if the latter were reformed in accordance with the University Bills of 1845 and 1846. Fortunately for the future of Queen's, these attempts all failed, and in 1849, when Robert Baldwin was anxious to secure the affiliation of Queen's with the University of Toronto, the proposal was rejected by Queen's.

The system of study developed at Queen's reflected the influence of Scottish Presbyterianism and of Scottish higher education. Most of the early professors were Scots and established much the same pattern as at Edinburgh, Glasgow, and Aberdeen. The teaching staff in 1846–47 consisted of the Rev. James George (St. Andrew's University and Glasgow University), the Rev. Hugh Urquhart, the Rev. John Machar (Aberdeen), the Rev. James Williamson (Edinburgh), and the Rev. George Romanes (Edinburgh).

The course of study for 1846–47 was broader than was the case with the early Anglican colleges in Canada and indicated the Scottish preoccupation with theology and philosophy. The subjects listed were: theology, church history and biblical criticism, oriental languages, natural philosophy, moral philosophy, logic, mathematics, and classics.[31]

Details of teaching in theology and church history listed in the syllabus for the previous year, 1845–46, suggest not only the strongly polemical character of theological study at Queen's but also signs of the trend toward philosophic idealism, later destined to flower at Queen's under John Watson. The courses in theology included not only

Lectures on the Person, Character and offices of Christ, as disclosed in various ways, both in the Old and New Testament—Lectures on the Principal Doctrinal Heresies of the Primitive Christian Church, and the various modifications of these heresies presented in modern times [including, no doubt, Arminianism]. Doctrinal tenets of the various Christian Churches. . . .

[31]*Queen's College Calendar*, 1845–47.

Lectures on the connection between Moral Philosophy and Christian Theology and particularly on the principles of moral obligation.[32]

That the discipline in theology and church history was rigorous is suggested by the information that the course in theology included "weekly written and *viva voce* examinations on the subjects of study and three Public Discourses composed and delivered by each student." "Oriental Languages" probably meant Hebrew, which was listed in the 1845–46 course as follows:

Lee's Hebrew Grammar . . . Critical Examination of Pentateuch—Series of Lectures on Biblical Criticism—and weekly Written Examinations on the subjects of the Lectures; also Hebrew Exercise with additions on prescribed subjects—delivered in public.

Natural philosophy at Queen's, and in other Canadian universities, meant physics. The course at Queen's in 1845–46 included "Mechanics, Hydrostatics and Hydro-dynamics, Pneumatics, Light, Heat, Fixed and Locomotive Steam Engines, Electricity, Galvanism, Magnetism, Electromagnetism and Electro-Chemistry."

The syllabus for 1861–62 indicates a continuing interest in the subjects listed in previous calendars, but a greater emphasis upon natural science. The list of members in the Faculties of Theology and Arts, for the 1861–62 session indicate the nature of the course.

The Very Rev. Principal Leitch, Primarius Professor of Divinity
The Rev. John B. Mowat, Professor of Oriental Languages, Biblical Criticism and Church History
The Rev. James Williamson, Professor of Mathematics and Natural Philosophy
The Rev. James George, Professor of Logic, Mental, and Moral Philosophy
The Rev. George Weir, Professor of Classics
George Lawson, Professor of Natural History

Science, taught by a layman, had now appeared at Queen's. Lawson's class in natural science was attended during the second year of the course by regular students in the Faculty of Arts. As texts he used Balfour's *Outlines of Botany*, Dallas's *Natural History of the Animal Kingdom*, and Page's *Introductory Textbook of Geology*.

During the period 1860–65, Queen's passed through a period of crisis and depression. It was marked by a bitter and unsuccessful

[32]*Ibid.*

attempt to secure a share of the endowment of the University of Toronto and by a shattering quarrel between two professors, George and Weir, which disrupted the faculty. About 1865, the University was pulled together by Principal William Snodgrass, "a burly Lowlander, whose practical, half-humorous sagacity all knew, and who hid under a heavy exterior a force and determination which were to tide the university over her third great crisis."[33] A new staff was built up. John Hugh MacKerras succeeded Weir as professor af classical literature in 1864. In 1867 Nathan Fellowes Dupuis began his long association with Queen's as professor of chemistry and natural science. Robert Bell, the great Canadian geologist, was professor of chemistry and natural science from 1863 to 1867, after which he began his career on the Geological Survey of Canada.

The establishment of Knox College was a result of the disruption of 1843 in Scotland when a large number of clergy seceded from the Church of Scotland to form the Free Church of Scotland. In Canada, a number of congregations also seceded from the Presbyterian Church of Canada in Connection with the Church of Scotland and formed the Presbyterian Church of Canada. When the first Synod was held in 1844, the new church had thirty-three ministers and thirty-nine congregations.

Since Queen's College remained in the possession of the old church, it was necessary for the seceding group to make some provision for the training of the ministerial candidates. At its opening session, the Synod decided to establish a college for this purpose. It was also decided to hold classes in Toronto for the first year at least. The Rev. Henry Esson was appointed professor of literature and science and the Rev. Robert Burns was appointed professor of divinity. Burns had been minister of St. George's Church, Paisley, in Scotland, prior to the disruption. Having joined the Free Church, he came out to Canada in 1845 and became minister of Knox Church, Toronto. Classes began in November, 1844, in a room in Esson's house, with fourteen students. In 1846, the Synod decided to call the new institution Knox College

Knox College had a chequered career in its early period. During its first ten years it occupied four different houses, and changes on the staff were frequent. The problem of finance was always difficult.

When the college charter was granted in 1858, the *Canadian Presbyter* noted that the College had been the subject of much discussion and of much anxiety in the church.

[33]W. L. Grant, and F. Hamilton, *Principal Grant* (Toronto, 1904), 197.

The College has had a variety of fortunes. . . . The church has been most prolific in legislation on its behalf. Many a committee has sat upon it, and many a lengthy and carefully penned report has been made of its state and prospects. Numerous are the recommendations, schemes and instructions of which it has been the subject. We do not know of a Synod since the year 1844 in which it has not been a prominent topic of discussion. . . . Every year we have to make an outcry about its empty exchequer; and it puzzles the brains of its wisest friends to know what is best to be done to improve its financial position.[34]

During the early years, the work of the College was hampered by the poverty of the church. For the first seven years, the average current expenditure on it was two thousand five hundred dollars. From 1852 to 1861, the amount was increased to four thousand seven hundred and fifty dollars. In the beginning, the Free Church of Scotland contributed one thousand four hundred and eighty dollars annually to the College. The grant was continued until 1854, when the Canadian Church assumed full responsibility for its educational work. In addition to Esson and Burns, the early staff of the College included the Rev. William Rintoul, the minister of Streetsville, who taught Biblical criticism and Hebrew.

In 1847, the Rev. Michael Willis was appointed professor of theology, and in 1857, he was designated by the Synod as the first principal of Knox. He had been born in Greenock, Scotland, and ordained as a minister of that branch of the Presbyterian Church known as Old Light Burgher. While principal he took an active role in many of the enterprises of the church. He took a particular interest in the Buxton Mission, established near Chatham, Ontario, for the rehabilitation of negroes who had escaped from slavery. He was a scholar of some eminence and in 1865 published *Collecterna Graeca et Latina: Selections from the Greek and Latin Fathers*. In 1870 he resigned the principalship and returned to Scotland.

The most distinguished of the early teachers at Knox College was also the shakiest in his theology. George Paxton Young (1819–89) was born at Berwick-on-Tweed and educated in Edinburgh High School and the University of Edinburgh. During his university course he was distinguished in his favourite subjects, mathematics and philosophy. Young studied at the Free Church Theological Hall and was ordained. He emigrated to Canada in 1847 and became minister of Knox Church, Hamilton, in 1850.

In 1853, Young was appointed professor of mental and moral

[34]Quoted in *The Centenary of the Granting of the Charter of Knox College, Toronto, 1858–1958* (Toronto, 1958), 3.

philosophy at Knox College. He lectured in almost every department of the college, but particularly taught "evidences."[35]

By 1864, his philosophic development made it impossible for him to give to the Westminster Confession "the sort of assent expected by the Presbyterian Church," and he resigned from his professorship and withdrew from the Presbyterian ministry. A volume of Young's sermons delivered to his Hamilton congregation and published in 1854, *Miscellaneous Discourses and Expositions of Scripture,* indicates that already he had begun to introduce into Canada historical and critical methods of analysing the Old Testament that were being developed in Europe. By 1864, philosophy and higher criticism had landed him in a position in which he could no longer accept orthodox Presbyterian doctrine. He was appointed to the staff of the Ontario Department of Education and during the next four years served under Egerton Ryerson, who gave him the task of reorganizing the grammar schools of the province. In 1868, he returned to the staff of Knox on the understanding that he would not be required to teach theology. In 1871, he was appointed to the Chair of Logic, Metaphysics and Ethics in University College.

Young was a magnificent teacher who left a lasting impression on his students. According to Professor John Irving, "It was the unanimous conviction of Young's students that he was one of the greatest teachers of philosophy the world had ever seen."[36] His reputation as a teacher was based not upon his time at Knox but on his career at University College where for eighteen years, with great eloquence and skill, he expounded the values of ethical idealism. This phase of his career will be discussed more fully in the next chapter.

In 1861, the fortunes of Knox were affected by an important development in the history of Canadian Presbyterianism. After several years of negotiation, the Synod of the Free Church in Canada united with the Synod of the United Presbyterian Church to form the Canada Presbyterian Church. Knox absorbed the divinity hall which the United Presbyterian Church had maintained in London, Ontario. As a result, two men came to Knox from the United Presbyterian Church: the Rev. William Caven, and the Rev. J. J. A. Proudfoot.

Caven, who had been minister of the church at St. Mary's, Ontario, was appointed lecturer in exegetics in 1864. Two years later he was

---

[35]Probably this course was based on Paley's *Evidences of Christianity,* a volume widely used in Canadian church colleges in the nineteenth century.

[36]John A. Irving, "The Development of Philosophy in Central Canada from 1850 to 1900," *Canadian Historical Review,* XXXI, 1950.

appointed professor of exegetical theology and in 1873 he became principal. Caven exercised a great influence upon his students, and, through them, upon the church. It was said of him that "he had all the traditional respect of a true Scot for education." After his death a collection of his papers and addresses was published under the title *Christ's Doctrine of the Last Things*.

Proudfoot was a son of the famous diarist, the Rev. William Proudfoot, who had been a missionary for the United Presbyterian Church in the London area. John Proudfoot had been born in Scotland and had come to Canada with his parents in 1832. In 1847 he was ordained a minister of the United Presbyterian Church. In 1867, he was appointed as lecturer in homiletics, pastoral theology, and church government, and gave instruction in those subjects for thirty-four years. One of his former students has given his impression of Proudfoot as a teacher:

Students who sat under his instruction remember well the genial, highly intelligent face, all aglow with enthusiasm, as he explained and illustrated his system, pressing it home upon the minds and hearts of his hearers. Or, perhaps, they remember better the day when his sermon lay upon the desk before him, and with true eye, unerring hand and keen blade, he proceeded to dissect, laying bare every flaw and fault. With what breathless interest he was listened to as he pointed out the merits of the sermon, cheerfully giving every meed of praise. At length the word "but" which marked a point of departure, and almost made the heart of the victim stop beating, introduced a most searching, incisive criticism, which was hard to bear, painful to remember, but of lasting benefit.[37]

King's College, Toronto was finally opened on June 8, 1843, with Strachan still as president and with divinity taught by an Anglican clergyman as part of its curriculum. The tone of the institution was indicated by remarks of the two Visitors at the opening ceremony, on June 8, 1843. Chief Justice John Beverley Robinson deplored the effect of the Act of 1837 in depriving the University of "its distinct religious character." The Hon. Justice C. A. Hagerman, the other Visitor, expressed his sense of the great importance of the provision made for the study of divinity and his hope that King's College might "year after year send forth from its halls an abundant supply of persons worthy to become the ordained Ministers of our Church."[38]

The course taught at King's was avowedly derived from that of King's College, London, an affiliate of the University of London. The entrance examinations required work in two Greek and two Latin

[37]*Knox Centenary Volume*, 9.
[38]*The Universities of Canada*, 18, 35–6.

authors (one prose writer and one poet in each language) and in mathematics, the first two books of Euclid elements and simple quadratic equations. The undergraduate course at King's included the works of four or five classical writers, and prescribed in each of the three years, mathematics, physics, and chemistry. Candidates read Whateley's *Rhetoric*, John Locke's *Essay Concerning Human Understanding*, Paley's *Moral and Political Philosophy* and *Evidences of Christianity*, and some Biblical literature.

The staff at King's included several men who subsequently had distinguished careers at the University of Toronto. John McCaul was professor of classics and vice-president. He was destined to have a long career (1853–1880) as president of University College. Henry Holmes Croft was professor of chemistry and experimental philosophy, a chair which he held first at King's and afterwards at the University of Toronto until 1880. James Beaven was professor of divinity, metaphysics, and moral philosophy. A graduate of Oxford and an Anglican clergyman, Beaven stood for all that was most objectionable to non-Anglican critics of King's. John Irving has written of him:

> Beaven brought with him to Canada the scholarship, the idiosyncracies, and the prejudices of an Oxford man of the early nineteenth century. He was absolutely for the Church of England and absolutely against nonconformists....[39]

During twenty-nine years of university teaching, Beaven was tireless in performing ecclesiastical duties for the Church of England. He was a canon of St. James Cathedral and from 1862 to 1873, precentor of the Synod of Toronto. He gave his services frequently and gratuitously to many struggling parishes in and around Toronto. As a teacher, Beaven displayed an austere, even forbidding personality, although actually he was kind, considerate, and patient with his students and not devoid of a sense of humour. In 1845, on the opening of a residence at King's College, he was placed in charge as dean and immediately established regulations governing the conduct of students of the type with which he had been familiar at Oxford during his undergraduate days. When the Chair of Divinity was abolished in 1849, Beaven became professor of metaphysics and ethics in the University of Toronto, a position which he held until 1872.

It was the status of divinity and the Anglican form of worship at King's which was a continuing cause of annoyance to the critics of the

[39]John A. Irving, "The Development of Philosophy in Central Canada from 1850 to 1900," *Canadian Historical Review*, XXXI, 1950.

college, including the Reform leader, Robert Baldwin, who was himself an Anglican. In 1851 Lord Elgin commented on this dissatisfaction and explained to the Colonial Secretary, Earl Grey,

> The main cause of this dissatisfaction was undoubtedly the attempt which was made, notwithstanding the tenor of the Act of 1837 to keep up a connexion between the Church of England and the University in various ways & chiefly by the establishment of a Divinity Professorship and a chapel Service.[40]

The trustees of Queen's College, in a memorandum to Lord Cathcart (1845), insisted that the Act of 1837 had only concealed, but not prevented, the "unduly acquired ecclesiastical superiority" which the original Charter of 1827 had conferred. They felt that since the Anglicans were still in control of King's, they would not abandon their original desire for exclusive privileges,

> inasmuch as the parties who obtained the original charter, though now constrained in some measure to act on the amended one, must be expected, according to the well-known principles of human nature, to endeavour to secure the operation of the principles of the charter which they sought, and which even yet they do not scruple to maintain they have neither repudiated nor abandoned.[41]

Four sweeping measures of amendment to the Act of 1837 were introduced in the legislature, between 1843 and 1849, two by Conservative and two by Reform administrations, but of these four, only that of 1849 passed into law.

In 1843 Robert Baldwin introduced into the Legislative Assembly a bill which was intended to make King's non-denominational and also to draw into incorporation with it the Colleges of Queen's, Victoria, and Regiopolis, a Roman Catholic college at Kingston which had been incorporated in 1837. This was the first suggestion of the principle of federating denominational colleges with non-sectarian universities. It was destined to play a role of central importance in the history of Canadian universities. Baldwin's measure had not been passed when the session of the legislature was brought to a sudden conclusion on December 9, 1843, by the quarrel between Governor Metcalfe and the majority of his advisors over the question of patronage. Baldwin and the Reformers retired from the Executive Council and W. H. Draper became the head of a Conservative administration, a position which he held until 1847.

[40]Public Archives of Canada (P.A.C.), G, vol. 461, p. 481, Elgin to Grey, Feb. 4, 1851; quoted in Elgin-Grey Papers (Ottawa, 1937), 1551.
[41]*The Universities of Canada*, 43.

In 1845, Draper introduced three bills into the Legislative Assembly, one to create The University of Upper Canada, one to vest in it the endowment of King's College, and one to repeal the Act of 1837 and to make certain amendments in the royal charter. The net effect would have been the complete secularization of the University. The bills passed second reading but were then dropped for the session.

Lord Cathcart, who became Governor General, and therefore *ex officio* university chancellor early in 1846, asked the opinions of the governing bodies of King's, Queen's, Victoria, and Regiopolis on "the present state of the charter of the University of King's College, as amended by the statute of Upper Canada, 7th William IV, chapter 16th."

Before the end of March, 1846, he had received diverse opinions from the four colleges. The Council of King's suggested various changes in the organization of the College. On the vital issue, the position of divinity in the curriculum, the Council did not contemplate any important change. The Professor of Divinity was to be appointed by the Anglican Archbishop of the Province, or by the Bishop of the Diocese of Toronto. The trustees of Queen's said that they would be willing to move to Toronto and establish a purely theological college in affiliation with King's, providing the government endowed "a theological professorship" at Queen's and gave to the Board and professors of Queen's a "fair and virtual influence" in the administration of the provincial University. Egerton Ryerson, the principal of Victoria, said that his college was unwilling to move to Toronto unless given compensation for its building at Cobourg. The Methodists, he said, had made greater efforts in the field of college education than the Anglicans, Presbyterians, and Roman Catholics, each of whom had received large appropriations from the state. The result was "dissatisfaction" which seemed likely to become "deep and universal." Presumably the deep and universal dissatisfaction would be relieved by extensive governmental assistance to Victoria. Bishop Alexander Macdonell of Kingston replied for Regiopolis, urging that his college be endowed out of the Jesuit Estates Fund. He hesitated to offer advice as to what amendments should be passed by the legislature in regard to King's but "expressed the opinion" that King's College charter should be repealed and the endowment distributed among the four colleges (King's, Queen's, Victoria, and Regiopolis) and a college of law and medicine which should be erected somewhere in the province.

In 1846 the Draper administration introduced measures calculated to create a non-sectarian "University of Upper Canada" and to transfer to it the endowment of King's College. This measure was described by Bishop Strachan as "in some respects better, because there are degrees of evil" but "nevertheless liable to the most serious objections."[42] The House resolved to postpone the second reading of the university bills to a future session.

The long and acrimonious struggle over the sectarian charter of King's College came for all practical purposes to an end with the passage of the University Act of 1849 (12 Vict., cap. 82), which completely secularized the institution, and changed its name to "The University of Toronto." The thoroughness of the secularization was indicated by section 29 of the Act of 1849 which declared,

> no religious test or qualification whatsoever shall be required of or appointed for any person admitted or matriculated as a member of such University, whether as a scholar, student, fellow, or otherwise; or of or for any person admitted to any degree in any Art or Faculty in the said University; or of or for any person appointed to any office, professorship, lectureship, mastership, tutorship, or other place or employment whatsoever in the same; nor shall religious observances, according to the forms of any particular religious denomination, be imposed upon the members or officers of the said University, or any of them.

In this way Anglican King's College was transformed into the non-sectarian University of Toronto.

In the meantime the University of Toronto and the denominational universities went their several ways. One object of the Act of 1849 had been to induce Queen's and Victoria to give up their degree-granting powers and affiliate with the provincial University, but this object was not achieved. Partly this was a result of the fact that the reform of the University of Toronto had come too late. In addition, none of the existing denominational colleges would consent to abandon the degree-granting power unless they were permitted as teaching institutions to share in the proceeds of the university endowment. From this they were expressly debarred by the Act of 1849. Queen's, Victoria, and Regiopolis retained their independence. The Anglicans soon added to the number of denominational colleges by the establishment of Trinity.

Bishop Strachan did not accept the University Act of 1849 without a struggle. He undertook to secure its disallowance by the Imperial government and went to England in April, 1850, to secure this object. His attitude, a combination of bitterness and courage, was indicated

[42]John Strachan, "Brief History of King's College," *The Universities of Canada*, 48.

by a pastoral letter to the clergy, two months before his departure for England:

> I shall have completed my seventy-second year before I can reach London, of which more than fifty years have been spent in Upper Canada; and one of my chief objects during all that time was to bring King's College into active operation; and now, after more than six years of increasing prosperity, to see it destroyed by stolid ignorance and presumption, and the voice of prayer and praise banished from its walls, is a calamity not easy to bear. I shall not rest satisfied till I have laboured to the utmost to restore the College under a holier and more perfect form. The result is with a higher power, and I may still be doomed to disappointment; but it is God's work, and I feel confident that it will be restored, although I may not be the happy instrument, or live to behold it. Having done all in my power, I shall acquiesce submissively to the result whatever it may be; and I shall then and not till then, consider my mission in this behalf ended.[43]

Strachan failed to secure the disallowance of the University Act but he was more successful in the second object of his trip to England. Already he had begun to lay plans for another church university in which secular learning might be cultivated in an atmosphere of Christian teaching, not only by candidates for Holy Orders but by all other students of the university. During the visit in England, the Bishop undertook to secure a charter and financial assistance for the new university.

Strachan was successful in securing large donations from societies and individuals in England. With these, supplemented by what had been given in the form of land and money in Canada, he and his supporters decided to begin the erection of a college building as soon as possible. The order for the preparation of plans was given in January, 1851, and in January, 1852, Trinity College was opened at the head of Strachan Avenue, facing Queen Street.

Strachan had greater difficulty in securing a charter to incorporate the University and to confer degree-granting powers. He made application to the Imperial government citing as precedents the charters granted to King's College in 1827, Upper Canada Academy in 1836, and Queen's College in 1842. The Colonial Secretary, Earl Grey, in view of the fact that the application for the Trinity charter had not been forwarded through the office of the Governor General, informed the Bishop that he would feel it his duty to "communicate with the Provincial Government on a matter of such importance before committing Her Majesty's Government to any settled course of action."

[43]Pastoral Letter, addressed to "The Clergy and Laity of the Diocese of Toronto," Feb. 7, 1850, *The Universities of Canada*, 119–20.

Unfortunately, the Provincial government, in the persons of Lord Elgin, the Governor General, and Robert Baldwin, the head of the administration, were none too sympathetic to Strachan's request. Elgin had a profound dislike for Strachan whom he described in a letter to Grey as "the most dangerous and spiteful man in Upper Canada."[44] This was probably a fair representation of Baldwin's attitude to Strachan also.

There was more than personal spite to the opposition of Elgin and Baldwin. Elgin explained to Grey on October 25, 1850:

It is to be remembered that the object of our recent legislation on the University question has been to set up one great Institution in the Province where a high Educational standard might be maintained and which should give degrees which shall be worth having—With this view we are endeavouring to induce Queen's College (the Presbyterian Seminary) and Victoria College (the Wesleyan) to renounce the power of giving any degrees but those in Divinity—and to affiliate themselves to the Toronto University. . . . Baldwin feels strongly that if just at this moment we are parties to setting up a Church of England College with a power to grant (not degrees in Divinity only, for that we should be glad to encourage) but all degrees, we shall be acting inconsistently and doing what we can to defeat our own policy—He points to the States where Charters are given to all who ask for them and where consequently University degrees are of no value.[45]

Strachan was advised that the Provincial government was unwilling to grant degree-conferring powers, although he was not told of their hope that Queen's and Victoria would surrender the powers already given to them. The Bishop made vigorous protests against a policy which discriminated against the Church of England and assured the Provincial Secretary that he did not believe it could be made to appear reasonable,

that the Government having readily granted Charters for Colleges to the other large bodies of Christians who have desired them, should now for the first time discover that this has been an erroneous policy and should be determined to grant no more exclusive Charters just at that point of time when such a decision would have the effect of leaving the National Church in a position inferior to that of other Religious Denominations, though in number she exceeds them.[46]

Elgin admitted to Grey on April 16, 1851, that if Queen's and Victoria refused to give up the degree-granting powers and to affiliate with the

[44]P.A.C., Elgin-Grey Papers, Elgin to Grey, Dec. 2, 1849, 552.
[45]Ibid., Elgin to Grey, Oct. 25, 1850, 726–7.
[46]Ibid., J. Leslie (Provincial Secretary) to Strachan, Jan. 11, 1851; Strachan to Leslie, Jan. 20, 1851, 800–3.

University of Toronto, there could be no justification for further resistance to the Bishop's application. With this view Grey concurred.[47]

At first Strachan had to be content with an Act of the Provincial legislature (14 and 15 Vict., cap. 32) which incorporated Trinity College without conferring the degree-granting power. Since Queen's and Victoria refused to abandon the degree-granting power, there was no good reason for withholding similar powers from Trinity. On January 16, 1853, a royal charter was issued giving Trinity the right to confer the degrees of "Bachelor, Master, and Doctor in the several arts and faculties." Strachan thus secured what he had referred to as "a perfect Charter."

As the fulfilment of Strachan's persevering efforts, Trinity, like other church colleges, stood for the close association between religious teaching and the arts. A later Provost of Trinity, T. C. S. Macklem, described the ideas of Strachan and the other founders:

> they were convinced, from the highest considerations and also from the experience of practical life, that the separation of religious and moral training from university education was a wrong step; and that if the State was compelled of necessity to sever them, then they, as individuals, must exert themselves by private effort to reunite them. They were of opinion that a university should, before all things, as General Simcoe said, "impart religious and moral learning," that all secular instruction of youth should have its basis on such learning; and, as Dr. Arnold, of Rugby, wrote, be made "subordinate to a clearly defined Christian end."[48]

Trinity was established during a time of intense conflict in Britain and in Canada between the high church and Evangelical sections of the Church of England. Strachan was well aware of the pitfalls in the form of differences in churchmanship which a Church of England university might encounter and, in order to avoid controversy, he was anxious that the churchmanship of Trinity should be moderate. When the appointment of the original staff of three was being contemplated he wrote, "We are anxious that the three belong to neither extreme of the Church, but that they should be true sons of the Church of England, not low, or what is called Evangelical, but equally distant from Romanism on the one hand and Dissent on the other."[49] In this opinion, Strachan was supported by the group of laymen, professional men, and business men who helped to establish Trinity. As the bio-

---

[47]*Ibid.*, Elgin to Grey, April 16, 1851; Grey to Elgin, May 9, 1851, 816–19.

[48]T. C. S. Macklem, "Trinity College," in W. J. Alexander, ed., *The University of Toronto and Its Colleges 1827–1906* (Toronto, 1906), 138–147.

[49]T. A. Reed, ed., *A History of the University of Trinity College* (Toronto, 1952), 46.

grapher of Sir John Beverley Robinson, the first chancellor, argued, "Certainly those of them who had sent their sons to King's College, under its very modified Charter in 1843, cannot fairly be accused of extreme Church views."[50]

When Trinity opened in January 1852, its staff of three consisted of the Rev. George Whitaker of Queen's College, Cambridge, as provost; the Rev. Edward St. John Parry of Balliol College, Oxford, professor of classics; and the Rev. George Clerk Irving of St. John's College, Cambridge, professor of mathematics.

Whitaker, the first provost, had graduated from Queen's College, Cambridge with a first class classical tripos and honours in classics and mathematics, and had been a lecturer and fellow at Queen's College. His was the task of formulating courses and of piloting the institution through the initial stages of its history. That he did this with success was attested by a formal tribute in *Rouge et Noir*, the Trinity magazine upon the occasion of his retirement in 1881: "In learning, ability and loftiness of character he had no peer amongst the clergy of this land. . . . He has laid, along with Bishop Strachan, Chief Justice Robinson and others, a solid foundation."

Two institutions which had already been organized provided a nucleus for the Trinity organization. The Diocesan Theological Institute of Cobourg, which had been founded in 1841 and opened at Cobourg in 1842, was moved to Toronto and became the Faculty of Divinity of the new university. The courses which had been taught at Cobourg provided the basis for the divinity system at Trinity. The syllabus had included courses in Greek Testament, the Thirty-nine Articles, the evidences of Christianity, Old Testament history, liturgics, church government, ecclesiastical history and the Greek and Latin fathers. Although the Cobourg Institute was small, beginning with seven students and eventually increasing to seventeen, it made a significant contribution to the establishment of Trinity.

The Upper Canada School of Medicine became the Medical Faculty at Trinity, but had a comparatively brief career there. Owing to friction between the Medical Faculty and the Council of the University, the medical staff resigned and the Faculty ceased to function in 1856. It was not re-established until 1871.

The curriculum in arts and divinity was characteristic of Anglican church colleges in Canada, and consisted chiefly of courses in classics, mathematics and divinity.

The matriculation requirements for the Faculty of Arts were

[50]Macklem, "Trinity," *Toronto and Its Colleges*, 138.

Scripture history, Greek New Testament, Latin and Greek authors, arithmetic, algebra, and books I and II of Euclid.

Candidates for the Faculty of Divinity were required to be graduates of Trinity or of some other university. Candidates without a university degree, being twenty-one years old, could be admitted on the recommendation of the Rector and the Bishop, if they passed preliminary examinations in Greek, New Testament, Scripture, church catechism, and on one Latin and one Greek author of the candidate's own choosing. Only divinity students were required to sign the Thirty-nine Articles in order to be admitted.

The contents of the arts course are indicated by the examinations prescribed in the calendar for 1854–55. It was a three year course and the candidates wrote two examinations: the "previous examination" at the end of the Lent term in the second year and the "final examination" at the end of the third year.

The previous examination consisted of papers on an historical book of the New Testament, Paley's *Evidences*, church catechism, a Latin and a Greek author, Latin prose, algebra, trigonometry, and Euclid.

At the end of the third year candidates were examined on Old and New Testament history, another historical book of the New Testament, two Greek and two Latin authors, Greek and Roman history, Latin composition, mechanics and hydrostatics, Euclid, algebra, and trigonometry. The only step beyond the confines of the classics-mathematics-divinity triangle was a venture into physics in "Mechanics and Hydrostatics," which were taught in that period as part of the course in mathematics.

Strachan's desire for middle of the road churchmanship on the part of the staff at Trinity failed to satisfy the Evangelical section of the Anglican community in Ontario. Particularly Trinity failed to satisfy Benjamin Cronyn, who became bishop of Huron in 1857.

Cronyn, a strong Evangelical, had never liked the teaching in theology at Trinity which was too high to accord with his views. In the Huron Synod, in June, 1860, when one of his clergy proposed that the Synod uphold the University of Trinity College, Cronyn asserted, "I cannot agree with the mover of the resolution in the exaggerated eulogium he has pronounced upon Trinity College. I have taken every pain for two years to inform myself concerning the teaching of the University and I cannot approve of it."[51] Bishop Strachan defended Trinity and the result was a controversy between Strachan, Provost

---

[51]A. H. Crowfoot, *Benjamin Cronyn, First Bishop of Huron* (London, 1957), 91–6.

Whitaker, and Travers Lewis, the bishop of Ontario, on the one hand, and Cronyn supported by Archdeacon Isaac Hellmuth on the other. Cronyn attacked a manuscript, "The Provost's Catechism," written and used by Whitaker in his teaching at Trinity. He made specific objections to Whitaker's teaching under such headings as "The Virgin Mary," "The Communion of Saints," "The Remission of Sins," and "The Sacraments." Cronyn's motion of censure against Whitaker, which he made as a member of the Trinity corporation, was rejected by the corporation in February, 1862. Strachan had already asserted in his charge to the Synod of the Diocese of Toronto, in June 1861, "If the Bishop of Huron is dissatisfied with Trinity, let him establish his own Divinity School. I did this at Cobourg. Let the Bishop of Huron do the same."[52] This was precisely what Cronyn did. The result was the establishment of Huron College.

Bishop Cronyn's objections to Trinity College resulted in the establishment of Huron College in 1863. Huron was the forerunner of the Anglican university which ultimately developed into the nonsectarian University of Western Ontario.[53] Cronyn was strongly supported by his brilliant and dynamic archdeacon, Isaac Hellmuth. Hellmuth, an able and exotic personality, was of Jewish origin and a graduate of the University of Breslau. Converted to Christianity, he had gone to England in 1841 where he studied for the ministry of the Church of England. He emigrated to Canada in 1844, was ordained to the Anglican priesthood by Bishop G. J. Mountain in 1846, and was Professor of Hebrew at Bishop's College from 1846 to 1854. He was then appointed Secretary of the Colonial and Continental Church Society. In April 1861, Cronyn, on a visit to Bishop Mountain in Quebec City, encountered Hellmuth and persuaded him to come to London as his commissary. In July 1861, Cronyn appointed Hellmuth as assistant at St. Paul's Cathedral and archdeacon of Huron.

Hellmuth was a vigorous and imaginative man who conceived a broad scheme for education under church auspices in the Diocese of Huron. He founded a boy's school, which became Hellmuth College, and also founded Hellmuth Ladies' College; but his most notable achievement in the field of education was Huron College.

Probably Cronyn had already begun to contemplate the establishment of a diocesan theological college, but the controversy with

[52]*Ibid.*, 95. Cronyn also objected to the broad church attitude of the Rev. Edwin Hatch who was at this time on the staff of Trinity. See Philip Carington, *The Anglican Church in Canada* (Toronto, 1963), 132–3.
[53]James J. Talman, and Ruth Davis Talman, *Western, 1878–1953*, (London, 1953), Chapter I, 3–54; A. H. Crowfoot, *Benjamin Cronyn*, 91–6.

Strachan and Strachan's brusque challenge to found his own theological college must have provided the final incentive. In October, 1861, Hellmuth was despatched to England to raise money for the College. On this visit he raised twenty-three thousand dollars, enough to enable him and the Bishop to proceed with their plans. The act incorporating Huron received the royal assent on May 6, 1863, and instruction began at Huron in January, 1864.

Huron College was primarily a result of the pressing need for clergy for the work of the frontier church. Like Strachan with King's and Mountain with Bishop's, Cronyn felt the need of an institution to produce an indigenous clergy. Bishop Charles Petit McIlvaine, the bishop of Ohio, indicated one of the main reasons for the establishment of Huron in his inaugural address at the opening of the College on December 2, 1863: "It is an effort to raise up a succession of clergy indigenous to the soil—men of the country to do the work of the country." McIlvaine pointed out that the supply of clergy from England would always be uncertain and inadequate and the preparation in English schools would not be as suitable as the education to be provided by the new Huron College. He concluded:

The remedy is in the rearing of a body of clergy for your parishes and missions out of the sons of the soil, whose thoughts and associations, and attachments, and habits have been formed in contact with the people of the land; whose sense of home, socially as well as officially, is there; and whose training as ministers has been guided with special reference to the circumstantial features of the work they are called to do.[54]

Not only was the College to be "indigenous," it was also to be Evangelical. Cronyn's immediate incentive had been the controversy with Trinity, which he regarded as too "high." Hellmuth was a strong Evangelical. It was significant also that the principal speaker at the official opening of the College was Bishop McIlvaine, a leader of the low church wing of the American church.

To begin with, Huron was merely a theological college. It did not commence like King's and Bishop's, as a combination of liberal arts college and theological seminary. Yet the intention of its founders was to provide a more liberal education than was usually included in a theological course. In this manner the way was prepared for the establishment of a university in the eighteen-seventies. Indeed, the Rev. Adam Townley, an opponent of Cronyn, charged in 1862, that

[54]The Right Rev. Charles Petit McIlvaine, "The Inaugural Address Delivered at the Opening of Huron College," (London, 1864), quoted in James J. Talman, and Ruth Davis Talman, *Western, 1878–1953*, 4–5.

the design was ultimately to expand the College into a university.[55]

Albert College, Belleville was the result of an early division in Canadian Methodism. In 1833, the Canada Conference of Upper Canada, which had been pioneered by Episcopal Methodists from the United States, voted to merge with the Wesleyan Methodists of Lower Canada. The united body was to be called the Wesleyan Methodist Church in Canada. A minority group of Episcopal Methodists in Upper Canada refused to join the merger. They claimed that the Methodist Episcopal Church had no right to dispense with episcopacy and substitute presidency, nor to place itself virtually under the authority of the British Wesleyans. According to the historian of Albert College, the Episcopal Methodists,

> wanted to be independent—independent of the government in Canada and of the Conference in Britain. The political trend of the country was towards self government: their church ought not to go backward here. They considered that their system of church direction had proven itself suitable to Canada and ought not to be given up. They would go on as they had and reorganize their church accordingly.[56]

In 1836 the continuing Methodist Episcopal Church held its first conference in Belleville. The early years were spent in the organization of the Church. The first task was to build churches. By 1844 the Book Room of the Methodist Episcopal Church was in business and in 1845 the new church paper, the *Canada Christian Advocate*, came out. By 1852, the Church was able to contemplate the establishment of a college. A pastoral letter from the Bay of Quinte Conference in that year read:

> The want of a seminary of learning has for some time been seriously felt among us. . . . We believe there are both ability and disposition among you to respond suitably to the call whenever we shall deem it expedient to appeal to your liberality. We shall then enjoy facilities for imparting a sound mental and moral as well as religious education to the children of our numerous friends, and especially to those young men who are desirous of qualifying themselves more fully for the ministry of our church.[57]

The objectives of the church in establishing Albert College were to provide a general education for young people in Upper Canada and training for the ministry. The *Canada Christian Advocate* referred to the need of improving the education of the ministry in which "something more than a common school education is required." The

[55]Talman, and Talman, *Western*, 8.
[56]Waldo Smith, *Albert College 1857-1957*, 1.
[57]*Ibid.*, 1.

Advocate asserted that the people were improving in intelligence and that it was necessary for their preachers to keep in advance of them if possible. It referred also to the loss suffered by the Methodist Episcopal Church when its young people had to go elsewhere for higher education, "under very different if not opposite influences."

Like the Baptists, the Episcopal Methodists were voluntarists, strongly opposed to the idea of state aid for church colleges. In 1855, when it become known that the proposed bill to incorporate the College contained a clause providing for a grant of three hundred and fifty pounds, strong letters of protest were written to the *Advocate* by the defenders of voluntarism. The Rev. Thomas Webster, who was later the historian of the Methodist Episcopal Church, wrote indignantly:

> Let us fling back the hush money into the Treasury of a corrupt Government and let them bestow it upon crouching sycophantic teachers of religion and corruption. . . . Let the Churches of England, Scotland, Rome and the Wesleyans, if they have no higher trust, fawn and lick the dust at the feet of every description of rulers who will pay them their price, but never let it be said that the Methodist Episcopal Church has abandoned the true principles of voluntaryism.[58]

Webster's sentiments were shared by the majority of the Board of Managers of the College and at their first meeting on August 8, 1855, they declined a government grant.

Albert College opened on July 16, 1857. From the beginning, it was co-educational. At first it seems to have been more of a school than a College, but it soon began to give College work. The curriculum included most of the subjects which were required as basic to a liberal education. A list of the original faculty indicates the character of the course. The Rev. J. H. Johnson was the principal and professor of ethics, belles lettres, and mental philosophy. J. N. Martin taught classics and natural sciences. Albert Carman taught mathematics and Gilbert Goldsmith English. Miss Eliza Deaver gave the "extras" which included French, German, Italian, Spanish, drawing, and embroidery.

Although the education of ministers had been one of the purposes in the establishment of Albert, there was, at first, no Chair of Theology, and the training was simply that of the grammar school plus philosophy and some elementary theology.

During the early history of Albert College it drew heavily upon the United States for faculty. This was a result of the shortage of faculty personnel in Canada and also of the American connections of the

[58]*Ibid.*, 3.

THE GOLDEN AGE

Methodist Episcopal Church. Albert Carman, a thorough Canadian, objected to the American influence and wrote in May, 1858:

> I cannot understand why the Board threw so strong an ingredient of Americanism into the Faculty. We are rid of two and still we have two too many. Would it not be gigantic mismanagement to take the government of the Institution from the hands of men born and educated in Canada and vest the authority in men whose predilections are unmistakably American? Yet such is the plot.[59]

The tone of the College in the early period was a combination of student exuberance and spiritual regeneration. During the first year the students were so uproarious as to constitute a serious discipline problem. In 1858, Johnson, who had become involved in a controversy with the Board over the question of discipline was succeeded as principal by Albert Carman. Carman was a graduate of Victoria where he had offered for his fellowship a thesis on music. He had been converted during a religious revival in Cobourg and had decided to become a church member. He was advised by his father, Philip Carman, to join the Methodist Episcopal Church "although in some localities it is not so popular or quite as good a trade as some other branches of the Christian Church."

The survival and early expansion of Albert College was largely the result of Carman's efforts. He had courage, perseverance, enterprise, and great gifts as a public speaker. He was a clear and careful teacher of mathematics. He left abundant evidence of his patient interest in the students and of his belief in his vocation in the school.

As a public speaker Carman was a fine advocate of the Christian religion and of Albert College. He had a clear mind and a mastery of English style. His numerous addresses and sermons were masterpieces of lucid thought and expression. According to Waldo Smith, Carman's oratory "was thought out, supported by intellectual content and directed to important objectives." When he addressed the Niagara Conference the reporter wrote in the perfervid language of the period:

> There followed period after period of the grandest thought, the most powerful appeals that moved all hearts. Such meetings as these, such addresses as these, such men as these cannot fail to accomplish the end they have in view in raising the endowment of Albert College.[60]

The problem of financing the College required all Carman's energy and devotion. The story of the early years is of constant battle to meet the scarcity of money. Since the supporters of the College were strongly voluntaryist, its needs had to be met by contributions from

[59]*Ibid.*, 13.   [60]*Ibid.*, 20.

men of very moderate means. Some of these contributions were in kind. During the winter of 1860-61, Philip Carman repeatedly sent shipments of food to help out. In November, he sent ninety-four pounds of beef, twenty-four of pork, and fifty-eight of butter. College treasurers were hard put to it to make ends meet. When the desperate Treasurer accepted eight hundred dollars from the government in 1858 there were bitter protests from the college constituency and some people stopped giving. Despite these hazards the College survived, mainly because of Carman's strength and courage.

In 1861, Albert College was affiliated with the University of Toronto, an arrangement which permitted its students to take the first two years of an arts course at Belleville. For the first year courses Toronto accepted examinations set by the Albert faculty and written in Belleville. Second year students took their courses at Belleville but wrote Toronto examinations at Toronto. The right to take the first two years of an arts course was of especial advantage to ministerial candidates studying at Albert.

On August 15, 1866, the College received its university charter and became Albert University with the power to grant degrees in arts.

During the period of controversy over the university question in Canada West, between 1827 and 1849, the Baptist denomination made no attempt to establish an arts college.[61] In this they differed from their fellow Baptists in Nova Scotia who established Horton Academy and Acadia College in this period. The Baptists of Upper and Lower Canada established a theological college at Montreal which had a brief history;[62] but they did not venture further into the realms of higher education.

The refusal of the Bapists of Canada West to establish a college was not the result of indifference. It was a result of their firm conviction that education both at the school and college level should be completely non-sectarian. During the controversy over King's College in the forties, the Baptists, true to their principles, stoutly opposed the principle of state-aided church colleges. They presented many petitions against King's and criticized Victoria and Queen's which

[61]See unpublished B.D. thesis at McMaster University by A. J. MacLachlan, "Canadian Baptists and Public Questions before 1850," 25–51.

[62]The Canadian Baptist College was established in Montreal possibly in 1836, and opened in 1838 with Dr. Benjamin Davies as its first principal. The College lost ground, partly as a result of friction between Baptists in Canada West, who were mainly immigrants from the United States and therefore "close communicants," and Baptists in Canada East, who were predominantly of British origin and "open comunicants." In 1850 the College was closed because of lack of support. See *The Universities of Canada*, 127–28.

also were attempting to secure support from the state. R. A. Fyfe, a prominent Baptist leader, wrote caustically in the Baptist *Register* on December 18, 1845, "The fact is that these two institutions have followed in the wake of the Episcopalians, and are demanding Government support, because they see the Episcopalians so impudently insisting upon it."[63]

Baptist ideas on university organization were indicated by resolutions adopted at the Second Annual Meeting of the Baptist Union, reported in the *Register* of July 17, 1845, and by Dr. Fyfe's article in the *Register* of December 18, 1845. The Baptist concept of a university was much the same as that of Baldwin and Lord Elgin. Their plan was to have a non-sectarian central arts college with denominational theological colleges clustered around it.

After 1850, there was some change of heart on the part of the Baptists in Canada West in regard to the question of church participation in secular education. The new policy was begun with the formation of the Regular Baptist Theological Education Society in February, 1853. The first venture of the Society was the foundation of a purely theological college, Maclay College, which was closed in 1856. Dr. Fyfe was appointed president of the Society which was reorganized in 1876.[64]

Fyfe, one of the leading personalities in the Baptist community in this period, was of Scottish extraction. He had been educated at the Canadian Baptist College in Montreal, Madison University, New York, and at the Newton Theological Seminary. He had acted as principal of the Canadian Baptist College in 1843–44 and afterwards had been pastor of several churches in Canada and the United States. He had already taken a prominent part in proclaiming the separation of church and state and had led the way in attacking the evils of the Clergy Reserves and sectarian control of King's.[65]

It was Fyfe who proposed that the Baptists should enter the field of secular education. In an article entitled "A Proposal," published in the *Christian Messenger* of December 13, 1855, Fyfe suggested that the Baptists should establish an academy in a western locality where Baptist parents might send their sons and daughters. He proposed that the academy should provide theological training and a good residential secondary school under Christian supervision. Young candidates for the ministry would receive a general education before

[63]MacLachlan, Canadian Baptists, chapter II, p. IV.
[64]R. Hamilton, "The Founding of McMaster University," unpublished B.D. thesis, McMaster University.
[65]For a brief biographical note on Fyfe see *The Universities of Canada*, 128–9.

proceeding to theology. In addition, young men and women proceeding to secular callings would be influenced by sane Christian training. He asserted that education under religious influence was the best training for other spheres of Christian activity as well as for the pulpit.[66]

Fyfe's "Proposal" led to the establishment of a co-educational school, the Canadian Literary Institute at Woodstock in 1860. The school opened on July 4, 1860, with Fyfe as principal and with forty pupils. The newly-constructed school building was destroyed by fire in January, 1861, but was rebuilt in 1862.

In establishing the Canadian Literary Institute, the Baptists of Canada West departed from the principle of abstaining from participation in secular education; but they adhered to their firm belief in the separation of church and state by refusing any government aid even at the municipal level. When the new building was under consideration after the fire of 1861, the Town Council of Woodstock offered to contribute six hundred dollars, but the administrators of the Institute, adhering to their Baptist principles, declined the gift with thanks, "refusing to accept state taxes."[67]

The struggle of the Canadian Literary Institute for existence was severe and protracted but the institution survived. Dr. Fyfe, the principal, who had been so largely responsible for the establishment of the Institute, was also responsible for its survival. In the words of a nineteenth century history, the Institute "was sustained chiefly by his indomitable energy, exceptional aptitude and unflagging zeal."[68]

The founders of Bishop's College showed the same desire as those of other Anglican colleges to have secular study pursued in a religious environment. Their petition, presented to Sir Charles Metcalfe, the governor of Canada, in 1843, said "for the education of the youth of this Province in the principles of true religion and in the various branches of learning and sound literature."[69]

Bishop's developed the arts course under close Anglican control. The arts course provided training for the clergy, and for members of other professions. Unlike King's Nova Scotia, in the early period, Bishop's admitted students of all denominations but they had to take divinity courses taught by Anglican clergy, and to go to chapel.

[66]Hamilton, "McMaster University"; *The Universities of Canada*, 130.
[67]Hamilton's phrase; J. L. Gilmour, "The Baptists in Canada," in Adam Shortt, and Arthur G. Doughty, *Canada and Its Provinces* (Toronto, 1914), XI, 368.
[68]*The Universities of Canada*, 129.
[69]D. C. Masters, *Bishop's University: The First Hundred Years* (Toronto, 1950), 15.

Bishop's represented the tradition of classics and mathematics, derived from Oxford and Cambridge by two of its founders, Jasper Hume Nicolls (Oxford) the first principal, and Bishop George J. Mountain (Cambridge).

Bishop's owed its inception to Bishop Mountain and to a group of laymen and clergy in the Eastern Townships. Mountain, the first president of Bishop's was an urbane and scholarly man. A fine Christian, and an old-fashioned high churchman, he made an effort to be fair to the Evangelical wing of his church as well as to the Tractarians. He was a firm believer in education carried on in a Christian setting.

A prominent member of the Eastern townships group was the Rev. Lucius Doolittle, the rector of Lennoxville and Sherbrooke. Doolittle, a graduate of the University of Vermont, had been ordained to the Anglican ministry in 1828 and, after service in the Gaspé region, had come to Lennoxville in 1833. In concert with his lay associates in Lennoxville, he gave both land and money in order to induce the Bishop to establish the college at Lennoxville. He served as bursar in the early period without remuneration. His portrait in Convocation Hall at Bishop's indicates a shrewd, determined, Yankee countenance and helps to explain his effectiveness as an early supporter of the institution.

The College was incorporated by an act of the Provincial legislature passed in 1843 (7 Vict., cap. 49) constituting "a Body Politic and Corporate, under the name of 'Bishop's College'." The corporation of the College was to consist of the Bishop of Quebec, the trustees of the College (not less than three) and the College Council (not less than three). The appointment and replacement of trustees and councillors was vested in the Bishop of Quebec.

Like most other denominational colleges, Bishop's from the first admitted students of all denominations without religious tests. The original petitioners in 1843 had pointed out "That the said Institution is intended to be in immediate connection with the Church of England and Ireland, but without excluding the youth of any other religious profession."[70] Bishop Mountain, when offering the principalship to Jasper H. Nicolls on January 17, 1845, wrote:

> The feature of the project which staggers you is, I am aware, the admission of Dissenters as students. They will all be required, however, to attend daily prayers in the College and will only by special permission in each case, go to any other place of worship on Sundays.[71]

---
[70]*Ibid.*, 15.   [71]Nicolls Papers, Mountain to Nicolls.

Bishop's opened in the autumn of 1845, under the principalship of Jasper Nicolls. Nicolls had been educated at Oriel College, Oxford (B.A. 1840) and had been a fellow of Queen's College, Oxford. He was principal of Bishop's from 1845 to 1877 and did much to give the College its distinctive character as a liberal arts college and training centre for Anglican clergy. Nicolls was a gentle, scholarly man with a quiet sense of humour. He was a strong Anglican with Tractarian leanings and was convinced that the world of secular learning could only be understood in a religious setting.

Nicolls' only academic associate, when the College opened, was Henry Hopper Miles, a Scot who had been educated at the Universities of Edinburgh and Aberdeen. Miles came to Bishop's as professor of mathematics. A full-blooded, rather irascible man, Miles was destined to remain at Bishop's until 1867 when he was appointed secretary of the Department of Public Instruction in the Province of Quebec, a post which he occupied until a few years before his death in 1895.

The course of study at Bishop's was humanistic and consisted almost entirely of Greek, Latin and mathematics with additional work for students in divinity. The outline of courses published with the *List of Officers* in 1851 indicates the nature of the course. It was heavily weighted with Greek, Latin, and mathematics in each of the four years, although some attention was devoted to Hebrew, history and moral philosophy. Additional courses were prescribed for divinity students: Greek text, systematic theology, "controversy with Rome," pastoral theology and so forth, while the Professor of Mathematics offered supplementary lectures in physics. An effort was made in 1849 to begin instruction in chemistry. Dr. S. C. Sewell, a physician, became temporary professor of chemistry but there was no money to pay him. After giving his services freely for some time, with apparatus supplied by the College, he resumed medical practice first in Montreal and then in Ottawa.

During the first ten years of its history, Bishop's did not possess the degree-granting power. In 1853, after an arduous campaign by Nicolls and Mountain, the College secured a Royal Charter with power to

> have and enjoy all such and the like privileges as are enjoyed by our universities of our United Kingdom of Great Britain and Ireland as far as the same are capable of being had or enjoyed by virtue of these letters patent.

Among the privileges given was the degree-granting power.

THE GOLDEN AGE   67

The curriculum of the College published in the *Historical Sketch of the University of Bishop's College* (Montreal, 1857) indicates the nature of the course more fully. The curriculum provided for a preliminary year in the school which was being organized in connection with the University, and three years in the University.[72] The course was as follows (for purposes of brevity I have listed authors but not the precise excerpts required from their works):

First Year (in the college, i.e. the school)
  Greek: Xenophon, Homer, Euripides
  Latin: Cicero, Virgil, Horace
  Mathematics: Algebra, Euclid, Plane Trigonometry
  Divinity: Part of the Gospels, The Pentateuch, Greek History
  Composition in all years: English, Latin, and Greek

Second Year (first year in the university)
  Greek: Herodotus, Euripides, Sophocles
  Latin: Virgil, Horace
  Mathematics: Differential and Integral Calculus, Analytical Geometry
  Roman History
  Rhetoric: Richard Whately's *Rhetoric*
  Divinity: The Gospels continued, The Old Testament Historical Books

Third Year (second in the university)
  Greek: Thucydides, Sophocles, Pindar, Demosthenes
  Latin: Livy, Juvenal
  Mathematics: Differential and Integral Calculus; Mechanics (part 1), Statics and Dynamics
  Divinity: William Paley's *Evidences of Christianity*, History of the Old Testament continued
  General View of European History
  Logic: Huysche's

Fourth Year (third year in the university)
  Greek: Aristotle's *Rhetoric*, Plato, Aristophanes, Aeschylus
  Latin: Cicero
  Mathematics: Euclid, Spherical Geometry and Trigonometry, Plane Astronomy, Mechanics (part 2), Optics and Optical Instruments
  Divinity: The Acts—Paley's *Horae Paulinae*
  History: England and her Colonies
  Moral Philosophy: Abercrombie on the Intellectual Powers and on the Moral Feelings

Supplementary lectures by the Professor of mathematics in physics, chemistry, and physical geography were also listed.

Divinity students were required to take additional courses based upon the New Testament Epistles; Butler's *Analogy*; Bishop Gilbert

---

[72]Later the school was called Bishop's College School.

Burnet's *Exposition of the Thirty-nine Articles*; Bishop John Pearson's *Exposition of the Creed*; Ernest's *Institutes*; Wheatley on Common Prayer; Richard Hooker's *Ecclesiastical Polity, Book V*; and the Hebrew Bible.

That the actual programme of teaching was less extensive than the list in the *Historical Sketch* is indicated by an explanatory note: "Some of the subjects contained in this course are not yet sufficiently provided for, though they are not wholly neglected, such as History and Moral Philosophy, and Chemistry."[73]

McGill was still in a sense a church college until the issuance of its second charter in 1852. Until 1852, the Bishop of Quebec was a governor of the University. When instruction finally commenced in arts the system appeared much like the other Anglican church colleges. The staff in 1844 consisted of the Principal, the Rev. John Bethune, an Anglican clergyman who was also professor of divinity; a second lecturer on divinity; the vice-principal, who was also professor of classical literature; the professor of mathematics; and a classical tutor.

Even after the beginning of instruction in arts the institution did not flourish. Quarrels continued between the Board of the Royal Institute of Learning and the Governors of the College. The Bishop of Quebec, George Mountain, fervently disliked Principal John Bethune. This was one of the reasons why Mountain established Bishop's College at Lennoxville in 1843–45. The student body in arts consisted of twenty students in 1843, seventeen in classics and three in mathematics. Twelve years later it had only risen to thirty-eight.

The real beginning of McGill as an important institution of higher learning occurred in the 1852–55 period. It was also in this period that McGill was completely secularized. In 1852 a group of public-spirited men, headed by Judge Charles Dewey Day, determined to revive the institution and secured an amended charter, dated July 6, 1852, which was more elastic and less cumbrous than its predecessor. Under an able and influential Board of Governors, the revival of McGill began.

In 1854, William Dawson, the superintendent of education for Nova Scotia, was appointed principal. The post would normally have fallen to the Rev. W. T. Leach, the vice-principal, but Leach, who was also rector of a city church was unwilling to give up his church in order to devote his entire time to McGill. This was a relief to the Governors who felt that "it was very desirable that no aspect of

[73]*Historical Sketch of the University of Bishop's College* (Montreal, 1857), 16.

denominationalism should be given to the university."[74] In 1855, Dawson, later Sir William, began the career of distinguished service at McGill which lasted until his retirement in 1893. That Dawson was to preside over a completely non-sectarian institution was indicated by the opening statement, in the McGill calendar for 1854-55, introducing the course of study.

> The arrangements have been made on a basis of the broadest liberality, to the exclusion of all sectarianism and party spirit. The advantages of the University are open and equal to all classes, and it is believed that our youth may receive in it the best instruction, whether of a general or personal character, without being exposed to the evils which too often attend an education and the formation of habits at a distance from home and in a state of society differing from that in which they are to live.[75]

Like their co-religionists in Canada West, the Presbyterians in Quebec City established a theological seminary, Morrin College, during the period covered in this chapter.[76] The foundation of the College was made possible by a "deed of gift" of Joseph Morrin, dated September 26, 1861. Morrin was a physician and surgeon, born in Scotland and educated in Quebec, Edinburgh, and London. He had a large practice in Quebec and was first president of the Medical Board of Lower Canada. A man of culture as well as of public spirit, Morrin was twice mayor of Quebec City. As mayor he appears to have been quite an entertainer. His New Year's Ball in 1856, judging by the florid description in the Quebec *Mercury*, was quite a lavish affair.[77] His decision to establish the College was partly the result of his desire to leave "some permanent memorial of his regard for the city of Quebec" and partly of his wish to mark "his attachment to the church in which he was reared and to which he had always belonged" —the Presbyterian Church of Canada in Connection with the Church of Scotland.

Morrin placed his gift, which consisted of "certain immovable properties and sums of money" in the hands of three trustees, including the Rev. John Cook, who obtained an act of the Canadian legislature creating "Morrin College" a corporation and vesting its management in a board of governors (24 Vict., cap. 109). The avowed object of the

---

[74]Sir William Dawson, *Fifty Years of Work in Canada* (London and Edinburgh, 1901), 96.
[75]*McGill College, Montreal, Officers, Professors—Course of Study Session 1854-5*, 4.
[76]*The Universities of Canada*, 154-55.
[77]Quebec *Mercury*, Jan. 3, 1856. The ball was attended by Kate Mountain, the daughter of Bishop G. J. Mountain.

institution was the instruction of "young men intended for the ministry of the Church of Scotland in Canada." The Governors, all Presbyterians, were authorized to make regulations for "the superintendence and management of all the property belonging to the corporation" and also for the control of the educational work done in the College.

Dr. Cook was named in the statute as the first principal and chairman of the Board of Governors. A distinguished Presbyterian, Dr. Cook had been born in Scotland and educated at Glasgow and Edinburgh Universities. He was for many years minister of St. Andrew's Church, Quebec City, and played a prominent part in bringing about the union of Presbyterians in Canada. He was one of the founders of Queen's University and was its principal in 1857-58. He remained principal of Morrin College from 1861 until his death in 1892.

Morrin College closed as a teaching body about 1899, but the Board continued to administer the property of the College consisting principally of its endowment and the college building which originally had been the Court House of Quebec. The Board continued to grant scholarships, at first to Presbyterian theological students and eventually to "worthy students of the City of Quebec, who are pursuing studies above the High School level, in any of the various courses."[78]

King's College, Fredericton, chartered in 1828 as the continuation of the old College of New Brunswick, had a career of thirty-one years as a moderately Anglican institution.[79] It will be recalled that by the Charter of 1828, students of any religious denomination were free to attend the College without subscribing to any religious tests with the exception of students in divinity. Members of the College Council were to be Anglicans, but the way was opened for professors of other religious faiths to teach at the College.

The faculty at King's was predominantly Anglican. The Rev. George Best, the archdeacon of Fredericton, was named president. The position of vice-president and acting head was filled by the erudite Dr. Edwin Jacob, a distinguished Oxford scholar and divine who also served as professor of classical literature, history, and moral philosophy. Dr. James Somerville, the former president of the College of New Brunswick, continued as professor of divinity and metaphysics. Paid a salary of only one hundred and fifty dollars, with permission

---

[78]I am indebted to Dr. Neil G. Smith of the Presbyterian College, Montreal and to Mr. W. MacKenzie Ross for information about Morrin College.
[79]Francis A. Firth, "King's College, Fredericton, 1829-1859," in Bailey, ed., *New Brunswick Memorial* (Fredericton, 1950).

to take any additional church preferment which might be offered, Somerville eventually worked himself into a state of nervous collapse and retired from ill health in 1840. George McCawley, a graduate of King's College, Nova Scotia, who had taught in the collegiate department of the College of New Brunswick, became professor of logic, mathematics, and Hebrew. In 1836 he became president of King's College, Nova Scotia.

Under this staff the curriculum was still of the type characteristic of Anglican Church colleges. It included classical authors, mathematics, mental and moral philosophy, the evidences and general principles of the Christian religion, logic, rhetoric, and history. With the appointment of new professors the curriculum was considerably expanded. Dr. Jacob adhered to the older system. He asserted that the College's concern was to impart intellectual and moral culture but believed that it was to be achieved almost solely through the study of the ancient classical languages and literature. His new colleagues, James Robb, William Brydone Jack, and Joseph Marshall, second Baron d'Avray were in agreement with Jacob on the fundamental aims but took a broader view as to how they were to be accomplished. They insisted that modern languages and courses with a "vocational value" should play a greater part in the curriculum.

James Robb was appointed the first professor of chemistry and natural history in 1837. He had graduated in medicine from Edinburgh, had studied at the Sorbonne and had travelled extensively in Europe collecting specimens which, along with those collected in New Brunswick, were assembled to form the museum for the College. As well as taking a prominent part in the cultural activities of the community, he engaged in research in geology and drew up a geological map of the province.

William Brydone Jack, a Scot, was appointed professor of mathematics and natural philosophy in 1840. Jack was a graduate of the University of St. Andrews where he had come under the influence of Sir David Brewster, one of the most famous mathematicians and "natural philosophers" of his time. Jack's vigorous personality was soon felt in the lecture room and in the community of Fredericton. He persuaded the College Council to acquire a fine equatorial telescope then the best of its kind in North America. In his efforts to expand the curriculum to include more "practical" subjects, he was the initiator of a course in surveying which led at a later date to the establishment of a department of engineering.

The most influential personality on the faculty was d'Avray who was appointed professor of modern languages in 1847, a chair which he held for twenty-two years. D'Avray had an exotic background. His father, the first Baron and a medical doctor, had had a romantic career in science and diplomacy. He had helped in the restoration of Louis XVIII to the French throne and had been rewarded with his title. Later he had served as tutor to the French royal family with whom the second Baron received his early education.

D'Avray became a most conspicuous figure in education at midcentury in New Brunswick. He held progressive and practical views on education. He instilled in his students the fine appreciation of literature which later flowered in the work of the Fredericton School of Poets. In the eighteen-fifties, besides being Professor of Modern Languages, d'Avray was Chief Superintendent of Education for the Province and editor of a newspaper, the Fredericton *Head Quarters*.

Despite the steady intellectual development of the university, it was under heavy attack in the New Brunswick legislature because of its Anglican character. Opposition culminated in the Act of Amendment to the charter (8 Vict., cap. 3) which was passed in 1845 and received the royal assent in 1846.[80] By this measure the College Council was broadened to include members of other religious denominations, although the Professor of Theology still had to be an Anglican clergyman. The reforms of 1846 did not end the attacks in the legislature. As a result the Lieutenant-Governor, Sir Edmund Head, appointed a royal commission to investigate the university question. The commission consisted of three local political figures, John Hamilton Gray, John S. Saunders, and James Brown, and two educationalists, J. W. Dawson and Egerton Ryerson. The recommendations embodied in the report of the commission, supplemented by proposals of the Council of King's College in 1857, became the basis of the university act which was passed by the New Brunswick legislature in 1859 and which received the royal assent in 1860. By this act the name of the institution was changed to the University of New Brunswick, and the system of university government was reformed. The secularization of the University was completed by the abolition of the professorship of theology.

King's College thus became a truly provincial and non-sectarian institution. During its period as a moderately Anglican institution,

---

[80]One of the objections urged against the measure was that it was beyond the competence of a provincial parliament to amend a royal charter. Eventually, however, the Colonial Secretary conceded that there was no valid constitutional objection to the measure. *The Universities of Canada*, 196

King's had gone far toward accomplishing the transition from a dominantly classical and mathematical system to one which was more comprehensive and modern. Francis A. Firth, the historian of the 1829-60 period at King's has appraised this achievement.

It may be said without fear of contradiction, therefore, that during the years when the University was known as the royal foundation of King's College, in the words of James Robb, the spirit of antiquity became united with that of modern life; the wisdom of Cicero, the philosophy of Aristotle, the poetry of Homer, and the eloquence of Demosthenes were consolidated and transmitted in due admixture and combination with the science of Bacon, of Newton, of Humboldt, of Owen and of Faraday. Thus the foundations laid in the College of New Brunswick were maintained and enlarged by the men of King's in preparation for the establishment of a truly liberal university.[81]

The most important development in higher education among Maritime Methodists in the period covered by this chapter was the establishment of Mount Allison.[82] Like other church colleges, Mount Allison was intended to serve two purposes: to provide a general course in arts and professional training for the Methodist ministry.

Previous to the establishment of Mount Allison, training for the Methodist clergy had been supplied in a variety of ways. From 1784 to 1800, when Nova Scotian Methodism was within the orbit of the Methodist Episcopal Church of the United States, its ministers were largely supplied from the United States. In 1800, the connection with the United States ceased and the Wesleyan Church in England became responsible for work in Nova Scotia. For the next forty years about seventy-five per cent of Methodist ministers came from Great Britain. Some Canadians were trained by actual missionary work under the supervision of the clergy. These candidates carried on prescribed reading for four or five years, wrote examinations, and were orally examined before the district meeting. A few candidates attended Wesleyan College in Connecticut where they graduated in arts.

Mount Allison Wesleyan Academy was originally established as a grammar school in 1839. In the parlance of the period, the term "Academy" meant a school, as distinct from a college. The foundation was made possible by the generosity of Charles Frederick Allison. Allison, a prosperous Sackville merchant, had been brought up an Anglican and had married Milcah Trueman of the same town who

---

[81]Bailey, ed., *New Brunswick Memorial*, 32.
[82]W. J. Falconer, and W. G. Watson, *A Brief History of Pine Hill Divinity Hall and the Theological Department of Mount Allison University* (Halifax, 1946).

has been described as "an elect lady and devoted Methodist." During an illness in 1833 he had a religious experience and became a strong supporter of the Methodist Church. His letter to the Chairman of the New Brunswick District in May, 1839, indicated the religious atmosphere in which Mount Allison was established.

My mind has been much impressed with the great importance of the admonition of the wise man—'Train up a child in the way he should go; and when he is old, he will not depart from it.' The establishment of schools in which *pure religion* is not only taught, but constantly brought before the youthful mind, and represented to it as the basis and groundwork of all the happiness which man is capable of enjoying here on earth and eminently calculated to form the most perfect character is, I think, one of the most efficient means in the order of Divine Providence, to bring about the happy result spoken of by the wise man.

It is therefore under this impression, connected with a persuasion of my accountability to that Gracious Being, Whom I would ever recognize as the source of all the good that is done in the earth, that I now propose through you, to the British Conference and to the Wesleyan Methodist Missionaries in the Provinces of Nova Scotia and New Brunswick, to purchase an eligible site and erect suitable buildings in Sackville, in the County of Westmoreland, for the establishment of a School of the description mentioned, in which not only the elementary, but higher branches of education may be taught; to be altogether under the control and management of the British Conference, in connection with the Wesleyan Missionaries in these Provinces.

If my proposal should be approved of, and the offer I now make accepted, I will proceed at once to make preparations, so that the buildings may be erected in the course of next year; and I will, as a further inducement, give, by the blessings of God, £100 per annum for ten years.

I shall be glad to hear that my offer is accepted, and to have the earliest intimation of your decision on this subject and, am,

Reverend and dear sir,
Yours Sincerely,
C. F. Allison[83]

Allison's offer was, of course, accepted. The corner-stone of the new institution was laid on July 9, 1840, and on January 19, 1843, Mount Allison Wesleyan Academy commenced teaching with Humphrey Pickard as principal.

The career of the first Principal indicates the close association between the Academy and Methodism. Pickard, who was born in Fredericton of New England Puritan stock, was a graduate of Wesleyan Academy, Wilbraham, Massachusetts, and of Wesleyan College, Middletown, Connecticut. Having been a business man in Fredericton for a few years, he had experienced a religious awakening

---

[83]*Ibid.*, 130; *Mount Allison University Calendar, 1963–64,* 28.

and had entered the Methodist ministry. He had been pastor of a church in St. John, New Brunswick, and editor of the *British North American Methodist Magazine* which was published in the same city.

The original curriculum indicates that as in other contemporary schools, the emphasis was heavily classical but that under the heading "Literary and Scientific" a considerable variety of other subjects were included.

COURSE OF STUDY 1843-44

Classical

Latin Grammar and Exercise	Greek Lesson
Latin Reader	Greek Grammar and Exercise
Caesar or Sallust	Jacob's Greek Reader
Virgil's Aeneid or Bucolics	Greek Testament
Cicero's Select Orations	Homer's Iliad
Horace	Graeca Majora
Cicero de Oratore	Aeschines and Demosthenes
Livy and Tacitus	De Corona
Roman and Grecian Antiquities and History, Ancient Geography, etc.	

Literary and Scientific

Algebra	Intellectual Philosophy
Geometry	Political Economy
Trigonometry, Plane and Spherical Mensuration of Superficies and Solids	Evidences of Christianity
	Natural History
	Chemistry
Mensuration of Height and Distances	Geology
Rhetoric	Mineralogy
Logic	Astronomy etc.
Moral Philosophy	History (added later)
	Botany[84]

In 1849, by an act of the New Brunswick legislature, the trustees of Wesleyan Academy were incorporated. In 1858, by an amending act of the New Brunswick legislature, the Academy achieved the status of a college. The act authorized the establishment of Mount Allison Wesleyan College which was vested with the power to confer degrees. The College opened under the presidency of Dr. Pickard with a faculty of five and a tutor. The first class in arts graduated in 1863.

As in the case of Victoria College, the Methodists in the Maritimes began by establishing a school which was intended to qualify men for any station in life. Mount Allison was not a theological seminary. However, during its first stage as a school, and from 1858, as a college,

[84]Falconer, and Watson, *Brief History of Pine Hill*, 32.

it permitted candidates for the ministry to receive academic training. In 1861, for the first time, formal instruction in theology was provided with the appointment of Charles De Wolfe as professor of theology.

De Wolfe's career, like Pickard's, indicates the close association of Methodism with Mount Allison. Born in Wolfville, he had been brought up a Baptist. While a student in law in Halifax, he experienced conversion, became a Methodist and soon a local preacher. In 1836, he gave up the study of law and became a candidate for the ministry. He studied in England, was ordained at the City Road Chapel, returned to Nova Scotia and soon became an outstanding minister. As professor of theology, he was vested with direction of all probationers and others hoping to enter the ministry. De Wolfe's appointment indicated the close co-operation between the Church and the College: Mount Allison provided the facilities for his work but he was paid by the Methodist Conference.

The establishment of Acadia College was the result of allegedly unfair treatment of a leading Baptist by the non-sectarian Dalhousie College. The application of E. A. Crawley, a leading Baptist minister and scholar, for appointment to Dalhousie was refused and instead two Presbyterians were appointed. Crawley, in letters to the *Nova Scotian* on September 23, and October 4, 1838, claimed that his rejection was because of his religious affiliation.[85] As a result, Crawley, John Pryor, who had just resigned as principal of Horton Academy in order to continue his theological studies, and the Rev. I. E. Bill, the pastor of Nictaux, decided to establish a college at Wolfville in connection with Horton Academy. They worked through the Baptist Education Society which had established Horton and which also established the college. The college was to be under the same government as the Academy. No restrictions of a denominational character were to be imposed on the professors or the students.

Although the college opened in 1839, there was a delay of two years before its incorporation. The bill to incorporate the institution as Queen's College passed the legislature in 1839, but was denied the royal signature since exception was taken to the name. On March 10, 1841, the Executive Committee of the Baptist Education Society changed the name to Acadia. The amended bill of incorporation passed the legislature on March 10 and secured the royal signature on December 10, 1841.

Acadia, as an extension of Horton, represented the determination to have higher education free of Anglican control. The Baptists would

[85]R. S. Longley, *Acadia University*, 28–9.

have been happy enough to participate in the work of non-sectarian Dalhousie but since this appeared to them impracticable after the Crawley incident, they had determined to "go it alone." Like Victoria, it provided a broader and more practical curriculum than was provided for in the more strictly classical curricula of the Anglican colleges. Like Victoria also, Acadia stressed the place of moral and religious instruction as part of the arts course. Religion was not to be taught to arts students as a separate course but it was to be an integral part of courses in arts subjects.

John Mockett Cramp, in his inaugural address as president in 1851, described the place of religion in the system at Acadia. Cramp called attention to

the importance of religious influence, pervading the whole course of study, and sanctifying, so to speak, all the arrangements. This College is open to all denominations, no religious tests being imposed either on students or Professors; nevertheless, we must claim the right of aiming to imbue literature with the spirit of religion, and of inculcating, from time to time, those principles of our common Christianity, and those moral lessons which are admitted by all who wish to shun the reproach of infidelity.

Cramp continued,

Habitual recognition of God, should distinguish every seat of learning, so that while the din of controversy is never heard, and party contentions are unknown, all may be taught that 'the fear of the Lord is the beginning of wisdom.' It has been well observed, that 'it is our educated young men who will give the tone to society, and control the destiny of the generation in which they live.' How desirable, nay even necessary, it is that the education they receive, while truly liberal in its plans and provisions, should be connected with that moral conservatism, without which, the advantages of knowledge itself may prove comparatively valueless.[86]

Acadia opened in 1839 with a staff of two professors, John Pryor and E. A. Crawley. The curriculum was basically classical but with the addition of rhetoric, logic, mathematics, and natural philosophy (i.e. science). Pryor taught the classics, and all the great Greek and Roman writers from Homer and Demosthenes to Cicero and Tacitus. He also taught natural philosophy during the first year.

Crawley taught rhetoric, logic, moral philosophy and mathematics. He has been described as a gifted teacher and a born leader. He did much to shape the early curriculum of the College and was a master of graceful and accurate English. Among the text books which he used were Richard Whately's *Logic* and Weyland's *Ethics*.

[86] T. A. Higgins, *The Life of John Mockett Cramp* (Montreal, 1887), 141.

Crawley participated in a famous debate with the redoubtable Joseph Howe at a place named Onslow on October 9, 1843, over the respective merits of provincial universities and small colleges. Howe had opposed the efforts of the Baptists to secure increased aid from the legislature for Horton and Acadia.[87] The result of the Howe-Crawley debate was indecisive, both sides claiming a victory.[88]

In 1840, the science part of the curriculum was greatly strengthened by the appointment of Isaac Chipman as professor of mathematics and natural philosophy. Chipman had been educated at Horton Academy, Colby College, then Waterville College, Maine. He was a thorough and skilful instructor. He collected hundreds of specimens for the classroom and the college museum and used the specimens to give his lectures a higher degree of vitality. In his comparatively brief period at Acadia (he was drowned in 1852) he did much to inspire his students with a deeper regard for learning and investigation.

In 1844, Acadia decided to become a theological seminary as well as a liberal arts college. Crawley accordingly became the first professor of theology.

In 1851, Acadia and Horton separated. Soon afterward the college came under the control of the Baptist Convention of Nova Scotia, New Brunswick, and Prince Edward Island.

John Mockett Cramp, who became president of Acadia in 1851 laid great stress upon the broadening of the course. In his inaugural address in 1851, he asserted:

A clear and comprehensive view of our present position and prospects will enable us to discern the path of duty. It is especially incumbent on us to bear in mind that the age is remarkably progressive, and that all institutions must keep pace with it, or sink in public estimation. The range of study is extending every year, as the boundaries of science expand, so that the instructor finds it necessary to incorporate additional branches in his course, and the student is compelled, if he would avoid the reproach of ignorance, to spend much time in making acquisitions for which there was no demand in the days of his predecessors; while the ancient standards of learning still retain, and must continue to retain, their place and preeminence.[89]

---

[87]In accepting government aid, Acadia followed the opposite principle to that of the Baptist colleges in Ontario, the Canadian Literary Institute, and McMaster University which rejected government aid, even at the municipal level.

[88]Longley, *Acadia University*, chapter V. After the debate the audience voted. Sheriff Blanchard, a friend of Howe's made the vote Howe 170, Crawley 159; Vice-Chairman King, who was pro-Crawley, counted Crawley 202 and Howe 161.

[89]Higgins, *Life of Cramp*, 139–40.

THE GOLDEN AGE

Acadia's answer to the need for a broad course is indicated by its programme of instruction for 1851 which included:

The Greek and Latin Classes

Mathematics, including Geometry, Algebra, Trigonometry, with their application to Mensuration of Surfaces and Solids, and to Navigation, Surveying, etc., Differential and Integral Calculus, Natural Philosophy, including Mechanics, Hydrostatics, Pneumatics, and Optics.

Chemistry.

Astronomy.

Intellectual Philosophy.

Moral Philosophy and Evidences of Christianity.

Logic and Rhetoric.

The French Language.

A monthly Lecture . . . . on subjects not included in the course.[90]

This impressive-looking programme was all taught by two men: Cramp and Isaac Chipman. Chipman taught mathematics and science, while Cramp taught the literary subjects.

Cramp was a gifted teacher; in the face of this staggering programme he was able to impress the students with his erudition in the fields of classics, philosophy, and theology. Higgins has described Cramp's versatility as well as his surprisingly sound grasp of the subjects he taught.

> If the class were required to translate a difficult Latin book, it was soon found that the teacher could go minutely into the grammatical structure of the sentences and make the meaning plain, and also give the history of the author and his contemporaries, and the circumstances under which the book was written.
>
> If it were an oration of Demosthenes, or a Greek play, not only were the Greek roots uprooted, but Grecian history, literature and mythology were all freely taxed, to make enigmatical references bear their part in the composition. If it were a lesson in moral science, not only were the thoughts of the text book thoroughly weighed, but the views of other authors on the same subject were placed side by side with them, to see how far they agreed, and where they differed. If it were a lesson in theology, for ministerial students, it was found that every doctrine of the Bible had been most deeply pondered, the circumstances of every inspired author thoroughly considered, the contemporary literature of each book gathered up, the errors or evils which needed correction, and called forth the warning, were alluded to.

Higgins concluded:

> All of which would call forth no special comment, if a specialist had been dealing with each subject. . . . But the wonder was to find any one man

---

[90] *Ibid.*, 146–7.

who could act so well the part of a specialist on such a variety of dissimilar subjects.[91]

In a public address delivered in 1853, Cramp described the theological course at Acadia, indicating the central place occupied by the Bible in his own thinking and that of Acadia. He said that Theology was the "Queen of the Sciences" and that its object was to learn the truth of God as contained in the Bible. He asserted:

the perpetual need of reminding the inquirer that if he would have pure theology, he must derive it from the Bible, and the Bible only, and of so ordering, so directing his studies that the holy book may be ever before him —the mine which he will ceaselessly explore—the fountain at which he will daily slake his thirst,—the authority from which there is no appeal. This will be the distinguishing feature of the instructions imparted in the Theological Institute.

In the same lecture, Cramp indicated the orthodox Protestant thinking of the institution.

The faculty, moreover, rejoice that Christianity is the revelation of God's grace to the guilty—that it makes known the way in which He can be just, and the justifier of him which believeth in Jesus, even by sending his own Son, and that 'by grace we are saved.'[92]

After the death of Chipman in 1852, Crawley, who had gone into pastoral work, returned to Acadia where he divided the teaching duties with Cramp. In 1853, Crawley was president of the College and also taught Hebrew and Biblical interpretation in the Theological Institute and taught logic, political economy and history in the College.

The subsequent history of the staff illustrates the vicissitudes of a small, struggling church college. Changes were frequent and periods of service at the College were brief. Artemas Wyman Sawyer was appointed professor of classics in 1855 at an annual salary of a thousand dollars. In 1856, A. P. S. Stuart came to Acadia as professor of mathematics and science, but in the same year Crawley resigned. Cramp was in charge of both the College and the Theological Institute with the title of President of the Faculty. He still had a very heavy teaching load. Gustav Pople was engaged to teach modern languages, but the experiment failed from lack of interest and lack of funds. Stuart resigned in 1858 as the result of a financial crisis at Acadia. Alfred Chipman was invited to be a tutor in science and mathematics with the understanding that he succeed to the chair of his late brother,

[91]*Ibid.*, 148.   [92]*Ibid.*, 161–3.

Isaac but he decided to devote his life to the ministry. D. F. Higgins became tutor and later professor of mathematics. In 1860, James DeMill succeeded Sawyer in the Chair of Classics.

The demands of a frontier church on a church college were indicated by a special course which Dr. Cramp put on for theological students "compelled to be satisfied with an English education." The course had no classics and consisted of mathematics, history, rhetoric, logic, moral science, political economy, chemistry, geology, and the evidences of Christianity. Cramp had some misgivings about the course. All candidates proceeding to a degree were required to take the classical course, but the needs of the ministry had compelled this relaxation of requirements for theological students.

Classics was still regarded as of central importance at Acadia. When honours work was first introduced it was in the field of classics. In 1862-66 a change in the curriculum enabled students of first class standing to graduate with honours by completing additional work in classics. The first honors students graduated in 1864.

After the reduction of Pictou Academy to the status of a grammar school at the end of the decade of the eighteen-thirties, Presbyterian institutions of higher education in the Maritimes had a chequered career.[93] After Thomas McCulloch had accepted the presidency of Dalhousie and had moved to Halifax in 1839, he continued the work of the Theological Hall, which had been a part of Pictou, until his death in 1843. McCulloch was succeeded as professor of theology by Dr. Keir of Princetown, Prince Edward Island. Keir's house at Princetown was the temporary abode of the College. He was assisted by the Rev. James Ross.

In 1848, the Secession Church, which had been identified with Pictou made a second attempt to establish a seminary teaching both arts and theology. The West River Seminary in Nova Scotia was opened under the principalship of the Rev. James Ross. Ross began by teaching arts subjects and in 1849 he began instruction in theology. The institution flourished briefly and in 1858 was moved to Truro.

In 1860, the Synods of the Secession Church (the Presbyterian Church of Nova Scotia) and of the Free Church united to form the Synod of the Presbyterian Church of the Lower Provinces. This settled the future of the Truro college. The theological section was moved to Halifax in 1860 and was combined with the Free Church College which had been established in 1848. The two colleges were

[93]Falconer, and Watson, *Pine Hill Divinity Hall.*

joined to form the United Colleges, usually referred to as "the Theological Hall."

The arts section of the Truro college remained at Truro for another three years. In 1863, when Dalhousie was reorganized, the Presbyterians adopted the traditional Presbyterian idea that the church should concentrate on teaching in theology and should leave arts to the secular authorities, either public or private. The arts students and three of their professors were moved from Truro to Halifax and joined to Dalhousie. Two of the Truro professors were paid until their retirement by the Synod of the Presbyterian Church of the Lower Provinces. The Synod of the Church of Scotland endowed the Chair of Mathematics of Dalhousie. Arts training was thus taken out of the hands of the Presbyterian Church which concentrated its attention upon instruction in theology.

The reforms of the 1827-30 period removing religious tests for students made King's College, Nova Scotia less exclusive but did not alter its Anglican character, since the President, Professors and Fellows must still be Anglicans.[94]

Under this new dispensation, the College made moderate progress despite repeated efforts by the British government to get King's to move to Halifax and amalgamate with Dalhousie. These attempts were successfully resisted by the Board of Governors. The final action of the Governors in resisting the proposal to amalgamate was the passage of a series of resolutions on March 6, 1837. In one of these the Governors affirmed their "confident hope" that King's "Will long continue to dispense the important benefits which it has afforded for nearly half a century to this part of his Majesty's Dominions."[95]

The modest record of King's as well as the character of its clientele was indicated by a statement of the Board, transmitted to the Secretary of State for the Colonies in November, 1835. In the period from 1802 to 1835 the College had produced one hundred and fifty-eight graduates, an average of about five per annum, including fifty-three clergymen; fifty-six members of the legal profession, thirty-nine in the army or navy or without profession, and ten members of the medical profession.

Dr. William Cochran in a memorial presented on the occasion of his resignation as vice-president of King's also gave an indication of the Anglican and Tory character of the institution. Dr. Cochran reckoned among his pupils now living in British North America, one

[94]Hind, *The University of King's College, 1890*, 69-105.
[95]*Ibid.*, 80.

bishop, one archdeacon, many missionaries and other clergy, one chief justice, six judges, one attorney-general, two solicitors-general, "very many eminent barristers, besides many of great worth in other professions."

There was a gradual curtailment of the financial support which King's secured from the British and Provincial governments and from the great British Missionary Societies, the Society for the Promotion of Christian Knowledge, and the Society for the Propagation of the Gospel. On August 2, 1832, Lord Goderich informed the Lieutenant-Governor that the grant of the Imperial Parliament to King's was to be one thousand pounds in 1833, five hundred pounds in 1834, and that it would then cease. In 1851 the Nova Scotia legislature repealed the act passed in 1787 endowing King's with four hundred pounds sterling per annum. The S.P.C.K. granted two hundred pounds sterling per annum in 1837 for divinity scholarships, but began to scale down the grant in 1843 and discontinued it in 1846. The S.P.G., which served as the distributor to the colonial church of funds granted by the British Parliament, in 1838 agreed to continue a grant of five hundred pounds a year to King's, despite the withdrawal of the British parliamentary grant. The S.P.G. discontinued this grant in 1846 but continued another annual grant of three hundred pounds for divinity scholarships and fellowships, which it had commenced in 1841, until 1871.

So long as King's was supported by the British and Provincial legislatures, its Board of Governors consisted largely of government officials. Having lost most of its government financial support, the College was relieved of this element of public control. A new act of incorporation which received the royal assent on April 14, 1853 (16 Vict., cap. 66) left the Charter of 1802 undisturbed, but altered the organization of the College. Previously, the Board of Governors had consisted of political officials: the Lieutenant-Governor, the Chief Justice, the Speaker of the House of Assembly and so on. The new Board of Governors was to be elected by the alumni of the College. All the Governors were required to be Anglicans. The Bishop of Nova Scotia was to be president of the Board and visitor. In addition to holding all college property, the Governors were to control the government of students and the appointment of the Professors, Fellows, and Scholars.

The old political Board which in 1851 had consisted of seven Anglicans, three Presbyterians, and one "not a member of the Church of England" was replaced by a new completely Anglican Board, elected by the alumni, on February 11, 1854. King's thus became a strictly denominational college, controlled by the Church of England and by its own alumni.

This did not mean that King's was cut off from all support by the legislature but it ceased to occupy a position of special privilege compared with that of other denominational colleges in Nova Scotia. In 1853, the Nova Scotia legislature placed King's upon the same footing as Acadia by a grant of a thousand dollars per annum and then left the College to pursue its own career.

The character of the course offered at King's was indicated by the list of its faculty in 1854. Like the other Anglican colleges it consisted in the original divinity-classics-mathematics core which had begun to be supplemented by science and modern languages. The faculty, still only five, fifty-two years after the grant of the royal charter, consisted of the Rev. G. McCawley, president and professor of classics; M. J. Hemsley, professor of mathematics; the Rev. G. W. Hill, professor of pastoral theology; Henry How, professor of chemistry and natural philosophy; and H. Shefelhagen, professor of modern languages.

When the first Bishop of Newfoundland, A. G. Spencer arrived in the colony in 1839, there were only eight clergy in his entire diocese. In order to provide much needed clergy the Bishop established "The Theological Institution" at St. John's in 1841. Its students lived in four private lodgings and attended lectures in a schoolroom in the Mall close to St. Thomas' Church. In 1844 the second Bishop, Edward Feild, described the college as "a poor wooden building in which six students attended daily to receive instruction from the clergyman of St. Thomas' Church."[96] In 1847 Feild obtained a house where the students could live together on the site of the future college. In a prospectus written in 1847, Feild said it was his wish to erect characteristic buildings of wood and stone "sufficient for a small college and collegiate school, with a chapel, hall, library, and lodgings for tutors etc."[97] The Bishop suggested that the institution be named Queen's College. By 1850 the first portion of the new buildings had been completed.

Like other Anglican colleges in British North America, Queen's was under the control of the Bishop. He called to his aid three of the resident clergy of St. John's to advise and assist him in its manage-

[96]J. J. Curling, and Charles Knapp, *Historical Notes concerning Queen's College, St. John's, Diocese of Newfoundland, 1842–1897* (London, 1898), 15; J. A. Meaden, *Queen's College Newfoundland* (St. John's, 1947), 4.
[97]Curling and Knapp, 14; Meaden, 5.

ment; but the Prospectus of 1847 made it quite clear that the Bishop was to "have power to appoint and remove, all the officers of the establishment, and to make, alter, and rescind the rules, etc."[98]

Queen's was primarily a theological college. Its chief purpose, as stated in Bishop Feild's *Directions and Regulations* in 1850, was "to prepare young men by a course of study, frugality, retirement and devotion[99] for the office and duties of Missionaries in Newfoundland."[100] The Bishop also wanted to make Queen's an imitation of King's College, Nova Scotia, with a liberal arts course as well as theology.[101] Perhaps with this end in view he specified that in addition to theology, instruction should be given in the Latin and Greek languages, English composition, and ancient and modern history. He further promised that encouragement would be afforded to the study of mathematics, logic, and music. The plan to form a liberal arts college did not materialize. A secondary school developed as a separate institution and was later called Bishop Feild College.

Bishop Feild's *Directions and Regulations* were formally read out to the students in the Hall of the College on January 19, 1850.[102] They indicated that the Bishop's intention was to maintain a meticulously-controlled institution. The reading, meals, clothing, furniture, the time of rising and retiring, the daily devotions and Sunday duties of the students were all prescribed. Liberals would have been shocked at the Bishop's rule concerning books and newspapers.

All the books of each Student must be submitted to the Principal's inspection whenever he may require it; and any books which he considers improper or unsuitable must be removed.
No periodicals or newspapers may be introduced, either for general or private use, without the Principal's sanction.[103]

The college menu was carefully described. The first meal of the day was to consist of bread and butter with coffee; the last meal of bread

[98]Curling and Knapp, 15; Meaden, 18.
[99]Bishop Feild's ideas on "frugality, retirement and devotion" were not entirely shared by the Anglican establishment at Quebec City. When Feild visited Quebec for a conference of Bishops, he was described by Bishop Mountain's wife as "a regular monk." [Nicolls Papers, Mrs. Mountain to Harriet Nicolls, Sept. 26, 1851.] In a subsequent letter written on Sept. 30, 1851, Mrs. Mountain made a further comment about Feild, "He is so kind and so complying in *most* things, though hard to convince that he is in the wrong, all meek and humble minded as I believe him to be; but we must excuse a *little* prejudice and warped judgment in a monk."
[100]Curling, and Knapp, *Historical Notes*, 35.
[101]Meaden, *Queen's College*, 18.
[102]Curling, and Knapp, 33–49.
[103]*Ibid.*, 36.

and butter with tea. Brewis (ship's biscuit soaked in water and boiled), meal, and corn cakes were to be served occasionally. Dinner was to consist, on ordinary days, of meat with vegetables and hard bread. Puddings and tarts were to be served occasionally. More Spartan fare was provided on days of fasting and abstinence for those who could not wholly fast. The missionary character of the college was indicated by the Bishop's further statement:

It will be wise to learn to forego the use of milk, because not only at sea, but in many out-harbors, we cannot procure it. For the same reasons the Students should accustom themselves to hard bread and fish, the only food to be obtained, at particular seasons, or, it may be, the greater part of the year, in the small and remote settlements.[104]

Tobacco in every shape was prohibited and the students were warned against eccentricities of dress. "No fancy waistcoats, or fantastic hats, or novel neckcloths" would be allowed. The hour of rising was six o'clock in the summer and half-past six in the winter. The Bishop expressed the hope that each student would partake of the Lord's Supper once a month and added, "The breakfast or other meal taken before receiving the Sacrament should be as sparing and simple as possible."[105]

An account of early college financing indicates the complete dependence of Queen's on the mother country in the early period. In the years before 1866, the College was kept up by an annual grant of three hundred pounds from the S.P.G.[106] In 1852 the S.P.C.K. made a grant of two thousand pounds.[107] In 1865, the S.P.G. agreed to continue the grant for the College, as well as large grants for the other expenses of the Newfoundland Church, for three years, on condition that the Bishop try to form an endowment fund within the three year period.[108] The Bishop set out to raise an endowment fund of six thousand pounds. It was characteristic of colonial church financing that the Bishop asserted in his letter of July 2, 1866, to the Church of England in Newfoundland, "*If* a real and good commencement be made in this country, I will cheerfully undertake to solicit further subscriptions in England."[109] By 1871, the Bishop was able to report that he had raised over six thousand pounds of which two thousand eight hundred and fifty had been raised in Newfoundland.[110] Five hundred pounds was contributed by the Bishop himself. The

[104]*Ibid.*, 38–9.
[105]*Ibid.*, 44–5.
[107]*Ibid.*, 19.
[109]*Ibid.*, 24.
[106]*Ibid.*, 19, 21.
[108]*Ibid.*, 21.
[110]*Ibid.*, 26–9.

total sum finally raised was seven thousand five hundred pounds. The money was placed in the hands of the S.P.G. to be invested so that the annual income could be paid for the maintenance of the College. By 1866, the College had trained twenty clergymen for work in the Newfoundland Church.[111]

St. John's College, an Anglican institution in Winnipeg, had its origins in a church school, the Red River Academy, which was established in 1833 by the Rev. David T. Jones.[112] Jones, who was supported by the C.M.S., had arrived at Red River in 1823 as the Chaplain of the Hudson's Bay Company and general missionary in the district. Red River Academy was intended to be, in Jones' words, "a respectable seminary on a large scale in this settlement for the moral improvement, religious instruction and general education of boys; the sons of Gentlemen belonging to the Fur Trade."[113] The school had a strong Evangelical background since most of the clergy associated with it had close connections with the C.M.S. which was dominantly Evangelical. However, the other great missionary societies, which were not Evangelical, the S.P.C.K. and the S.P.G. also gave it support. Red River Academy, which began as a co-educational institution, had many vicissitudes. It was reorganized by Bishop David Anderson, a man characterized by his "evangelical outlook and zeal," who became the first bishop of Rupert's Land in 1849. In Anderson's regime, the Academy became a theological seminary as well as a secondary school. In his charge to the clergy in 1850, Anderson said he had renamed the school "St. John's Collegiate School" and that, as a part of it, there would be an institution for the training of a native ministry, St. John's College. In the 1854–56 period, the S.P.G. paid the stipend of the Rev. Thomas Cochrane as being in charge of the "Collegiate School for the training, among others, of candidates for the Ministry." Cochrane, the son of a C.M.S. missionary at Red River, had been educated at the C.M.S. school in England for the sons of missionaries. In 1855, Anderson organized the first collegiate Board with a distinguished company of members. After 1856, the

[111]*Ibid.*, 22.
[112]Red River Academy was itself the successor to an earlier school established by the Rev. John West, chaplain to the Hudson's Bay Company, 1820–23, on the site later occupied by St. John's College in North Winnipeg. The boys were taught by George Harbridge and the girls by his wife. There were three other Anglican schools in the district prior to the establishment of Red River Academy. See A. B. Baird, "History of the University of Manitoba," published in *Manitoba Essays* R. C. Lodge, ed., (Macmillan and Co., 1937).
[113]T. C. B. Boon, *The Anglican Church from the Bay to the Rockies* (Toronto, 1962), 27–8.

Bishop became more heavily involved in the expansion of work in the diocese and the bright hopes for St. John's faded. From 1856 to 1866, the school was closed and higher education lapsed in the Red River settlement.

The College was reorganized by Bishop Robert Machray, the second bishop of Rupert's Land, in 1865-67. After his arrival at Red River in 1865, he outlined his plans for the College, which, he proposed, was to consist of a theological school and a higher school for the Red River settlement. The C.M.S. placed the prospective head of the institution, the Rev. John Maclean on its staff as a "theological tutor." Maclean became warden of St. John's College as well as rector of St. John's Cathedral. The College began work on November 1, 1866.

At a conference of the clergy and laity of the Diocese of Rupert's Land in 1867, Bishop Machray made a vigorous appeal to the church to go into action: "Next to the Ministry of the Word and Sacraments comes the Office of educating the young, so that they may receive a sound and religious education."[114] He said that there were three senior theological students and twenty-six pupils in the college school, of which seven attended a junior theological class.

By the year of Confederation, Canadian Protestants had established twelve church colleges: Acadia, Albert, Bishop's, the three King's Colleges, McGill, Mount Allison, Queen's, Trinity, St. John's, and Victoria. In addition four theological seminaries, Huron, Queen's Newfoundland, Knox, Morrin and a succession of small Presbyterian colleges in Nova Scotia had been founded. Although we can speak of twelve church colleges started before 1867, three of the twelve, King's Fredericton, King's Toronto, and McGill had already ceased to be church colleges. The process of secularization had already begun. Later it was to become the lot of other church colleges. Affiliation with secular universities, the other destiny of church colleges, had still to be tried, although Baldwin, Elgin, and others had already suggested it in connection with the secularization of King's Toronto.

[114]*Ibid.*, 96.

4. Changing Ideas (1867-1890)

IN THE YEARS AFTER CONFEDERATION the church colleges were influenced by significant adjustments in Protestant thought in Canada. The impact of new ideas in science and Biblical criticism began to weaken the hold of the older faith. The new ideas were chiefly British in immediate origin. The conception of man as a sinner who could only be redeemed by divine grace was partially abandoned. It was coming to be replaced by the humanist conception of man as essentially good and capable of improvement, largely through his own efforts. Two volumes were of especial importance in the development of this humanist attitude: Darwin's *Origin of Species*, which had been published in 1859, and *Essays and Reviews* in 1860. In *Essays and Reviews* a group of English scholars undertook to introduce to the British public the German critical approach to the Scriptures.

Both Darwin and the Biblical critics tended to foster a humanist conception of man. While Darwin dethroned man from the position of a special creation, he flattered human pride by establishing him as the highest of the mammals and one who had come out on top in the struggle for survival through his own adaptability. In stressing the environmental and purely human aspects of Hebrew religious development, the Biblical critics tended to supplement the humanism which Darwin had helped to foster. Both the scientists and the Biblical critics tended to destroy the orthodox conception of the Bible as an inspired and authoritative volume. The result was a growing skepticism in regard to the supernatural aspects of Christianity.

One result of this trend toward skepticism was the effort of such British idealists as Edward Caird and T. H. Green to preserve the ethics of Christianity while sacrificing the ideas of an inspired Scripture and miraculous interventions upon which Christianity had been regarded as depending. Edward Caird (1835-1908) was Professor of moral philosophy at the University of Glasgow (1866-1893) and master of Balliol College, Oxford (1893-1908). T. H. Green (1836-1882) was Whyte's Professor of Moral Philosophy at Oxford. They were leaders of a group in Britain who were dissatisfied with the prevailing philosophies in their own country and turned to Germany for light. They believed that they found it in the philosophy of Kant, as modified and supplemented by Hegel.[1]

For a time after 1860 the churches in Canada were not much affected by the challenge of the Biblical critics and the biologists but the universities soon felt the impact.

An early advocate of the new ideas was George Munro Grant who became principal of Queen's in 1877. While still a Presbyterian minister in Nova Scotia, Grant developed the ideas which he later put forward at Queen's. In a sermon preached at Pictou in 1862, and later in Halifax, Grant criticized the attitude of the churches to the discoveries of science.[2] He felt that God spoke to man through the physical universe as well as through the Scriptures. Both were capable of critical examination and there could be no real contradiction between them when properly understood since both were part of God's universe. Grant therefore demanded freedom to examine both and to announce his findings. He asserted:

> If both are from the one author they will not contradict each other. So do not put me to the rack, as the Papists did with Galileo, if I find that the earth goes round the sun. And do not persecute and call me hard names, as many of the evangelicals are in the habit of doing, if I cannot find traces of the Noachian deluge in America, or if I find bits of pottery in Egypt or flint weapons in France which I believe were fashioned by men more than six thousand years ago. In neither case am I an infidel, but the reverse. I would be an infidel if I refused to believe what is shown unto me by the light that lighteth every man that cometh into the world. I may be mistaken in my inference, but show me that I am. Or your inferences from the Bible may be unwarranted. And until we settle which is right, had you not better give and take the benefit of the doubt.

Grant's appointment at Queen's appears to have been regarded as a triumph for the liberal side of the ecclesiastical and university world. His reputation was indicated in the students' song at his inauguration,

> For cash to build new halls and found new chairs,
> We here at Queen's have long remained in want,
> At least propitious Fortune hears our prayers
> And from her treasures send "a liberal Grant."[3]

Grant's inaugural lecture at Queen's was a notable indication of the influence of the new thought in biology and Biblical criticism.

---

[1] See article on T. H. Green in C. D. Warner, ed., *Library of the World's Best Literature*, XII (New York, 1913).
[2] W. L. Grant, and F. Hamilton, *Principal Grant* (Toronto, 1904), 77–80.
[3] *Ibid.*, 78–9, 206.

Grant reiterated the idea that there was a place for the Biblical critics and the scientists, but he said that people should be critical about them. The testaments and God, said Grant, were not going to be harmed by investigation. He suspected both "the orthodox" and "the advanced thinkers." Both types were, to some extent, wrong. Truth lay between them. He urged his hearers to cultivate both criticism and science. Darwinism, he said, could do no harm to theology. The true believer in God was never upset by the discoveries of the scientists. He denied that the Bible was "an inspired scientific text book." Any human system, including the explanation of nature derived from the Scriptures, was merely a convenience and should not be regarded as a substitute for truth. Professed believers should be judged by their actions and not by their opinions. The wise man, asserted Grant, will judge believers "not by their words but by their fruits; for, as Bunsen says, action and not thought is 'the final object of man, the highest reality of thought, and the safest if not the only safe standard of truth.' "[4]

Salem Bland, a distinguished Methodist minister and academic, has asserted that Grant exercised an important influence in spreading the ideas of Biblical criticism. Bland, a Queen's graduate, attended sessions of the Queen's Alumni Conferences at which Grant gave lectures. He was very much influenced by Grant's teaching "in the dangerous waters of modern biblical criticism" and concluded his description of the lectures with the assertion, "In the altered atmosphere of all the evangelical churches of Canada today, in regard to biblical criticism, Principal Grant seems to me to have been one of the largest factors."[5]

In Canadian universities, British idealism repeated its role of attempting to preserve the ethics of Christianity in a period of widespread doubt in reference to the supernatural aspects of Christianity. British idealism secured important spokesmen in Canada with the appointment of three philosophy professors in 1871–72: George Paxton Young to the University of Toronto, John Watson to Queen's, and John Clark Murray to McGill. All three attempted to repeat the role of the British idealists in devising a rational defence for the ethical values of Christianity. A volume based on the lectures of George Paxton Young entitled *The Ethics of Freedom* is an illuminating case study in the thought of these Canadian idealists.[6] Young's lectures

[4]*Queen's College Journal*, Dec. 15, 1877.
[5]Quoted in Grant, and Hamilton, *Principal Grant*, 490–91.
[6]George Paxton Young, *The Ethics of Freedom: Notes Selected, translated and arranged by his pupil, James Gibson Hume* (Toronto, 1911), 55–63.

indicated his ideas in regard to the ethical standard. He flatly contradicted the position of the English utilitarians "in setting up as a standard of right the tendency of action to produce pleasure." He declared that man's chief good was not the pursuit of pleasure but "the realization of the moral ideal." Man's knowledge of the moral ideal, argued Young, would always be imperfect but the ideal could be known "in so far as the moral nature has unfolded itself and thus exhibited the capabilities that are in it." It was the function of conscience to reveal to man the moral law.

Young thus contrived to preserve the moral law despite the onslaughts of the utilitarians. Moreover, he attributed to it an authority which orthodox Christians had accorded to the Scriptures or to the Church. The distinguishing characteristic of the moral faculty, argued Young, was its authority.

> It merely pronounces that the highest of the ends that may be before the mind, should be sought; and this declaration is *ipso facto* one of absolute authority. . . . In other words, the moral faculty, even if not sovereign "de facto" is conceived as sovereign "de jure," its sole function being to act as sovereign, to guide, command, prescribe. If it has not authority it is nothing. A *nominis umbra*. It is either authoritative, or there is no such faculty in man.[7]

In seeking to replace orthodox Christian thought with ethical idealism, Young, Watson, and Murray had a powerful impact on a whole generation of Canadian university students, including the Protestant clergy. Early Wycliffe students took courses from Young at Toronto; Watson was particularly important in his influence upon the Presbyterian clergy.[8]

The church colleges felt the influence of these changes of thought in the Anglo-Saxon world. Their character as church colleges before 1867 had depended upon the orthodoxy which characterized their teaching in theology and which also provided the atmosphere in which secular teaching was carried on. The changes in theological thought after 1860 gradually altered the whole tone of thought in the church colleges.

While the character of their thought was thus beginning to change, the church colleges continued to deal with the problems of organiza-

---

[7]*Ibid.*, 63.
[8]John A. Irving, "The Development of Philosophy in Central Canada from 1850 to 1900," *Canadian Historical Review*, XXXI, Sept., 1950, 252–87; "Philosophical Trends in Canada between 1850 and 1950," *Philosophy and Phenomenological Research*, XII (2), Dec., 1951, 233–8.

tion and support which had always confronted them. In the struggle for survival some church colleges affiliated with larger universities.[9] Others remained independent and tried to strengthen themselves by developing cognate services. Acadia established Faculties of Education, Music, Fine Arts, and Household Science; Bishop's added Faculties of Medicine, Law, and Dentistry.

The establishment of the University of Manitoba in 1877 provided the means for three denominational colleges, St. John's, St. Boniface, and Manitoba College to combine in the establishment of a larger, composite institution.[10]

Manitoba College had been founded to train clergy for service in the Presbyterian Church and laymen for public service in the professions or politics. The College developed out of Kildonan School where the Rev. John Black and David B. Whimster had begun advanced classes in 1869. In 1871, the Rev. George Bryce, a widely-read young scholar, replaced Whimster and Kildonan School was converted into Manitoba College. In 1872 the Rev. Thomas Hart joined the staff. The College was moved from Kildonan to Winnipeg in 1874 and by 1877 had developed to the point at which it could join with the older colleges on terms of full equality.

Manitoba College was an offshoot of the Presbyterian theological and classical colleges of the East. John Black was a graduate of Knox College, Bryce of University and Knox Colleges, and Hart of Queen's and Edinburgh. The Rev. James Robertson, a leader of the Presbyterian Church in the development of Manitoba College was a graduate of University College and Princeton University.

Like Queen's, Manitoba combined teaching in classics and mathematics with a Scottish concern for mental and moral philosophy. Of the early teachers at Manitoba College, George Bryce was a brilliant and versatile figure, prominent in the life of the college, the Presbyterian Church, the Manitoba and Winnipeg school systems, and a prolific writer, particularly on the history of western Canada. Dr. Andrew Baird, one of Bryce's colleagues, recalled, "Dr. Bryce was admirably fitted for his work as a pioneer . . . he was versatile and capable of giving help and even leadership in all sorts of spheres. Always cheerful, always ready, there were few benevolent or religious enterprises in which he had no hand."[11] Thomas Hart was a quieter

---

[9]For example, Victoria, Manitoba, St. John's, and Wesley affiliated with larger institutions.
[10]W. L. Morton, *One University* (Toronto, 1957).
[11]A. B. Baird, "The Story of Manitoba College," radio script, Feb. 12, 1930.

but equally valuable type, an admirable complement to Bryce. With fewer outside commitments than Bryce, Hart

was always on hand and kept the wheels going round. One of the gentlest and kindliest of men, one whose rebuke even to slackers in his class was so mild and even so diffident, was so memorable that men who had no gift for Greek which was compulsory in those days plugged faithfully because even their modest degree of success so pleased their beloved teacher.[12]

In Chapter III the distinction was noted between the Queen's and Knox conceptions of the appropriate role of the church in higher education. Queen's had stood for the union of theology and the liberal arts in a denominational university. Knox represented the idea that the role of the church was to train the clergy, leaving liberal arts to the secular universities. Manitoba, in a sense, represented both traditions. It provided training in the liberal arts for candidates proceeding to the other professions as well as training the clergy; but under the influence of Black, Bryce, and Robertson, it was primarily in the Knox tradition and made training in theology its principal concern.

After the reorganization described in the last chapter, St. John's was incorporated by act of the Manitoba legislature on May 3, 1871. In 1874 regularly endowed professorships were established in systematic and exegetical theology, ecclesiastical history, and music. On June 12, 1876, when Bishop Machray handed the College over to the care of the Synod, he said, "When we look to the future a further question is pressed upon us—namely, Education. I feel increasingly the importance of our being able to raise up a Ministry of our own. . . . The building up of this College has been my great effort."[13]

The University of Manitoba was established in 1877 as a non-denominational, provincial, but not a state-supported university. The preamble to the University Act of 1877 stated that the University was to be an examining and degree-granting, but not a teaching body. The teaching was to be entirely in the hands of the federating colleges: St. John's, Manitoba and St. Boniface. The government of the University was to be carried on by the Chancellor and the Vice-Chancellor, both appointed by the Lieutenant-Governor-in-Council, and a council of twenty-six members, of whom twenty-one represented the three colleges. Academic matters were delegated by the council to a board of studies, consisting of two representatives nominated by each college and two nominated by the council.

[12]*Ibid.*
[13]Quoted in T. C. Boon, *The Anglican Church from the Bay to the Rockies* (Toronto, 1962), 96.

An examination of the curriculum of the University is relevant in this volume since it was co-operatively produced by three church colleges. After a series of meetings held at St. John's, the Board of Studies decided to adopt the classical curriculum of the English colleges. St. Boniface agreed to introduce more mathematics and natural science and Manitoba to give a greater emphasis to classics.

The Board of Studies then elaborated a curriculum leading to the degree. The matriculation, or university entrance examination was known as the "preliminary examination." It was required of all non-collegiate and of most college students. Students wrote an examination at the end of the first year, known, as at Trinity, as the "previous examination." Students, entering the second year, might take the special or honours course, or the general course. They wrote the "junior examination" at the end of the second year and the "final examination" at the end of the third or final year.

The subjects on which papers were written in the preliminary examination were Latin, Greek, modern languages including English, and mathematics—thirteen papers in all. In the previous examination the papers were in Latin, Greek, modern languages, mathematics and the rudiments of one of the natural sciences. The final or senior examination in the general course consisted of papers in Latin, Greek, mathematics, natural science, and assigned subjects in logic, metaphysics, and ethics—a total of eleven papers. Papers might be set and answered in English or French. From the first, a generous latitude was allowed St. Boniface, and the other colleges, in the prescription of texts and courses of study in philosophy and history. A college might substitute, on approval by the council, for an objectionable text one of equivalent standard.

The purpose of the special or honours courses was "a more thorough knowledge of some one department of knowledge" together with high scholastic standing. In the 1877–89 period honours courses were offered in mathematics, classics, natural science, modern languages, and mental and moral science. For entrance to the honours course the candidate offered standing in the previous examination for the ordinary degree as well as standing in mathematics, chemistry, logic, and ethics. In each course papers were prepared in the department of specialization and in the prescribed ancillary subjects. The result was intensive courses of study which only the best students could master.

The establishment of the University of Manitoba was an important landmark in the history of church colleges in Canada. It meant that the component colleges were able to continue the liberal arts course in a church atmosphere, while sharing in the benefits of membership in a larger body. The unique Canadian achievement in higher education, the working out of a relationship between church colleges and secular universities had begun.

Although it did not join the university until 1888, Wesley, the Methodist College, was begun in 1873, when the Conference of the Wesleyan Methodist Church opened the Wesleyan Institute, a secondary school. Its rise, like that of Manitoba College, marked the inflow of members of its denomination from eastern Canada and the British Isles. In 1877, Wesley College was incorporated and provision was made for its affiliation with the University of Manitoba. Wesley was unable to meet the qualifications for affiliation until after the union of the Wesleyan Methodist Church and the Episcopalian Methodist Church in 1884 had enabled the Methodists to put Wesley on a proper footing. A canvass for funds, begun in 1886, made it possible to expand the school into a college and in 1888 to affiliate with the University.

Wesley, an offspring of Victoria, represented the same tradition of denominational independence and the same distrust of a state or church monopoly of higher education. It represented too, a firm belief in the teaching of the liberal arts in the same college with theology. Wesley was in the tradition of Egerton Ryerson in emphasizing the teaching of the liberal arts without regard for denominational ideas of religion and churchmanship. Like most of the other church colleges, it admitted all students without religious tests. The first calendar announced, "Wesley College welcomes to its advantages students of any denomination whatever." The College developed the tradition of an autonomous, academically self-sufficient college within the University.

To a large extent the early success, indeed the survival, of Wesley College was a result of the character and ability of its first Principal, Dr. Joseph Walter Sparling. Sparling had been born and brought up on a farm near St. Mary's, Ontario. He had been educated at the St. Mary's High School and Victoria College. Ordained to the Methodist ministry at Belleville in 1871, he had served in the Methodist pastorate in Montreal, Aylmer (Quebec Province), Ottawa, and Kingston.

As Principal of Wesley, Sparling was a very successful financial administrator. He was tireless in canvassing the western Methodist constituency to support the College. One of his colleagues wrote later, "Every congregation, large and small, from the head of the Lakes to the snow-capped peaks of the Rockies, was yearly made, by the financial appeal, college conscious."[14] He had great physical vigour and an Irish geniality which enabled him "to find ready access to the pockets, purses, and fortunes of men."[15] Sparling was principal at a time when the institution was entirely dependent upon the liberality of individual subscribers. Yet he left it with a valuable property on Portage Avenue "and without one dollar of debt against it."[16] His gifts as an educator consisted less in the ability to teach than in the unerring skill with which he chose his staff. He was almost solely responsible for the choice of his faculty. He chose able colleagues and elicited their loyalty and unsparing co-operation. The appraisal of Sparling by J. H. Riddell, one of his successors as principal, was measured and just:

> He lived through eventful days in the Middle West. His sanity, good judgment and unfailing optimism, did much to lay broad and deep the foundations of religious and educational life on the prairies and beyond. He was a wise administrator and beyond that a broad-minded capable citizen.[17]

Sparling's two colleagues in 1888 were R. H. Cochrane who taught mathematics, classics and some English, and G. J. Laird, who taught science and moderns. Cochrane, a former high school teacher in Ontario, appears to have made a fine impression on his students. Fifty years later one of them, Dr. W. A. Cooke, wrote:

> The students were impressed with the information that Prof. Cochrane was the most efficient and successful high school teacher in Ontario. We did not doubt this when he was leading us to a finer appreciation of English literature, and believed it with conviction, when in mathematics he got away down to the foundations, as it seemed to us, of that department of human thought. To some of us it seemed that we had never had a teacher before.[18]

G. J. Laird, who had a Breslau degree, represented the German tradition in Canadian education. In 1892 J. H. Riddell was appointed to teach classics and so began a long career in the service of Wesley College.

The shift of Manitoba College toward a primary emphasis on theology was gradual in the years after the establishment of the University of Manitoba. Previous to 1883, Manitoba College was an arts college exclusively, though with the help of Black and Robertson it had been able to prepare men in theology. During 1883, at the request of the

[14] J. H. Riddell, *Methodism and the Middle West* (Toronto, 1946), 168.
[15] J. H. Riddell, *Address delivered at the Semi-Centennial Anniversary of the University of Manitoba*, Oct. 6, 1927.
[16] *Manitoba Free Press*, June 7, 1912.
[17] Riddell, *Methodism and the Middle West*, 325.
[18] *Winnipeg Free Press*, May 28, 1938.

Presbytery of Winnipeg, the General Assembly established a theological department and appointed the Rev. John Mark King as principal of the College and professor of theology.

King was largely responsible for the continuing success of Manitoba College in the vital area of college finance and in the increase in the number of students. He represented the German tradition in biblical scholarship. Dr. Baird recalled of him:

A graduate of the University of Edinburgh who had distinguished himself in the departments of philosophy and mathematics, and who had supplemented this with post-graduate training in the University of Marburg in Germany, he came to Manitoba in the fulness of his powers. He had quite unusual gifts as a teacher. His mind was analytical and delighted in making distinctions between things or opinions which are liable to be confused with each other but which ought to be kept separate. Quite beyond his gifts as a teacher was the impression made by the intensity and weight of his moral character. He demanded much of his students, but first of all he gave himself to them without stint. Many of us loved him, some feared him, assuredly nobody ignored him. As an administrator he extricated the College from debt, set it firmly on its feet financially and left it with a considerable endowment. The admiring enthusiasm of a Scottish friend who knew his record at first hand applied to him the encomium bestowed upon the Emperor Augustus "He found Rome brick and left it marble." In a moral and spiritual sense this was not far from the truth about Dr. King.[19]

The Theological Department was gradually strengthened by additions to the staff, notably Dr. Baird who joined the staff in 1887 and was appointed professor of Hebrew and church history in 1891 and the Rev. E. Guthrie Perry who became professor of Old Testament language and literature in 1905. Baird was conservative in his approach to the Scriptures; but Perry, a Ph.D. of Leipzig, expounded a more critical approach to the Scriptures. Despite this increasing emphasis on theology, Manitoba remained an arts college until 1914.

During the years between 1877 and the end of the century, St. John's enjoyed a phase of progress. During this period Bishop Machray improved the financial condition of St. John's and strengthened its staff. In 1883, one wing of the new building on the west side of Main Street was erected. Academically the years between 1880 and 1900 were years of some brilliance for staff and students. The Bishop himself occupied the Chair of Church History and Liturgics until 1883 when he appointed his nephew and namesake, Canon Robert Machray, who had just returned from Cambridge. The eloquent J. D. O'Meara, a graduate of Toronto and Huron College, was appointed

---

[19] A. B. Baird, "The Story of Manitoba College," 5.

professor of systematic theology in 1873. Canon S. P. Matheson, later to be the Anglican primate of all Canada, was professor of exegetical theology. Other members of the faculty were Canon J. F. Coombes, the professor of music and the Rev. J. F. Cross who became Machray Fellow in Mathematics when he returned from Cambridge in 1898.[20]

Emmanuel College, Prince Albert began its career as an Anglican divinity school to provide workers for service in the Diocese of Saskatchewan among Indians and settlers of European origin. It was opened by Bishop John McLean, the bishop of Saskatchewan in 1879. He indicated his objects in a report to the Synod of the Diocese in 1882.

> The origin of Emmanuel College was in the sense of need I entertained for a trained band of interpreters, school-masters, catechists and pastors, who being themselves natives of the country would be familiar with the language and modes of thought of the people.[21]

Bishop McLean realized that he could not count upon getting missionaries from England or eastern Canada for the rough, hard work of pioneering, and so he determined to train his own men. In the initial period Emmanuel was largely an Indian college. During the first year of its operation it had eleven students: four Crees, two Cree half-breeds, one Sioux, and four of European parentage. In 1881, Emmanuel opened a boys' school in connection with the College. In addition to classes for boys the College offered courses preparing young men for the matriculation examinations of the University of Manitoba. The theological course leading to Holy Orders was formally instituted in 1881.

In 1883, Bishop McLean decided to establish a university of which Emmanuel was to be a part. He and his associates petitioned the Dominion Parliament and, in 1883, secured the passage of an act establishing the University of Saskatchewan[22] in that section of the Northwest Territories which was in the Diocese of Saskatchewan. The members of the university corporation were to be the Bishop and certain clergy and laity of his diocese. The Bishop intended to have Emmanuel incorporated by the university Senate. He thought that the College would teach arts subjects as well as theology.

Meanwhile Emmanuel was prospering. In October, 1883, the Bishop

[20] Boon, *The Anglican Church*, 111–12.
[21] Jean E. Murray, "The Early History of Emmanuel College," *Saskatchewan History*, IX (3), autumn, 1956, 81.
[22] This Anglican university should not be confused with the provincial University of Saskatchewan established in 1907.

reported that there were thirty-four students at the College. Eight of the students were being trained as missionaries, including representatives of the Cree, Blackfoot, and Chipewyan tribes. This phase of the history of Emmanuel ended after the death of Bishop McLean on November 6, 1886. His successor, Bishop W. C. Pinkham, thought that McLean's plans for the College and the University were in advance of the needs of the country. He turned Emmanuel into an Indian school and allowed the university powers to fall into abeyance. Emmanuel was not revived as a college until twenty years later.

In 1885, in the southern part of Saskatchewan, Bishop A. J. R. Anson of Qu'Appelle initiated an educational experiment in a tradition rather different from the conservative Evangelicalism of Bishops Machray and McLean. St. John's College, an Anglican institution was opened at Qu'Appelle Station in November, 1885, "with three Farm students, three Theological Students—besides some 'Brothers.'" Bishop Anson had been impressed by what he heard of "a wonderful work of some Farming Brothers in connection with the Oblate Fathers in assisting settlers" which he thought "might be with the greatest advantage copied in some manner by our Church." In the circumstances of his diocese, the Bishop favoured a common fund, out of which his clergy should receive not a fixed stipend, but rather their expenses, and he thought that it would be possible to effect economies by several of the clergy sharing the same establishment, rather than to expect each parish to provide a clergy house. The scheme proved abortive. The brotherhood broke up and St. John's College had ceased to exist by 1895.[23]

In the period after 1867, Victoria College continued to progress. As indicated in Chapter III, the appointment of Nathanael Burwash to the Chair of Natural Science in 1866 marked the beginning of a policy of appointing Victoria graduates to the staff. Two more Victoria graduates joined the staff, A. H. Reynar in 1868 and Abraham Robert Bain in 1870.

Reynar, a graduate of 1862, had been selected in 1866 to teach French, German, and English literature. After two years preparation in France and Germany, he joined the staff as professor of modern languages and English literature. An expansion of the work of Reynar's department followed his appointment. In the previous year courses afforded by the department had been limited to rhetoric and

[23]L. G. Thomas, "The Church of England and Higher Education in the Prairie West before 1914," *Journal of the Canadian Church Historical Society*, III (1), Jan. 1956, 7.

English composition in the first two years, French in the second and third years, and German in the fourth year. In the year 1869–70, a two year course in the English language and composition was introduced and this was further extended in 1870–71. In 1870–71 also, the course in German was enlarged to two years. In 1872 the programme of the department was recast to include rhetoric and English composition in the first year, English literature, English composition and French in the second year, English literature, French and German in the third year, and German in the fourth year.

A. R. Bain had a chequered academic career which was less unusual at the time than would have been the case later when rigid specialization became the rule in universities. He graduated from Victoria in 1858 and from 1860 to 1868 served his apprenticeship as classical tutor and rector of the grammar school. Having been appointed professor of mathematics at Victoria in 1868, he spent the next two years in the study of mathematics and astronomy, first with Peirce at Harvard and afterwards with Chauvenet at Paris. In his first two years at Victoria (1870–72) Bain revised the curriculum of his department, enlarged the scope of honours work, and introduced the latest English text-books and methods. For twenty-two years he filled the Chair of Mathematics at Victoria; but after its affiliation with the University of Toronto he was transferred to the Chair of Ancient History and entered on his duties in 1894 after two years' post-graduate study at Oxford in his new field.

As Victoria graduates, Bain, Reynar, and Burwash all carried with them the impress and the methods of the old staff. Bain and Burwash had studied under all the older men, Nelles, Kingston, Wilson, Beatty, Whitlock, and Harris. Reynar missed only Beatty. While this triumvirate carried forward the old traditions of Victoria, they also added new ideas. As Burwash himself reported:

They had all come in contact with the spirit of the new age in Science and Literature as it was now developing in Europe and America, and they all had practical experience of the new system of primary and secondary education as it was rapidly evolving in this country, and were earnest students of the new problems which were to arise from the relations of that system to the university work of the Province.[24]

An important step forward in the teaching of science at Victoria was taken with the appointment of Eugene Haanel, as professor of natural science in 1872. Haanel was one of the great teachers at Victoria. A native of Breslau, he had emigrated to the United States

[24]Burwash, *History of Victoria*, 234.

where he had engaged in railway work in the South, served through the American Civil War, and taught at several small American colleges including Albion College, Michigan. He had been converted during the pastorate of a Methodist minister, the Rev. B. F. Cocker at Ann Arbor, Michigan, and had been licensed as a local preacher. He had returned to Breslau to complete his Ph.D. While his specialty had been physics and chemistry he had given attention to microscopic work in biology and blow-pipe work in mineralogy. During the American phase of his career he had worked on the State Geological Survey of Michigan, under Dr. Winchell. He had an excellent command of English. Burwash has described Haanel the teacher:

> As a lecturer he was clear, forcible, and often eloquent. In illustrative experiment he was a master. We have never seen a failure even in the most intricate experiments in which he followed Faraday, Tyndal, or the German physicists. He carried the severe discipline of his military training into the organization of his laboratory work, and a weak, careless, or inefficient student found no mercy at his hands, and with such he was not popular; but the best students received his most generous service and could not do too much for him in return.[25]

Although Victoria had been established as a denominational college, it had never provided special training for candidates for the ministry. The Victoria conception of its role had been to provide a liberal arts training of a practical type for all young people including candidates for the ministry. In the eighteen-seventies Burwash was responsible for a change in this policy. Burwash was really a theologian and had been appointed to teach natural science on a purely temporary basis with the understanding that he was to organize a theology department as soon as circumstances would permit. As a pastor in Hamilton, he had formed a class of young men preparing for the Christian ministry. Some of them had accompanied him to Victoria as students. They formed the nucleus for private classes in theology which Burwash conducted for two years. He also formed classes in Hebrew. In the year 1870–71, the work was first recognized in the calendar in a suggestion of studies for conference students, including theology, biblical literature, the English language and church history, church polity, Greek Testament, and Hebrew. In the same year, the Board formally authorized a department of theology with the following staff: "the Rev. S. S. Nelles, D.D., President and Professor of Ethics, Evidence of Natural and Revealed Religion, and Homiletics; John Wilson, M.A., Biblical Antiquities and New

[25]*Ibid.*, 239–40.

Testament Exegesis; Rev. N. Burwash, B.D., Hebrew, Biblical History, and Theology; Rev. A. H. Reynar, M.A., Rhetoric and Church History."

Although this statement looked impressive, the proposed staff in theology was really a collection of part-time teachers since they all had heavy duties in the Faculty of Arts, to say nothing of Nelles' duties as president of the University. The first step in the direction of a full-time teaching staff in theology was taken in 1873 when Burwash resigned from the Chair of Natural Science and became a full-time teacher in theology.

In the years after 1867, Albert College continued to develop its work in arts and theology. A list of its faculty in 1869-70 indicates that there had been a considerable expansion in its programme since 1857.

    The Rev. A. Carman, Metaphysics and Mathematics
    The Rev. George Hapgood, Ancient Literature
    R. B. Carman, Chemistry and Mineralogy
    Thomas Nicol, Physiology and Ethnology
    The Rev. Joseph Wild, Hebrew
    The Rev. John Macount, Botany and Geology
    Thomas McIntyre, History of English Literature
    James Thomson Bell, Mineralogy and Agricultural Chemistry
    Mrs. M. A. Smith, Preceptress
    G. S. Wright, Tutor in Modern Languages
    St. George B. Crozier, Music

Work in theology was extended. Hebrew had been taught since at least 1865. Carman was anxious to establish a theological department, beginning with one chair. In spite of doubts on the part of the Board of Management he contrived to raise the necessary funds. The Rev. E. I. Badgley was appointed in 1870 to teach natural theology and evidences.

By 1876 the college calendar indicated Faculties of Arts, Divinity, Engineering, Law and Music together with a Department of Agriculture and a grammar school. Engineering and agriculture were two year courses; the other courses took four years.

The most distinguished member of the staff was John Macoun, the professor of natural history and botany. Macoun had come from the north of Ireland to Canada in 1850 and, after various kinds of work, had qualified at the normal school in Toronto. In 1860 he was appointed to a school in Belleville. Macoun picked up a practical knowledge of botany and geology. He made long field trips along the shore of Lake Ontario and into the rear townships and became recognized as an authority on the flora and geology of southern

Ontario. He was appointed to the staff at Albert College in 1868. In 1872 he was included in Sir Sandford Fleming's famous expedition to the Pacific. Macoun made further trips to the Northwest. While on the teaching staff at Albert he wrote a number of brochures on botany. Subsequently he published *Manitoba and the Great Northwest* (1882), containing comprehensive information about the resources of that area, and in 1895 *The Forests of Canada and Their Distribution*. In 1879, he was appointed explorer for the Canadian government in the Northwest Territories. In 1882 he became botanist to the Geological Survey of Canada. In 1885 he was promoted to be assistant director and naturalist to the Survey, a position which he occupied until his death in 1920.

In 1874 Carman, the real founder of Albert College, left to become a bishop of the Methodist Episcopal Church. The new Principal, J. R. Jacques, had been born in England but educated in the United States where he had had a career as minister and teacher. He came to Albert from Wesleyan University, Bloomington, Illinois. Jacques was a fine linguist, at home in Hebrew, Greek, Latin, French, German, Spanish, and Italian.

Like other principals of church-related colleges, Jacques took an active part in the life of the Episcopal Methodist denomination and encouraged his students to do the same. Students were required to attend church twice on Sundays, the denomination to be as the parents directed. Although the tone of the College was still Evangelical, one does not hear of revivals in the Jacques period to compare with the one which had occurred in 1858. At this time the Episcopal Methodists had secured land on the St. Lawrence for camp meeting revivals and church services but there was evidence that the revivals carried less appeal than in earlier years. Under Jacques' leadership Albert College sponsored a different type of religious refresher, "the Sunday School Parliament." For a week people came together for lectures on the Bible, theology and teaching methods. Cultural subjects had a place and there were discussion periods. The emphasis was upon teaching rather than on conversion.

During the eighteen-seventies and eighties, steps toward the unification of Methodists in Canada strengthened the position of Victoria College. In 1874, Wesleyan Methodists of western Canada, the Wesleyan Methodists of the Maritime Provinces and Newfoundland and the New Connexion Methodists of Canada united. In 1882–83, a general union of Canadian Methodism occurred. One of the results of the union was a consolidation of the educational institutions of the church. On the petition of the General Conference of the united church an act was passed in 1884 establishing one university for the united Methodist Church under the name of Victoria University. Albert College abandoned its university status and reverted to its original status as a secondary school, now in affiliation with Victoria. Some of the theological courses, including Hebrew, were continued at Albert. Albert became the most important single source of undergraduates for Victoria and an important agent in preparing candidates for the preliminary examination for the Methodist ministry.

Under the provisions of the Act of 1884 a number of other secondary institutions were affiliated with Victoria, including the Stanstead Wesleyan College (Stanstead, Quebec), the Columbian Methodist College (New Westminster, B.C.), the Wesleyan Ladies' College (Hamilton), the Ontario Ladies' College (Whitby), and Alma College (St. Thomas). All these schools served as feeders for Victoria and provided a field for Victoria graduates to begin their work as teachers.

During the period of consolidation and expansion of the Victoria constituency, further significant additions were made to the staff. In 1881–82, Andrew James Bell, a graduate of the University of Toronto, and a Ph.D. of Breslau, was appointed to assist Professor Wilson in classics. He thus began a career of over forty years of distinguished service at Victoria. He was appointed a professor of Latin language and literature at Victoria in 1889. In 1908, he was appointed by the University of Toronto to the Chair of Comparative Philology, a post which he held concurrently with his professorship at Victoria. In 1882, Arthur Philemon Coleman, a Victoria graduate and a Ph.D. of Breslau, was appointed professor of natural history and geology. He was destined to have a long and distinguished career as a geologist, first at Victoria and afterwards at the School of Practical Science, Toronto, and at the University of Toronto.

George Coulson Workman, a Victoria graduate, was appointed associate professor of Hebrew at Victoria in 1882. In 1884, he left on an extended leave of absence for study in Germany. The story of his subsequent career at Victoria will be described below. In 1887, the Rev. Frances Huston Wallace was appointed professor of New Testament exegesis and literature. A graduate of University College in classics, he had been ordained to the Methodist ministry and had studied at Drew Theological Seminary and later in Germany. He had an honoured place at Victoria as professor and from 1900 as dean of the Faculty of Theology. Professor Sissons recalls that he was the last of the professors to kneel at College Prayers in Chapel.

When the University of Toronto was established in 1849, it had been the hope of its founders that the denominational colleges would affiliate with the University which would be enabled to become an illustrious and variegated body. As shown in Chapter III, this hope had been disappointed at the time but at long last the early hopes of Baldwin and Elgin began to be fulfilled in the movement toward university federation which began in Ontario in the eighties and nineties.

The story of university federation in Toronto is part of the history of church colleges as well as of the history of the University of Toronto and therefore must be briefly traced. The first step to federation was taken in 1881 when the Roman Catholic college, St. Michael's, was granted limited federation by the University of Toronto. Subsequently, three theological colleges: Wycliffe, Knox, and the Toronto Baptist College, a forerunner of McMaster, were affiliated by statutes passed by the university Senate. Each of the three colleges was given representation on the university Senate. Six subjects taught in the theological colleges were permitted as options in the third and fourth years of the arts course in the University. The subjects thus accepted were Biblical Greek, Biblical literature, apologetics, ethics, didactics, and church history. St. Michael's also shared in this concession.

In 1884 a more extensive scheme of university federation was considered. A rapid increase in registration at the University of Toronto had given rise to a demand on the part of supporters and alumni of additional aid to the University from the Ontario legislature. The demand was vigorously opposed by supporters of Queen's, Victoria, and Trinity.

The result was a series of conferences in 1884 in which representatives of the University of Toronto, the three church universities, and the affiliated denominational colleges all participated. The group passed a series of resolutions which could provide the basis for university federation. The first resolution read:

It is proposed to form a confederation of Colleges, carrying on, in Toronto, work embraced in the Arts curriculum of the Provincial University, and in connection therewith the following institutions, namely: Queen's University, Victoria University, and Trinity University, Knox College, St. Michael's College, Wycliffe College, and Toronto Baptist College, shall have the right to enter into the proposed confederation, provided always that each of such institutions shall, so long as it remains in the confederation, keep in abeyance any powers it may possess of conferring degrees other than degrees in Divinity, such powers remaining intact, though not exercised.[26]

---

[26]*The Universities of Canada*, 390–95.

The scheme of federation contained in the resolutions was given a mixed reception. It was adopted by the Senate and by Convocation of the University of Toronto but rejected by the authorities of Queen's and Trinity. The General Conference of the Methodist Church of Canada after a long debate, in September, 1886, authorized the Victoria Board to proceed with university federation. The resolution was passed in opposition to the wishes of President Nelles and three of his staff (Burwash, Bain, and E. I. Badgley). Encouraged by the action of the two universities, Toronto and Victoria, the Ontario government in 1887 secured the passage of an act (50 Vict., cap. 43) which embodied the principles contained in the Resolutions of 1884 and laid the groundwork for university federation.

The University Act introduced the federal principle. It provided that the affiliating colleges should hold in abeyance the right to grant degrees except in theology. Each college was to turn over to the University instruction in certain subjects, mainly the sciences, and to retain instruction in other subjects, mainly languages. Control of examinations was given to the university Senate; but each church college retained some control through representation on the university Senate and by control of the examinations in certain religious knowledge options.

The act was particularly significant for the church colleges because it attempted to reconcile the claims of God and of Caesar in higher education. It embodied the principle that religion has a place in higher education; that the state must enlist the moral and financial support of the churches in the course of higher education; and that the churches may avail themselves of the superior advantages afforded by the state in new and expanding fields of learning.

In the specific case provided for in the act, the church colleges were to secure for their students instruction in the physical and social sciences in the University or in University College, provided that there were no religious tests for staff or students in the church colleges. Any religious instruction secured by students of University College was to be optional. The federating universities were to make their own arrangements in regard to religious instruction.

The act accepted the principle of state supervision in return for state support. The Ontario government accepted financial responsibility for the provincial University but required large concessions in the matter of control. The government appointed the President and professors and provided for their retirement. The Minister of Education and nine others appointed by the government were to be members of the university Senate, the governing body in the University. The act said nothing about the internal organization of the federating universities.

Finally, the Act of 1887 embodied the principle of state responsibility for professional training. Education was included as a subject to be taught by the University, although many years elapsed before instruction was provided. Medicine and law, after an exile of twenty-five years returned to the University; although Osgoode Hall continued to function as an independent institution.

The only institution to avail itself of the Act of 1887 in the period immediately following its passage was Victoria University. Victoria federated with the University of Toronto after vigorous opposition from a large group of its supporters who feared that federation would reduce it to the position of a mere theological school. Their leader was Henry Hough, a former president of the Alumni Association. Although President Nelles had been opposed to the scheme prior to its acceptance by the General Conference in 1886, he gave loyal support to the decision to federate once it had been taken. He felt that there was a great future for Victoria as a Christian institution within a pluralistic university. In his last baccalaureate address, delivered in May, 1887, he urged the graduating class to stand by their university as a Christian institution, and continued:

Tell them [the Methodist people] that Missions are good, that pulpit service is desirable, that Sunday Schools are excellent, that Young Men's Christian Associations are useful. But tell them, and in telling them you speak my sentiments, that nothing is so good as a Christian university, for it is pregnant with all these.[27]

After Nelles' death on October 17, 1887, his successor as president, Nathanael Burwash, took up the scheme of federation with vigour and piloted Victoria into federation. On November 12, 1892, the Act of 1887 was proclaimed and the work of the University of Toronto as a federated institution began.

The new curriculum in arts at the University of Toronto at the beginning of federation indicates the division of teaching between the University and Victoria. There were eight Honours Departments: Classics; Modern Languages; Oriental Languages; Logic, Metaphysics, and Ethics; Political Science; Mathematics and Physics; Chemistry and Mineralogy; and Natural Science. Victoria continued to teach in the first four departments and the latter four passed entirely to the University.

[27]Burwash, *History of Victoria*, 265.

The coming of federation necessitated a number of changes in the staff at Victoria. The surrender of teaching in the sciences and mathematics by the College involved the positions of three professors: Bain, Haanel, and Coleman. Bain continued at Victoria as registrar and professor of classics. Haanel accepted an appointment on the staff of the University of Syracuse. Coleman was transferred to the University of Toronto and entered upon his work in the School of Practical Science in 1891.

In 1891, Lewis Emerson Horning returned to Victoria as professor of German and old English. Horning had served his apprenticeship at Victoria as assistant professor of classics and modern languages from 1886 to 1889 and had been on leave of absence since 1889 for post-graduate study at Oxford. In 1905, he was appointed professor of Teutonic philology and played a large part in the success of Victoria.

In 1892, John Fletcher McLaughlin was appointed professor of oriental languages and literature. A Victoria graduate, McLaughlin had spent two years in post-graduate study at Oxford. He built up a vigorous Department of Orientals at Victoria and profoundly influenced the life of the University.[28]

Queen's University had passed through a time of depression during the 1860-65 period. After Confederation, the University experienced another crisis owing to the failure of the Commercial Bank in 1867 and the decision of the Ontario government to withdraw the annual grants to denominational colleges. The failure of the Commercial Bank reduced the investments of the University by two thirds, while the curtailment of grants to church colleges deprived it of five thousand dollars a year. The annual income of the University fell from thirteen thousand six hundred to seven thousand seven hundred dollars a year.[29] Faced with disaster, Queen's was again rescued by its Principal, William Snodgrass, and by the Professor of Classical Literature, J. H. MacKerras. They appealed to the Presbyterian Synod which met in Kingston in 1869 and secured a resolution to replace the lost revenue with an endowment of one hundred thousand dollars. Snodgrass and MacKerras undertook the rigorous task of canvassing some eighty-six pastoral charges. They raised an endowment which provided sufficient interest to replace the lost government grant.

The national union of all the Presbyterian Churches in Canada in

[28]Sissons, *Victoria University*, 195.
[29]Grant, and Hamilton, *Principal Grant*, 198.

1875 profoundly modified the position of Queen's in relation to the church. In the new body, the Presbyterian Church in Canada, former members of the various secession churches far outnumbered the adherents of the Old Kirk. The former, constituting the so-called voluntary section of the church, were opposed to the maintenance of arts colleges by churches. It was the adherents of the Old Kirk (the Synod of the Presbyterian Church of Canada in Connection with the Church of Scotland) which had maintained the close association between the church and Queen's. The footing of Queen's, therefore, became a delicate point in the negotiations leading to the Union of 1875.[30] An arrangement was effected which left Queen's nominally Presbyterian, but which virtually transferred it into a private institution. Hitherto, the governing body, the Board of Trustees, had been elected by the Synod from a list of persons nominated by the individual congregations. After union, the Board became a self-perpetuating body. Theoretically the corporation of the University consisted of the communicants of the Presbyterian Church in Canada; but practically, the Church as a body had no control over the University. The stipulation that trustees must be members of the Presbyterian Church remained in force until 1889 when it was modified. The trustees continued to furnish the General Assembly of the Church with an annual report. The Church undertook to contribute to the support of the Theological Faculty.

We have already shown how dissatisfaction with Trinity on the part of Bishop Cronyn and Isaac Hellmuth led to the establishment of Huron in 1863. In the eighteen-seventies a similar feeling of dissatisfaction among the Toronto Anglican Evangelicals led to the establishment of Wycliffe. The founding of Wycliffe was part of a prolonged struggle between the Evangelical and high church elements in the Diocese of Toronto. The Evangelicals were dissatisfied with their position in the Diocese and in Trinity College. They felt that too many offices in the Diocese were held by members of the high church party, to their own exclusion. They maintained also that the teachings of Trinity approached far too closely the high church position.[31] In order to strengthen their position the Evangelical party

---

[30]That the members of the Church of Scotland were anxious to maintain Queen's as a Presbyterian institution was indicated by a pamphlet published in 1871, *Presbyterian Union and the College Question* (Kingston, 1871), by an alumnus of Queen's College. The alumnus argued that the Church of Scotland must reject union with the Canada Presbyterian Church if its members insisted upon secularization of Queen's.

[31]*Wycliffe College Jubilee Volume* (Toronto, 1927), 1-76.

in 1869 formed the Evangelical Association of the United Churches of England and Ireland in the Diocese of Toronto. Its professed principles were to secure the rights of the Evangelical laity and to propagate the principles of the Reformation. Its officers included Dean Grassett of St. James Cathedral; Daniel Wilson, at the time professor of history and English literature at University College; and S. H. Blake, the hard-hitting brother of Edward Blake.

The Evangelical Association was merged in 1873 in the Church Association of the Diocese of Toronto. This new association was formed as a result of a severe Evangelical defeat in the Synod of 1873, when the majority vote excluded representatives of the Evangelical clergy and laity from all offices and committees of the Synod. The objects of the Association were similar to those of the earlier Association: "To maintain the principles and doctrines of our Church as established at the Reformation, and to preserve the simplicity of her Protestant worship and the purity of her Scriptural teachings," and to oppose "tractarianism, ritualism, rationalism, or whatever other movements threaten to undo the great work of the Reformation."

The Association was bitterly attacked by the Bishop of Toronto, A. N. Bethune. Some clergy in the Association were even impeached by the Bishop and summoned to trial by an Episcopal commission for disparaging the government and discipline of the Church, although the trial petered out.

As a further step in its campaign, the low church group in 1876 established the *Evangelical Churchman*, with Robert Baldwin, the second son of the Hon. Robert Baldwin, as chairman, to expound Evangelical opinions. The *Evangelical Churchman* opened its campaign by demanding that an Evangelical school be established for the training of low church Anglican clergy. The Evangelical movement received a great impetus as a result of a series of mission services conducted in 1877 by the Rev. W. S. Rainsford. Steps were soon under way to establish the Evangelical school. About the end of April, 1877, the Rev. James P. Sheraton arrived in Toronto from Nova Scotia to edit the *Evangelical Churchman* and to head the Evangelical school.

The school was incorporated as the Protestant Episcopal Divinity School. Later its name was changed to Wycliffe College. Its establishment was a step of great significance. It involved the secession from any support to Trinity College of the whole Evangelical wing of the Church of England in Ontario. The new school was destined to be a rallying point for the Evangelical party in the church from the time of its establishment.

The founders of Wycliffe were largely the group which had already established the Church Association.[32] The group included representatives of the older Toronto families such as Robert Baldwin, Edward Blake, S. H. Blake, Colonel G. T. Denison, and F. W. Jarvis; but it also included many of the rising business men who had combined with the older families in building Toronto. The list of founders included C. S. Gzowski, the engineer and railway promoter, and the financiers, J. H. Mason, W. H. Howland, and T. S. Stayner.

The organization met with stiff opposition from the high church party. Stormy scenes occurred at the Synod of the Diocese of Toronto in June of 1877.[33] Bishop Bethune in his opening charge to the clergy deplored the establishment of the new college as a dividing force within the church. S. H. Blake, the vice-chancellor of Ontario, made a speech criticizing the method of preparation at Trinity and pleading for recognition of the Protestant Divinity School. Professor Wilson cited history in support of the Evangelical group, but in spite of these eloquent pleas, Bishop Bethune declared that he would not ordain any students of the School.

Eventually, the struggle was avoided and less hostile conditions were restored in the Church of England. The Protestant Divinity School opened without opposition in October, 1877. In 1879, Bethune was succeeded as Bishop of Toronto by A. Sweatman, a churchman of more moderate opinions. Under Sweatman, more peaceful relations were restored between the Evangelical and high church groups in the Diocese of Toronto and the Protestant Episcopal Divinity School was able to proceed without further open challenge. About 1882 supporters of the School began to call it Wycliffe College and on January 9, 1885, an order was made by the judge of the county court of the County of York "authorizing the Trustees of the Protestant Episcopal Divinity School Corporation to use the name Wycliffe College for the purpose of designating the said Corporation."

Unlike Trinity, Wycliffe remained purely a divinity school and did not develop a faculty of arts. Wycliffe imitated Knox in sending its students to University College for their arts training. This process was facilitated by the fact that the first Wycliffe building, opened on College Street in 1882, and the second building, completed on Hoskin Avenue in 1891, were both in close proximity to University College.

Huron College which had been established in 1863 as a theological seminary became in 1878 the nucleus for the establishment of Western

[32]*Ibid.*, 61–76.
[33]*Mail* (Toronto), June 20, 21, 1877.

University.[34] Western was a church-related university in the period 1878-1908. As an Anglican institution it had a desperate struggle to secure adequate finances. The movement to establish a university began with a meeting of the alumni of Huron College on February 20, 1877, to consider the transference of the College into a university. They passed twenty-three resolutions including one stating their purposes to establish

a University and University College to facilitate the obtaining of the highest scholastic training and instruction in evangelical truth for the future clergy of this Diocese and Dominion, and to meet the educational wants of the fast developing West by supplying it with an undenominational School of Arts, Law, Medicine and Engineering.[35]

The meeting formed an organization, "The Association of the Professors and Alumni of Huron College" to put the project into effect. Strong leadership in the movement was provided by Isaac Hellmuth, the second bishop of Huron. Hellmuth undertook to use his personal influence to secure a charter for the University. The provincial statute providing for the Charter of the Western University of London secured the royal assent on March 7, 1878. The governing body, the Senate, was to consist of the Bishop of Huron, the Principal of Huron College, several persons specified in the statute, and ten senior graduates of the University. The Senate was not to exact religious qualifications from any student except in the Faculty of Divinity. The courses of study and the examinations, so far as possible, were to be those of the University of Toronto. The University Constitution of 1879 provided that the Chancellor, the Provost, and the members of the Senate should be members of the Church of England and "of Protestant and Evangelical principles." In 1881, Huron College handed over to the Senate, its entire income and resources and became the Faculty of Divinity of the University. In 1881, the University began teaching with a professional staff of four professors and eight lecturers, all Church of England clergymen. In 1882, the University Act was amended so that all members of the Senate should be Anglicans.

Western University suffered a blow in 1883 with the resignation of Hellmuth from the Bishopric of Huron. His drive and energy had been largely responsible for the establishment and early progress of the University. His successor, Bishop M. S. Baldwin, a strong Evangelical and a magnificent preacher, was less successful in his university policy and the Senate was soon in financial difficulties. The Council

[34]Talman, and Talman, *Western, 1878-1953*, 18-66.
[35]*Ibid.*, 14.

of Huron College on April 24, 1885, passed a resolution to withdraw from affiliation with the University. The Senate in 1885 suspended the Arts Faculty which remained in abeyance for ten years.

The Charter of McMaster University in 1887 was the culmination of long debate among Baptists in Ontario about the best policy for Baptists in regard to university education. The debate occurred at a time when university federation was being widely discussed in Ontario. Many Baptists favoured participation in the scheme. The debate also involved the question of Baptist policy in reference to the Canadian Literary Institute at Woodstock.

The fortunes of the Canadian Literary Institute in the eighteen-seventies were an important prelude to the establishment of McMaster. Fyfe continued as principal until his death in 1878. The Institute maintained three Departments: Preparatory, Literary, and Theological. The Institute contemplated the addition of some university arts courses. In 1875 it secured affiliation with the University of Toronto and began teaching the second year of university work. The policy of the Institute was to affiliate with the state university for all work of university grade but to conduct the work with Baptist money. However, the university work had soon to be abandoned and the affiliation soon lapsed.[36]

In the eighteen-seventies too, the Institute began to contemplate the advisability of moving the Theological Department to Toronto. It had been found that many candidates for the ministry who took their secondary work at Woodstock and then proceeded to the University of Toronto for arts did not return to Woodstock for their training in theology.

In July, 1879, the Institute decided to move its Theological Department to Toronto. Senator William McMaster, the munificent promoter of Baptist institutions of education, donated a site and erected a building which was named McMaster Hall. A charter was obtained for the theological college under the name, Toronto Baptist College. The College opened on October 4, 1881.[37] The Literary Department continued at Woodstock. In 1883 its charter was amended to change the name to Woodstock College.

Toronto Baptist College began to move toward the teaching of university work in arts. Its policy was to recommend that candidates

[36]R. Hamilton, "The Founding of McMaster," unpublished B.D. thesis (McMaster).
[37]*Ibid.*

for the ministry with deficient academic training should attend Woodstock College and then take a full or partial arts course, preferably at the University of Toronto, before entrance to the Baptist College. In many cases this was impossible and the general tendency of the authorities of Toronto Baptist College was to add arts subjects to the theological curriculum.

Between 1884 and 1887 the Baptists, particularly the authorities of Toronto Baptist College, were drawn into the discussions about university federation in Toronto. For a time, it was uncertain whether the Baptists would establish a college as part of the University of Toronto or develop an independent Baptist university.

Early in 1884 the movement for the federation of all degree-conferring colleges of the Province of Ontario with the University of Toronto assumed definite form. Negotiations had made some progress of a kind satisfactory to the Baptist representatives, Dr. Castle and Dr. Malcolm MacVicar, by the time of the meeting of the Baptist Union in Brantford in May, 1884. It seemed likely that Toronto Baptist College would join the federation on terms similar to those eventually accepted by Victoria, Trinity, and St. Michael's. It was proposed that a literary college should be established to teach those subjects left to the denominational colleges. Arts students of Toronto Baptist College would take the balance of their subjects at University College, would write University of Toronto examinations, and would secure Toronto degrees. Negotiations in regard to university federation, involving as they did many diverse interests, continued to proceed slowly. According to D. E. Thomson,

> It became increasingly evident to the Baptist representatives, however, that the federation, if effected, was scarcely likely, at any rate in the division of subjects between University College and the other schools, to prove ideal from a denominational standpoint. The delay, too, was thought injurious to every department of our educational work, more especially to the work at Woodstock, as it was found impossible under conditions of suspense to secure general support for the advance movement necessary to bring the school up to modern requirements.[38]

An important development occurred in 1885 when Theodore H. Rand was appointed to the Chair of Apologetics and Ethics at Toronto Baptist College. Rand, a leading educationalist from the Maritime provinces and a former professor at Acadia, was a strong

---

[38]D. E. Thomson, "McMaster University, 1887–1906," *McMaster University Monthly*, XVI, 24.

opponent of federation and exercised a powerful influence on the thinking of the Baptist denomination in Ontario. Senator McMaster, also expressed a preference for an independent institution.[39] In 1886, Rand was appointed as principal of Woodstock College. One of the terms of his acceptance of the position was that he might develop the College as rapidly as circumstances would permit until it reached the status of a university.[40] This agreement practically meant the abandonment of federation by the Baptists.

In 1885, an important change was made in the organization of Toronto Baptist College giving the Baptist Church an important measure of control.[41] Prior to 1885 the church had no legal control over educational work. Woodstock College was under control of its subscribers and Toronto Baptist College of its Board of Trustees, a self-perpetuating, closed corporation. According to D. E. Thomson,

It was beginning to be felt, however, that the Churches, through their general organization, which was being gradually improved and simplified, ought to have a more direct voice in shaping our educational policy.[42]

The charter of Toronto Baptist College was accordingly amended in 1885, to provide for a Senate which was to control the educational side of the work.[43] The trustees were left in charge of property and finances. The Senate was composed in part of college representatives elected by the three Baptist Conventions—East, West, and Manitoba. Woodstock College continued under the control of its subscribers until 1887.

After the turning point in the movement toward federation, the Baptists proceeded rapidly with plans for an independent Baptist university. In December, 1886, the Boards of Trustees of Woodstock College and Toronto Baptist College developed a plan to combine and to secure a university charter. The act to unite the two institutions and to incorporate them as McMaster University received first reading in the Ontario legislature on March 15, 1887. A large delegation headed by Principal Castle of the Toronto Baptist College and

[39]*Ibid.*, 8. Thomson, the author of the above article, was Senator McMaster's solicitor.
[40]*Ibid.*, 24; Hamilton, "The Founding of McMaster University," 27–8.
[41]48 Vict., cap. 96.
[42]Thomson, "McMaster University, 1887–1906," *The Universities of Canada*, 132.
[43]The senate was granted by the statute a concurrent power in the appointment and dismissal of members of the teaching staff of the College, and was invested with the "control and management of the system and course of education" pursued in it and of the examinations conducted in connection therewith.

Principal Rand appeared before the Private Bills Committee to plead the cause of McMaster. Castle and Rand both stressed the fact that the Baptists were not asking for state support but simply for the right to develop their own independent institution. In the debate on the bill, the Minister of Education, George Ross, expressed regret that the application for a charter was being made at an inopportune time. He said that independent colleges have a tendency to be narrow in outlook and to be content with a lower standard of education. He hoped that if the bill passed, the Baptists would see the way clear to enter the university federation. In spite of these cool sentiments, the bill secured its final reading on April 22, 1887.[44]

McMaster University began with a comparatively liberal charter. Professors must be members of an Evangelical church, but not necessarily Baptists. No religious tests were required of students, other than those in the Faculty of Theology. Professors in theology must be members in good standing of "Regular Baptist Churches." What constituted a "Regular Baptist Church" was exhaustively and precisely defined in the Trust Deed of the University.[45]

The grant of a charter did not end the controversy as to whether the new university should affiliate with the University of Toronto. A vigorous controversy on this issue raged for the next two years. The opponents of federation were horrified at the proposal to affiliate with what they regarded as a godless university.

Federation had its advocates including John Boyd, chancellor of Ontario.[46] Boyd argued that the influence of McMaster in the University of Toronto would be quite as potent as if it remained independent. He insisted that federation would not limit McMaster's freedom. The work of training and educating its students would be left entirely in the hands of its own professors who could teach all the subjects taught in University College and any additional subjects they might desire. Other advocates of federation were Archibald Blue, the deputy minister of agriculture for Ontario, and H. A. Calvin, the Kingston lumber king and the mainstay of Baptist work in Kingston.

While the Baptists were considering the question of federation in 1887–88 they were also arguing about the choice of a site for McMaster University. Toronto and Woodstock both had their advocates. E. W. Dadson, editor of the *Canadian Baptist* favoured Woodstock.

[44]Hamilton, "The Founding of McMaster University," 30–9.
[45]*Ibid.*; also W. S. W. McLay, C. W. New, and G. P. Gilmour, *McMaster University 1890–1940* (Hamilton, 1940), 10.
[46]Hamilton, *"The Founding of McMaster University,"* 44; McLay, New, and Gilmour, 9.

The advocates of Toronto included Chancellor Boyd, Archibald Blue, and W. K. McNaught, a prominent manufacturer.

Both the questions of federation versus independence and Toronto versus Woodstock were settled by a regular Baptist Convention convened at Guelph on March 27, 1888. The proposal to federate with the University was finally decisively defeated. A motion proposed by Dr. Thomas Trotter and passed by a large majority declared "that McMaster University be organized and developed as a permanently independent school of learning, with the lordship of Christ as the controlling principle."[47] On the following day, March 28, 1888, the question of a site was settled. The Convention decided to maintain Woodstock College as a secondary school and to move the Arts Department to Toronto.

McMaster University began its career fortified by a bequest of some nine hundred thousand dollars, the largest of the many donations given to the institution by Senator William McMaster. The University began its work in arts on October 10, 1890, at first teaching only the first two years of the university course. Academically the University opened its doors more auspiciously than other church colleges. It had a staff of about twelve instructors in arts, some of whom also taught theological subjects. During the first year the student body numbered sixteen.

McMaster's concept of itself was indicated a few years later by D. E. Thomson who had appeared before the Committee of the Ontario Legislative Assembly on behalf of the University in 1887 and who was for many years chairman of the Board. Writing in *The McMaster University Monthly* in October, 1906, Thomson described what he called McMaster's "distinctive characteristics," under the following heads:

1. *It is Christian.* In the earnest pursuit of scholarship and practical efficiency, it is not forgotten that Christian character is the chief attainment. Christian ideals of public and private duty are constantly enforced. Such principles as personal responsibility, liberty of conscience and universal brotherhood underlie and color everything in the college life. The institution aims at sending out into the world men and women of personal integrity, lovers of social justice and peace, ambitious to do good to all men as they have opportunity.

2. *It is independent.* The denomination in the past lent powerful aid in the struggle to remove all sectarian tests from what is now the state university,

---

[47]Hamilton, "The Founding of McMaster University," 51. See also McLay, New, and Gilmour, 11, and D. E. Thomson, "McMaster University, 1887–1906," 26.

and later to uproot the system of government aid to denominational colleges so long prevalent. Our people are unalterably opposed to church and state connection. This throws the responsibility for the support of the institution wholly upon the good old Baptist principle of voluntaryism, which involves as its correlative, independence of outside control.
3. *It is a residential institution.* It seeks to repeat in a new land the glories of Oxford and Cambridge in this respect, believing that the residential feature makes for the highest sort of manly culture.
4. *It stands for a strong, general course as against early specialization.* It has always insisted that a well rounded general course furnished at once the most symmetrical culture, and the best basis for later specialization. This feature has won for the institution the warm appreciation of leading educationists.[48]

The movement to establish a college in Montreal for the training of Presbyterian clergy was begun by a small group of clergy and laity including the Rev. D. H. MacVicar, Principal Dawson of McGill, and John Redpath. Presbyterian College, Montreal secured a charter similar to that of Knox College, Toronto and teaching began in the basement of Erskine Church.

A decisive step in the establishment of the College was taken in 1868 when D. H. MacVicar was appointed professor of divinity and, in effect, principal. MacVicar had been born in Scotland and had come to Canada with his parents as a child. He had been educated at the University of Toronto and at Knox College. In 1859 he had entered the Presbyterian ministry. From 1868 until his death in 1902, the fortunes of Presbyterian College depended mainly upon MacVicar's energy and devotion. His appointment represented the triumph of the party which desired the appointment of a Canadian. The minority party in the Synod had felt it an indispensable condition for success that some scholar of established standing should be brought across the ocean. In the early period of the history of Presbyterian College, almost the whole burden of teaching fell on MacVicar. Lectures on exegetics were given by a minister of a Montreal Church while MacVicar gave instruction in mathematics, Latin, Greek, logic, and moral philosophy, besides all the regular subjects of the theological curriculum, particularly systematic theology, apologetics, and church history.

MacVicar was a fine teacher, an able administrator, and a man of great courage. He was a remarkable preacher. When Ralph Connor was a boy, MacVicar assisted Connor's father, the Rev. Daniel Gordon in a pre-communion service in Glengarry. MacVicar's sermon on that

---

[48]D. E. Thomson, "McMaster University, 1887–1906," 27–8.

occasion served as the model for the Fast Day sermon preached by the "college professor" in Ralph Connor's novel, *The Man from Glengarry*.[49]

Presbyterian College was in a sense a branch of Knox College. In addition to MacVicar himself, his two early colleagues, John Campbell and John Scrimger, were both Knox graduates. In 1873 MacVicar was officially made principal and Campbell was appointed professor of church history and apologetics. Campbell, born in Edinburgh, had spent his boyhood in London and on the continent where he acquired proficiency in French and German. A graduate of the University of Toronto, as well as of Knox, he had also studied at New College, Edinburgh. About the same time the Rev. John Scrimger became lecturer in Old and New Testament exegesis.

The tone of the theology of Presbyterian College is indicated by John H. MacVicar's life of his father, which has been already cited. Principal MacVicar's theology was the solid, Calvinist theology of the reformed faith. His lectures always showed the influence of such divines as Charles Hodge and Jonathan Edwards as well as Calvin himself. The *Life* indicates the character of his lectures and of his theology.

In the earlier days—those described by Ralph Connor—the doctrine of election, perhaps, received larger attention in the class room than later on, though it was never tabooed. He believed too intensely in the sovereignty of God to pass it over in silence; but he grew accustomed to expect questions at this point. There was sure to be some one ready to voice a personal difficulty about reconciling the mission to preach a free gospel with the inscrutable decrees. I do not remember that in my own day he ever made Rowland Hill's reply, when advised to preach to none but the elect, that "he would certainly do so if some one would chalk them all on the back first," but probably every class that passed through his hands can remember the peculiar use he *would* make of chalk in an effort to demonstrate on the blackboard the necessity of preaching the Gospel to all in order to reach the elect. He would make a rough sketch of the interior of a church, with the pulpit well in view, and people sitting in the pews.

"Now," he would say, "Jones here may be elect, Smith over there may not. The preacher in the pulpit knows nothing about that, however, and the only thing he can do is to preach the Gospel to both."[50]

Dr. MacVicar was anxious that his students should preach the Gospel of salvation. His son later recalled that he admonished them,

You are not sent to preach science, or literature, or crude speculations, much less to amuse and entertain the people and carry on the work of the

---

[49]John H. MacVicar, *Life and Work of Donald Harvey MacVicar* (Toronto, 1904), 53–4; Ralph Connor, *The Man from Glengarry* (Toronto, 1901), 253–6.
[50]MacVicar, *Life*, 121–2.

churches after the manner of lyceums and theatres; you are sent to preach the Gospel, to proclaim the great doctrines of grace in the proportions and relations to each other in which you find them stated in the Word of God. I need scarcely remind you, after the discussions to which you have listened in my lectures on Theology, that in your public ministrations peculiar prominence should be given to the subjects of the atoning sacrifice of our Redeemer and the work of His Holy Spirit.[51]

A distinctive feature of the work of Presbyterian College was its function in training ministerial candidates for work among French Canadians. The College was identified with the work of Father Charles Chiniquy who had left the Roman Catholic church in 1858 and had begun his career of proselytization among his French-Canadian compatriots. The College helped to train Chiniquy's colleagues in this work.

All the early staff were keen on French work. MacVicar, a strong opponent of the Roman Catholic Church, was a member of the undenominational French-Canadian Missionary Society. For a brief period previous to the Union of 1875, he was convenor of the Committee on French Evangelization in connection with the Canada Presbyterian Church. After the union, he remained in this position and filled it until his death in 1902. Campbell identified himself with a French Protestant congregation in Montreal and supported MacVicar in the work of proselytization. Scrimger, too, was a strong advocate of the French work. Other early members of the staff were directly identified with the work in French theology: the Rev. Charles Doudier, the Rev. C. E. Amaron, and the Rev. B. Ourière.

The nature of the French work at Presbyterian College is indicated by an except from the college calendar of 1876–77:

All French Students and Students preparing for French Work are required to attend the Homiletical Lectures in French, and English Students who understand French are urged to do the same. Students taking this course and passing examination in it are exempted from examination in the Biblical History of the first year, the Apologetics of the second, and the Exegesis of the third. In the honour (*sic*) work they may also take the examinations in Latin, Greek and Hebrew authors, and Calvin, in French, instead of English. In the first year they may exchange Blaikie's "For the Work of the Ministry" for the French edition of Vinet's Homiletics; in the second year, Farrar for Guizot, Méditations sur la Religion Chrétienne; and in the third year, Walker for De Félice, Histoire des Protestants de France. . . .

French students are not required to give more than one of their College Exercises in English, and at least two of them must be in French. These French Exercises will be prescribed by the French Lecturer.[52]

[51]*Ibid.*, 124–5.
[52]*Annual Calendar, Presbyterian College, Montreal* (Session 1876–77), 11.

It is difficult to estimate the importance of the French work at Presbyterian College. In the report of the College in 1896, it was stated that of eighty-seven students enrolled (including students in arts proceeding to the ministry) there were ten French students and two Italians. This would suggest that the French work, although not very large, had reached respectable proportions.

Presbyterian College adhered to the Knox College principle that the function of the church college was to train the clergy in theology, leaving a secular institution to provide instruction in arts. The College was affiliated with McGill University and encouraged its students to take their arts training at McGill. The college calendar for 1876-7 contained the admonition:

> The Senate of the Presbyterian College, having a full knowledge of the nature of the training given, and the religious influence exerted on Students in the McGill University, confidently recommend parents to send their sons to it, whether they are designed for the Christian Ministry or for any of the learned Professions....[53]

Theological students taking arts were permitted to substitute Hebrew for modern languages in the first two years and were permitted to omit certain subjects in the third and fourth years—astronomy and optics, experimental physics and rhetoric in the third year, and experimental physics in the fourth year.

The establishment of Montreal Diocesan College for the training of Anglican clergy was mainly the work of Ashton Oxenden, the second bishop of Montreal. Oxenden introduced the question at the Synod of the Diocese of Montreal which met in 1870. The matter was delicate because of the historic connection between the Diocese and Bishop's University, and because of Oxenden's own position as a member of the governing body of Bishop's. In his charge to the clergy at the Synod of 1870, the Bishop discussed the problem frankly:

> The Training of our Candidates for Holy Orders is not altogether on a satisfactory footing. The fact of our Theological College being at a distance places us at a disadvantage. And I should be thankful if I could gather my candidates for the sacred ministry around me here at Montreal, where I could watch their characters and conduct, and superintend their preparation for the ministry. I feel unwilling however without more mature consideration to interfere with the present arrangement as regards the college of Lennoxville. But if it should eventually be found desirable to move the theological department nearer home, I doubt not that I should obtain from the Churchmen of the Diocese the needed help to enable me to carry out the project. My present conviction is that, if we had in this city a Theo-

[53]*Ibid.*, 16.

logical Institution, with a building worthy of its character, it would prove an immense blessing to the Diocese.⁵⁴

Oxenden had several reasons for dissatisfaction with Bishop's. One was the element of distance which he mentioned in his Charge of 1870. He repeated this complaint in the *Life* which he published shortly before his death, asserting of Bishop's, "In consequence of its nearness to Quebec, and its distance from Montreal, the college was comparatively useless to our diocese."⁵⁵ Oxenden was dubious about the high church character of the teaching at Bishop's. In 1871, he wrote, "The chief reason why the Institution [Bishop's] has lost the confidence of Churchmen here, is that it has earned the character (somewhat unjustly perhaps) of nurturing extreme opinions in its students."⁵⁶ While Oxenden appeared to exonerate Bishop's of the charge of extreme opinions he probably continued to regard it as a high church institution. Apart from the question of its teaching, he felt that it was too closely identified with the Diocese of Quebec. He reported in the *Life*:

I . . . generally attended its meetings, as my Predecessor had done; but I confess that I found them anything but agreeable, as there existed there a strong sympathy in favour of Quebec, and sometimes a direct antagonism to Montreal. Some of these meetings were most distasteful to me, as I felt myself in a false position; and they were rendered the more so by the presence of one or two who made no concealment of their opposition to any step which seemed to favour the diocese of Montreal.⁵⁷

In the early spring of 1873, the Bishop wrote that "the theological institution [is] in the offing," and a little later, with a view to allaying the suspicions of the S. P. G., always alert to any thing which might damage Bishop's, that his institution was "not . . . a rival to Lennoxville, but as a supplement to it."⁵⁸ The College opened in 1873 under the principalship of Rev. J. A. Lobley, late of Trinity College, Cambridge. After a year, Oxenden could write of the new institution, "Its success has been beyond my expectations chiefly owing to the great efficiency of our admirable Principal, Mr. Lobley, who is likely to

⁵⁴Ashton Oxenden, *My First Year in Canada* (London, 1871), 120–21; John Irwin Cooper, *The Blessed Communion: The Origins and History of the Diocese of Montreal 1760–1960* (Montreal, 1960), 97–9.
⁵⁵Ashton Oxenden, *History of My Life* (London, 1891), 216–17, quoted in F. D. Adams, *A History of Christ Church Cathedral Montreal* (Montreal, 1941), 153–4.
⁵⁶Oxenden, *First Year in Canada*, 39.
⁵⁷Oxenden, *Life*, 216–17, quoted in Adams, 153.
⁵⁸Cooper, *The Blessed Communion: The Origins and History of the Diocese of Montreal 1760–1960* (Montreal, 1960), 98.

become one of the leading men of the Diocese."[59] In addition to theology, Lobley gave a species of arts course, but encouraged his students to secure a B.A. degree at some university. In 1875 he reported that several of his students were graduates of Bishop's.

Montreal Diocesan College took its tone from its founder, Ashton Oxenden. Oxenden was a moderate churchman with Evangelical leanings. Like Bishop G. J. Mountain, a former bishop of Quebec, Oxenden preached moderation and deplored divisions within the church. He adjured his clergy in 1871:

Try to forget, my Reverend Brethren, any little specialties, either of doctrine or practice, which have in days past ranged you on separate sides; and think only of the greatness of those matters on which you are sent here to deliberate, and of His honour which should be dearer to you than all else. Look at each question which shall come before you, not as to how it will affect yourselves, but how it will affect the Church at large.[60]

There was a significant difference between Mountain and Oxenden, although both were moderate churchmen. Mountain regarded the Evangelicals as the principal dividers and inveighed against "party" meaning the low church party. Oxenden regarded the high church element as the main dividers and talked about people with "extreme opinions" meaning extreme high church opinions. Mountain was neutral against the Evangelicals and Oxenden was neutral against the high church wing of the Church of England.

Principal Lobley was rather too high to suit Oxenden. In an effort to be fair to him Oxenden wrote, "He was a little too much of a Churchman for some of my friends in Montreal, but he was a good and able man etc."[61] Dr. Henderson who succeeded Lobley as principal in 1877, was much closer to Oxenden's type of churchmanship. Abbott-Smith, a contemporary of Henderson's in Montreal, described the new Principal as,

a graduate of Trinity College, Dublin, an Irish Evangelical of the Old School, an accurate scholar, a clear and painstaking teacher and a man of deep piety whose gentle and modest bearing could not hide his real ability and strength of character.[62]

Oxenden wrote with approval of Dr. Henderson "under whose steady and unflagging superintendence the College still flourishes."[63]

[59]*Ibid.*, 98.
[60]Oxenden, *First Year in Canada*, 127.
[61]Oxenden, *Life*, 216–17.
[62]G. Abbott-Smith, *I Call to Mind* (Toronto, 1947), 70.
[63]Oxenden, *Life*, 216–17.

Under Bishop William Bennett Bond, who succeeded Oxenden in 1878, the College progressed and for a time preserved its Evangelical character. Bond confirmed Henderson in the principalship because he possessed, "the eminent qualifications of a Trinity College Dublin degree [and] a practical and varied experience of missionary work."[64] In 1879 Bond secured an act of incorporation (42 and 43 Vict. Cap. LXXII) which gave the College a legal base. At this time the title "Montreal Diocesan Theological College" appeared. In 1880, the College secured affiliation with McGill University. This enabled students from Montreal Diocesan to obtain an arts degree in Montreal before beginning their studies in divinity. The resources of McGill, in terms of staff and library, were placed at the service of the College.

Bond's difficulties over the degree-granting power indicate the existence of some opposition to Montreal Diocesan from the supporters of Bishop's. In 1881, Bond attempted to secure legal recognition of the Diocesan College's right to grant theological degrees and was opposed by Bishop J. W. Williams of Quebec. The subject of theological degrees was accordingly referred to the Provincial Synod of the Ecclesiastical Province of Canada. While awaiting its decision, Bond received a letter from Sir William Dawson, the principal of McGill, suggesting that, if necessary, McGill might come to the assistance of Montreal Diocesan, by granting degrees in divinity.[65] This proposal proved unnecessary since the Ecclesiastical Province of Canada secured legislation providing for the granting of degrees by the Metropolitan Archbishop of the Province acting on the advice of a board of examiners.

According to John Cooper, the historian of the Diocese of Montreal, this episode over the degree-granting power, represented the final *rapprochement* between the Anglican community and McGill. This result he attributes largely to the fact that Dawson and Bond had a great deal in common. "Not least was the belief that science was the handmaid of religion, and that each revelation of the physical world was simply another manifestation of the wonderful works of God."[66]

The College continued to progress in the eighteen-eighties, partly because its staff was reinforced by a number of clergymen and laymen who gave their services free. In 1882, Bishop Bond taught pastoral theology. Later L. H. Davidson gave instruction in legal matters coming within the province of a clergyman. Canon Lennox Mills, later the bishop of Ontario, taught church history over a period of

[64] Quoted in Cooper, 129. [65] *Ibid.*, 130.
[66] *Ibid.*, 131.

years. The Henderson period ended with the death of the Principal in 1896, only a few days prior to the opening of the new block of college buildings on University Street on October 21, 1896.

Wesleyan Theological College, Montreal was established as the result of a petition presented to the Canada Wesleyan Methodist Conference in 1872 by five members of the Methodist Church, including James Ferrier, the merchant and politician and David Torrance, who was subsequently president of the Bank of Montreal.[67] The memorialists asserted that for many years they had been "deeply convinced of the vast importance of establishing a Theological Institution in the city of Montreal, both for its advantages to the Connexion generally, as well as to strengthen the interests of Methodism in this city." They asked that immediate steps be taken to establish the institution and promised to raise forty or fifty thousand dollars for the purpose. They offered to hand over the entire government of the College to the conference.[68]

After consideration of this petition by a large committee of ministers and laymen, the Conference resolved to accept the offer of Ferrier and his associates. It also decided to assume control of the appointment of the professors as well as of the Board of Management.

The Rev. George Douglas was appointed the theological tutor in the proposed College. In 1873 the institution began instruction in the basement of Dominion Square Church, with a student body of six. A year later, the first report of the College was read to the conference. Douglas had lectured in "Theology, Anthropology and Homiletics," and courses in psychology, moral philosophy, logic and two of the natural sciences had been taken by the students from Wesleyan at McGill University.

The early development of the College was largely the work of George Douglas (1825–94) who became principal in 1874. Douglas, a Scot, had come to Montreal with his parents in 1832 and had gone to England to study for the Methodist ministry in 1849. Ordained in 1850, he had held charges in Montreal, Kingston, Toronto, and Hamilton. He was an eloquent preacher and a firm believer in the fundamental importance of religious training in education. In an address on education he insisted, "It is the moral and religious which supply the only stimulus to, and realm for, indefinite mental development."[69]

[67]The other signatories were W. Clendinning, John Torrance, and James Ferrier, Jr.
[68]This section is based mainly upon material kindly supplied to the author by the United Church Archives, Toronto.
[69]George Douglas, *Discourses and Addresses* (Toronto, 1894), 305.

He maintained that the finest elements in European and British cultures were the reflection of underlying Christian influences:

> Look at the influence which the coming of Christianity exerted, opening the vista of the ideal and the infinite. Genius rekindled her fires at this altar and the sacred portraits of Titian, and the cartoons of Raphael, and the crucifixion scenes of Van Dyke, and the cantatas of Ambrose, and the Gregorian chants of Gregory, tell how divine ideals winged immortal genius for higher flights in art and song than the ages had ever witnessed before. And then, if we come down to the history of the Motherland and look at the brilliant galaxy which culminated in the Elizabethan period, what is the admission of cold and cynical Hallam, no friend of Christianity? Why that the power that woke the genius of England, which warmed and vitalized it into peerless achievement, was the translation into the vernacular of the blessed Bible.[70]

Douglas argued that the church should undertake to foster the vital connection between religion and culture. He pointed out that some Canadian literature showed "a sympathy with the scientific atheism which is abroad, and an ill-concealed insolence towards evangelistic Christianity." He therefore concluded:

> I take these as a solemn warning of the evil of divorcing intellect from conscience, and as a solemn admonition to the Church to guard her rising manhood by providing those appliances which will train in loyalty, with truth divine, as well as for the highest possibilities of intellectual achievement.[71]

By enactment of the General Conference in 1878, Wesleyan Theological College was affiliated with Victoria College and with McGill University. The College was incorporated in 1879.

Like Presbyterian College in Montreal, Wesleyan was intended to provide ministers for work among French-speaking as well as among English-speaking Canadians. In 1878, in the *Journal of the Second General Conference of the Methodist Church of Canada*, the report of the Wesleyan Theological College said that the object of the institution was "in general, in training candidates for the ministry, and more particularly, in educating young men for the French mission work, and of giving greater prominence to the educational interests of Methodism in the Province of Quebec." The report asserted that the College was established in a centre "where we have to contend, not only with the gigantic superstitions of Romanism, but also with the insidious influences of "latitudinarianism." According to the report, friends of the College believed that the institution had before it a great field of usefulness in opposing "both these forms of error,"

[70]*Ibid.*, 306.   [71]*Ibid.*, 307–8.

and "that a Methodist College right here in the commercial metropolis of the Dominion, teaching Methodist theology, and surrounded by Methodist influences, must do much to further the cause of Christianity."[72]

Despite its high hopes for the training of ministers for service in French Canada, the real future of Wesleyan Theological College lay in its work among English-speaking Canadians. The Report of 1878 indicated that only three candidates for the French work had attended classes at the College and the work never assumed significant proportions. The College made an important contribution to the cause of English-speaking Methodism in Canada. When Douglas died in 1894 the College had an enrolment of seventy-two and a building free from debt on the McGill campus. According to the editors of Douglas' sermons, twenty per cent of the Methodist ministers serving in Canada in 1894 were graduates of the institution.[73] In its fifty-three years of service prior to the end of its career as a separate institution in 1926, Wesleyan Theological College trained about nine hundred ministers for service in the Methodist Church.[74]

At Bishop's University, the humanities and theology continued to dominate the picture. There was little sign of the shift to either the physical or the social sciences until after the turn of the century. Bishop's remained very much a church college. Indeed, an act passed in 1870 (34 Vict., cap. 48) bound the University more closely to the Synods of the Dioceses of Quebec and Montreal. The act provided that the corporation should consist of five trustees and members of the council to be chosen from such members of the Church of England, "as the bishops may deem fit; the number of such remainder to be in the proportion of three trustees and three members of council for every five named by every synod."

In this period Bishop's began the process of attempting to strengthen its position by adding new faculties to the university. The Bishop's Medical Faculty was established in 1871. It functioned in Montreal where it fought a rather acrimonious battle for survival against the already entrenched Medical Faculty of McGill. In 1880 Bishop's established a Law Faculty in Sherbrooke at the request of the St. Francis Bar. The Law Faculty made a brave beginning with a staff of five under Dean Robert Newton Hall.

[72]Report of the Wesleyan Theological College, 1878.
[73]George Douglas, *Discourses and Addresses*, xxxviii.
[74]See Report of the College to the General Council of the United Church of Canada, 1926.

Under the principalship of J. A. Lobley (1877–85) Bishop's had a faculty consisting mainly of Anglican clergy, each man teaching a variety of subjects. Lobley himself was professor of classics and also taught mathematics, logic, rhetoric and literature. The Rev. Dr. Scarth, the rector of St. George's Church, Lennoxville, taught pastoral theology and church history. Henry Roe, the professor of divinity taught courses in Hebrew, Greek text, Pearson on the Creed, Brown on the Thirty-nine Articles, Paley's *Evidences*, and Hooker's *Ecclesiastical Polity*. One of Roe's students wrote, "He was the whole show, taking almost every subject for every year men [i.e. men of every year]."[75]

In an effort to broaden the curriculum Bishop's employed the device of appointing teachers from Bishop's College School, which was run in conjunction with the University, as members of the university staff at a small increase in salary. The Rev. Philip C. Read was appointed rector of the school in 1877. In the following year he was also appointed professor of logic and moral philosophy in the University. After giving up the headship of the school, Read was appointed professor of classics in 1883. One of his students reported, "He had the faculty of imparting knowledge. We were always glad when he preached in Chapel . . . Vim, vigour and punch . . . interesting."[76]

R. W. Hudspeth, a master at the school, was appointed lecturer in natural sciences, at a salary of one hundred dollars a year, in 1881. Although an able man Hudspeth seemed unable to arouse much interest in science, perhaps because the humanistic tradition of the University was too much for him. He was reappointed, this time as lecturer in physics and chemistry, at the same salary in 1890.

Another subject not destined to be given prominence at Bishop's until much later had its tentative beginning in 1889 with the appointment of G. B. Woolcombe, as lecturer in political economy, also at a salary of one hundred dollars a year.

Two important personalities at Bishop's during the Lobley régime were Lobley himself and Henry Roe. Lobley, a graduate of Trinity College, Cambridge, was a fine scholar and a conscientious, hard-working man who seems to have captured the affection of his students. One of them, G. Abbott-Smith later wrote of the Principal:

One of the finest scholars that the Motherland has ever sent to Canada, he was a stimulating teacher with the faculty of inspiring his students with a

[75] Masters, *Bishop's University: The First Hundred Years*, 65.
[76] *Ibid.*, 65.

love of their work.... One could wish for no higher human ideal of devotion than that which Dr. Lobley exemplified in his life and his work. He gave himself unreservedly to those whom he served and, humanly speaking, wore himself out before his time in that self-sacrificing service.[77]

Roe, a graduate of Bishop's, was appointed professor of divinity in 1873, and dean of divinity and vice-principal in 1882. Prior to his appointment at Bishop's, he had been one of the ablest and most effective of the clergy in the Diocese of Quebec. A pronounced high churchman and a rigid disciplinarian, he eventually resigned as dean in 1891 because of a difference of opinion with Principal Thomas Adams over a question of discipline. Roe considered the Principal's policy too soft.

The union of all Presbyterian Synods in Canada to form the Presbyterian Church in Canada in 1875 led to a further consolidation of the churches' educational facilities in the Maritimes. Previously the Synods of Nova Scotia and New Brunswick in connection with the Church of Scotland had sent their theological students to Great Britain or to Dalhousie. In 1875 they appointed a professor to The Theological Hall. In 1878 the Board of the Hall purchased in Halifax a fine building, Pine Hill, the former home of a Mr. Albro. In 1879 the institution was incorporated as "The Presbyterian College, Halifax," a name which it was destined to retain until 1926.

The original staff of three professors reflected the three component elements of the Presbyterian Church in the Maritimes. The Principal and Professor of Systematic Theology was the Rev. A. McKnight who had belonged to the Free Church. Allan Pollok, the professor of church history and pastoral theology, had belonged to the Church of Scotland. Dr. John Currie, the professor of Hebrew, had been a member of the former secession church.[78]

Under the presidency of Artemas Wyman Sawyer (1869–93) Acadia achieved a significant broadening-out of its art programme. Sawyer represented the New England influence upon higher education in the Maritimes. Born in Vermont and a graduate of Dartmouth College, he had been professor of classics at Acadia from 1855 to 1860. During this period he had demonstrated that he was a superb teacher with an unusual ability to make his students think and express their thoughts in words. Sawyer had caught the spirit of Dr. Charles W. Eliot of Harvard and his presidency at Acadia was chiefly notable for the introduction of a considerable number of electives in a hitherto more rigidly prescribed curriculum. While a firm supporter of the classical

[77] Dr. G. Abbott-Smith, quoted in *Ibid.*, 64.
[78] Falconer, and Watson, *Pine Hill Divinity Hall*, 16–17.

system, Sawyer believed that other subjects too should be stressed. In 1874, he recommended the appointment of John Freeman Tufts, a graduate of Acadia and Harvard, as professor of history. In announcing the new appointment, he prophesied that in the future more attention must be given to modern subjects. He advocated a system of electives which would enable students to give more time to the study of modern languages, science, education, and history.

Science continued to be stressed although the Department had periodic crises. That greater emphasis was to be given to science was indicated by the appointment of William Elder as professor of geology and chemistry in 1869. At the Convocation of 1870, Elder spoke for ninety minutes on the value of scientific study. He asserted that freedom of enquiry and independence of thought were as needful for science as they were for the apprehension of revealed truth. [One can imagine the sensation of a modern university convocation if a junior member of the academic staff made a speech of ninety minutes.]

After this vigorous advocacy of the cause of science Elder left Acadia in 1872. There seems to have been some doubt as to the future of science at Acadia at this time, but it was resolved by a resolution of the Board in 1873 that "the continuation of the department of Science is essential to the prosperity of the college."[79] George T. Kennedy of Montreal was appointed professor of natural science in 1874. In 1880, he was succeeded by Albert Coldwell, an Acadia graduate of 1869, who held the Chair of Science for twenty years.

Another significant addition to the course occurred in the field of English language and literature. After 1858, when Daniel Welton became tutor in English, some attention had been given to the subject, but generally as a part of courses in belles lettres and philosophy. In 1880, Jacob Gould Schurman was appointed professor of English literature, logic, and political economy. Schurman, a graduate of Acadia, had studied at Edinburgh and on the continent. He was young, enthusiastic and an excellent teacher. In his brief stay at Acadia (1880–82), he made English literature a popular subject of study. He was succeeded by Elias Miles Kierstead who remained at Acadia as professor of English literature and logic until 1905.

There was an increasing demand for electives at Acadia in the eighteen-eighties. This resulted in a change in the curriculum, the grant of permission to substitute a modern language for Greek. To provide for increased enrolment in modern languages, Luther E. Wortman was appointed professor of languages and history in 1886. In 1891 seniors and juniors were given permission to elect a science or

[79]Longley, *Acadia University*, 84.

mathematics. Francis R. Haley, an Acadia graduate of 1884, was appointed professor of physics in 1891, a chair which he held until 1930.

In 1893, the number of electives was again increased. The course for freshmen and sophomores was still rigidly prescribed, with the exception of the choice between Greek or a modern language; but in the junior and senior years the curriculum permitted three electives which might be chosen from classics, mathematics, German, French, constitutional history, and science. At the same time there were significant additions to the library in the fields of philosophy, modern languages, history, science, classics, and mathematics.

During the eighteen-seventies and eighteen-eighties the Theological Institute tried to cope with the problem of maintaining an adequate staff. In the early eighteen-seventies teaching was in the hands of President Sawyer and two venerable ex-Presidents of Acadia, Cramp and Crawley. In 1876 the Rev. Daniel Welton joined the staff of the Institute as Professor of theology and church polity. He spent the next two years in study at Leipzig, where he secured his Ph.D. Welton then returned to Acadia as professor of Hebrew and systematic theology. In 1881, Cramp died and Crawley retired. The burden of work at the Institute fell on Welton but he soon left to go to the new Baptist College in Toronto, one of the forerunners of McMaster.

Despite these set-backs the work of the Institute continued and in 1889 the Board of Acadia contemplated the expansion of the work of the Institute into the field of post-graduate training. To be sure, shortage of money meant that the expansion would be modest. The Board appointed a committee to see if some post-graduate training in theology was possible "without materially increasing the expenses of the college." As a result, E. M. Kierstead offered a course in homiletics. In 1892 Acadia introduced a course leading to the degree of Bachelor of Theology.

One important step was taken in the early eighteen-nineties. In spite of the fact that Acadia had been established and remained a denominational university, no formal instruction in the study of the Bible was given to arts students for more than fifty years. In the eighteen-nineties there were demands among the supporters of the University for compulsory courses in Bible for all freshmen and sophomores at Acadia. These compulsory courses were now introduced. They were made possible when G. P. Payzant of Windsor, Nova Scotia, financed the establishment of two theological professorships.

5. The Onset of Liberalism (1890-1920)

AT THE BEGINNING of Chapter IV, I suggested some of the changes in thought which church colleges continued to develop. In the years after 1890 these changes had an increasing impact upon these institutions.

This was especially true at Victoria where the faculty had been largely trained in Germany, so that they were especially familiar with German ideas of higher criticism.[1] In the period 1881-92, all the major appointments (including A. P. Coleman, G. C. Workman, L. E. Horning, and F. W. Wallace) were given to men who had done postgraduate work in Germany. The one important exception was J. F. McLaughlin. George C. Workman was a particularly advanced exponent of the critical approach to Scripture, judged at least by the current Canadian standards of his time. This was made clear by his famous lecture on Messianic Prophecy, delivered in 1890. He adopted the "Grammatico-Historical" principle of interpretation, claiming that every passage of Scripture must be understood as meaning only what the writer consciously intended to convey. He eliminated from Messianic Prophecy a large number of Psalms and individual texts limiting it to those passages in which the prophecy presented the Messianic hope of future deliverance to the people of Israel. He set aside many Old Testament passages quoted in the New Testament and described in the New Testament as being fulfilled. His lecture was an example of the anthropological approach to revelation which I have already described.[2] Workman's lecture created a controversy which ended in his resignation from Victoria College after the Principal, Nathanael Burwash, had suggested that he be transferred from theology to arts. He afterwards taught at the Wesleyan Theological College in Montreal with the same result. A more discreet man than Workman was J. F. McLaughlin, the professor of Old Testament at Victoria. According to C. B. Sissons,[3] McLaughlin's professorship "was exercised with

[1]See pp. 89-92 of this volume.
[2]Nathanael Burwash, *The History of Victoria College* (Toronto, 1927), 408-9. J. H. Riddell, *Methodism and the Middle West*, 229.
[3]Sissons, *A History of Victoria University*, 195-6.

distinction and without doctrinal dispute through forty years, although his theology was as modern as that of Workman." McLaughlin's Sunday afternoon Bible class was a great institution at Victoria.

The climate of opinion at Victoria in regard to the Bible is suggested by a bibliography of suggested reading for the clergy published in June, 1909, in *Acta Victoriana*, the student monthly magazine. It was compiled by Clyo Jackson who had received suggestions from the members of the Victoria staff and who had made extensive use of two lists published in the *Methodist Review Quarterly*. Jackson's list may be regarded as representative of the position of the Victoria staff in 1909 in regard to the problem of higher criticism. *Acta* had defended Victoria in February, 1905, against the charge of advocating extreme views on higher criticism, and had suggested that the College belonged to the "moderate wing." Jackson's bibliography of 1909 indicates that this claim was probably justified. The list included a mixture of critical and conservative books, although the bias of the compiler was obviously on the side of higher criticism. Among the critical works were the "International Critical" commentary, "more valuable to the scholar than to the preacher"; commentaries by S. R. Driver on Genesis, Isaiah, and Deuteronomy, the last of the three "specially recommended"; commentaries by A. S. Peake on Job, E. H. Plumptre on Ecclesiastes and James, and by T. K. Cheyne on Isaiah. Moderately critical scholars such as Bishop Westcott on John and Bishop Lightfoot on Galatians and Philippians were listed. Conservative commentaries, such as Ryle on Ezra-Nehemiah, Moule on Philippians, and Plummer on James, were also included. The viewpoint of the compiler of the bibliography was shown by his comment on the Cambridge Bible, "Scholarly yet popular. Some volumes represent a somewhat obsolescent standpoint."

In 1909, the same year in which *Acta Victoriana* published the above-mentioned bibliography, the Carman-Jackson controversy occurred. It was a further landmark in the progress of the higher criticism at Victoria and in the Methodist Church generally. Dr. J. A. Carman, the general superintendent and a conservative in his attitude to the Scriptures, crossed swords with the Rev. George Jackson, the pastor of Sherbourne Street Methodist Church, over a lecture on Genesis which Jackson had delivered at the Y. M. C. A. in Toronto. The controversy was vigorous since Jackson, in the words of J. H. Riddell, was "generally provocative in his statements" and "sometimes belligerent," while Dr. Carman, the conservative, was described as "positive, assertive, dogmatic." Despite the reputation thus achieved by Jackson as a critic, he was appointed professor of English Bible at Victoria in 1909. As a sequel to this controversy a resolution was introduced at the General Conference of 1910 deploring the teaching of higher criticism in Methodist colleges, but it was headed off by a more innocuous resolution introduced by A. D. Watson, M.D., and Dr. J. W. Sparling of Wesley College, Winnipeg. The net result was to clear the way for the teaching of higher criticism in Methodist colleges. According to Dr. Riddell, the general effect of the controversy was "a wholesome liberation of the thinking of that church (the Methodist Church) from a purely dogmatic approach."[4]

In other Canadian colleges too, the new ideas were having some effect. In 1902 the faculty of Wycliffe College were already wrestling with the works of S. R. Driver. A student's lecture notes indicate that H. J. Cody in his course in Old Testament dealt with Driver's views in regard to the authorship of Isaiah, as well as with more conservative opinion. That Dr. Cody himself was conservative is suggested by the student's notes on the dating of Deuteronomy. Driver had presented the argument that the book was written by the priests in the time of Hezekiah and attributed to Moses. "Prof. Cody thinks such reconstruction an impossible reconstruction. Practical difficulty: the difficulty of saving the moral character of the writers. It is not so that people issued books under other people's names. Here is a crucial point that it came from Moses. If it did not and came from them they were frauds."

Montreal Diocesan College was still largely conservative in the eighteen-nineties. Bishop Carmichael in his lectures on Isaiah adhered to the view that there could not have been two Isaiahs. Yet liberal views were introduced in the College by Frederick Julius Steen who held the Chair of Apologetics and Church History from 1896 to 1901. Steen has been described as "thoroughly conversant with the results of the far reaching work of modern and contemporary students."[5] In 1901 Steen was compelled by the board of Montreal Diocesan to resign from the College because of his advanced ideas. Archbishop Bond also inhibited him from preaching in the Diocese of Montreal on the ground that his views on the inspiration of the Bible and on a number of theological questions were erroneous. In 1902 the inhibition was withdrawn and he became senior assistant minister and

[4]Riddell, *Methodism*, 288–90; Sissons, *Victoria University*, 233–40.
[5]Frank Dawson Adams, *A History of Christ Church Cathedral Montreal* (Montreal, 1941), 100–103; *Recollections of the Right Rev. John Cragg Farthing, Bishop of Montreal, 1909–1939*, 115–17; G. Abbott-Smith, *I Call to Mind* (Toronto, 1947), 74–6.

vicar of Christ Church Cathedral where he had been special preacher since 1898 but he was not re-appointed to the faculty of the College. Yet afterwards, opinions similar to Steen's were expounded at the College by G. Abbott-Smith who had been appointed professor of New Testament literature in 1898. Abbott-Smith introduced higher criticism into his lectures, claiming that the clergy should be more aware of these ideas since they would have to contend with them. The Valedictorian of 1905 at Montreal Diocesan, W. O. Raymond, introduced liberal views of the Scripture in his address.

There is some evidence that evolutionary thinking had begun to influence the Montreal Diocesan constituency. An example was an article by the Rev. W. P. R. Lewis on "Spiritual Evolution: One Aspect of Human Character" which was published in the *Montreal Diocesan Theological College Magazine* in March, 1899. Mr. Lewis asserted that man is born with some "indelible, ineffaceable, immutable qualities" but he stressed the fact that he must also go through a process of progressive improvement.

Let us not forget that . . . each man's life is the scene of constant development. All the progressive and eager characteristics of a living soul demand it. Our life as we use it changes. In our acquirements, attainments, in what we hope and believe, in what we have said and done, we have brought about an unmistakable, a distinct and everlasting change. Every one of us is doing it, day by day. It must be so, for we have been given the inestimable privilege of ever travelling on to greater and better things. . . . Forces without and within change us. Our social place, our friends and loved ones, our environment generally; by travel, reading, intercourse, thought, our characters are changed, we obtain new ideas, better discernment, larger outlook.

At Bishop's University, F. J. B. Allnatt (professor of pastoral theology in 1887 and afterwards dean), although moderately conservative in his attitude to the Scriptures, was somewhat influenced by critical ideas in regard to the Old Testament.

At Manitoba College, the Presbyterian theological institution in Winnipeg, Professor Andrew Baird, a strong conservative, was engaged in refuting the higher critics of the Old Testament in the eighteen-nineties.[6]

To be sure the older ideas did not immediately disappear. In the year before George Munro Grant's inaugural lecture at Queen's a

---

[6]Andrew Browning Baird, *Notes on Introduction to the Old Testament, Printed for the use of the Students in Manitoba College, Winnipeg* (Toronto, 1898).

writer in the *Queen's College Journal* urged that the university should sponsor a day of prayer. The writer reported that a day of prayer had recently been held at Princeton and had resulted in sixty conversions. A subsequent visit from the Evangelists, Moody and Sankey, had given the movement of revival fresh impetus. The writer concluded, "Why should not Old Queen's have that spirit pass through her walls and leave the impress of its touch. It would increase the number of students and quadruple her power for good in the world."[7]

The address by Dr. Ross, professor of apologetics and New Testament criticism at Queen's, at the opening of the Theological Hall in 1893, suggests that the theology professors at the University were more conservative than the philosophers and the Principal. Dr. Ross rejected the evolutionary explanation of the emergence of the Hebrew religion and of Christianity. He insisted that Moses' conception of God was not the product of human intellectual evolution but of divine revelation. He insisted upon the central place of the inspired Bible as the source of human knowledge about God and declared:

Apart from what is revealed in the Bible, we would have no reliable knowledge of God as creator, orderer, sovereign, saviour, judge. The sacred writers were conscious that they were divinely inspired and this they testified to. They were the vehicles of revelation made to them by Him who seeth the end from the beginning. The writers were led by the spirit to compose the records which disclose the progressive evolution of God's redemptive dealings with mankind.[8]

Judging by the articles and editorials which appeared in the *McMaster University Monthly* in the eighteen-nineties, the tone of that University was conservative in theology and Evangelical. The *Monthly* chronicled the activities of the Fyfe Missionary Society, a student organization, with care. It commented on the death of Charles Haddon Spurgeon, the great Baptist preacher, and noted the progress of the Grande Ligne Mission in Quebec. It published articles critical of Darwin and the higher critics.[9]

Professor Sissons reports a gradual decline in the evidences of religious zeal at Victoria. There was a prayer meeting every Saturday

[7]*Queen's College Journal*, Feb. 12, 1876.
[8]*Ibid.*, Nov. 18, 1893.
[9]Typical of the articles in the *McMaster University Monthly* was the report of the Fyfe Missionary Society in the issue of Nov., 1891; an article by H. C. Priest, "Evolution and Ethics," in June, 1894; references to a pamphlet by Professor Goodspeed on "Some Unsolved Problems of Higher Criticism," in Feb., 1895; and the reference to an article by Dr. Sayce on higher criticism, in the column *Editorial Notes* in the issue of Jan., 1896.

evening from five to six in the period from 1867 to 1880;[10] but this did not continue after Victoria moved to Toronto in 1892.

The files of *Acta Victoriana*, for 1904-9, indicate the cross-currents of opinion at Victoria and the effects of critical as well as of Evangelical thought. There were still signs of the old Methodist tradition. In 1904, the Victoria Band, consisting of faculty members and students, was still holding Evangelistic services in Toronto and other places.[11] Victoria was still sending out candidates for the mission field, seven in the autumn of 1906.[12] Victoria men participated in the annual conferences organized by the Student Volunteer Movement at Lakeside, Ohio, where the claims of the mission field were presented by John R. Mott and others.

While *Acta* provided evidence of the continuance of the older Evangelical thought at Victoria it also (in 1904-9) provided many signs of the movement toward liberal theology. Among many people in Canada the adoption of a critical attitude to the Bible had resulted in a changed theology. The old theology had said that sinful man could be saved from eternal damnation only by divine grace. This was replaced by the proposition that man, who was essentially good, had a fair prospect of imitating the example set for him by Christ. A number of articles published in *Acta* indicated that Victoria men or other writers who appeared to be endorsed by *Acta* shared the view that the essential function of the Christian was to imitate the example of Christ. They believed too in the possibility of progress by the Christian toward a more complete fulfillment of this purpose. They showed little sympathy for the concept that man was a sinner saved by grace.

Some examples of the effects of higher criticism and of the adoption of a liberal theology may be cited from *Acta Victoriana*.

In December, 1904, *Acta* published an obituary article describing Principal Caven of Knox College as one who had been notably successful in living the life indicated by "the Great Exemplar." The March, 1905, number contained an article praising Professor McLaughlin's Sunday afternoon Bible class partly because he was able to provide "relief from intellectual difficulties." (i.e. He expounded higher criticism.) In October, 1905, *Acta* described the Eastern Student Convention for young women, "who wished to be led into the doing of God's will," which had been held during the summer at Silver Bay, New York. John R. Mott, a man who still had much ortho-

[10]Sissons, *Victoria University*, 155.   [11]*Acta Victoriana*, Oct., 1904.
[12]*Ibid.*, Oct., 1906.

doxy in his thought, appeared to be critical of Evangelicalism and of its stress on conversion. Robert E. Speer, another Christian leader, emphasized the idea of progressive improvement and appeared to envisage the Christian life as largely a matter of morality. Being a Christian was a process of imitating Christ. He urged, "Let us not be impatient if things come slowly. We are in school to be made like Christ, so let us go forward and do the work of Christ."

The same idea, that the Christian should try to imitate Christ's example, was stressed by an undergraduate, Miss E. L. Hildred in describing the Eastern Conference of the Y.W.C.A. at Silver Bay, New York. She wrote:

> It was in the platform meetings that we realized what that Christianity was, that had done so much for the world. There we saw visions of the Christ life, and vaguely felt what it would be to make our lives conform to the pattern placed before us.[13]

Miss Hildred felt that our lives are inspired by God to live a life of Service for others.

Some articles showed the impact of scientific thought, particularly that of the biologists, upon the minds of students. David Boyle, in an article entitled "Things We Want to Know About Early Man," suggested questions he would like answered in a forthcoming lecture at the University of Toronto on "Palaeolithic Man."[14] Boyle accepted the evolutionary theory of man's development but did not view it uncritically. He wanted the term primitive man defined. He was willing to accept the idea that contemporary savages were examples of primitive man but wanted to know more about their predecessors. He wondered how civilized man had secured his religious sense and did not think it could have been by a process of heredity. He noted that the language of "savages" is often richer and more specialized than one would have expected.

Another writer, A. Kirschmann,[15] criticized A. R. Wallace, the co-author of the theory of evolution, on the ground that he did not push his theory far enough. In his volume, *Man's Place in the Universe*, Wallace had argued that the earth was the only planet in the solar system, and that the solar system was the only system in the universe which could sustain life. Kirschmann contended that Wallace should have applied the evolutionary theory of the adaptability of organisms and the theory of the variation of the species to the universe in general.

[13]*Ibid.*, Oct., 1906. [14]*Ibid.*, Feb., 1905.
[15]*Ibid.*, Dec., 1905.

In spite of influences tending to weaken the holding of conservative faith at Victoria, there was still a good deal of formal religious activity in 1913,[16] although all students were free to embrace or avoid the religious exercises and studies of the College. The services included the regular chapel service from Monday to Friday from 9:50 to 10:10; weekly meetings of the Y.M.C.A.; and meetings of special groups such as the Missionary Society and the Student Volunteer Movement. However, Sissons says it is doubtful whether religion had as large a place in the life of Victoria as even ten years earlier.

It would be dangerous to generalize about the influence of more liberal ideas about the Scriptures upon the development of church colleges. But in some cases, at least, federation with a pluralistic university came less to be feared by church colleges which were themselves becoming more liberal. This was probably the case with Victoria and later with Trinity. Other church colleges, more resistent to change, were confirmed in the desire for independence by the fear of intellectual infiltration. Such was the case with McMaster.

It was in this atmosphere of transition that Trinity reconsidered the question of federation. There had been previous advocates of federation at Trinity, notably the Rev. Herbert Symonds, a young lecturer at the College during the provostship of Dr. Charles Body (1881–1900). Symonds had come to Canada in the eighteen-eighties to learn farming but had soon abandoned it in order to enter Trinity as an undergraduate. From 1887 to 1892 he was a lecturer and then a professor of divinity on the staff of Trinity University. Symonds, one of the most progressive members of the staff, exercised a considerable influence on the policy and teaching of Trinity. He urged that Trinity should seek federation with the University of Toronto if it could be brought about without sacrifice of principle. In 1894 he published a booklet, *Trinity and Federation*, which created a profound impression among supporters of Trinity. Many of the principles which he advocated were incorporated in the subsequent articles of federation.

The principal architect of federation at Trinity was the Rev. Thomas Macklem who became fourth provost in May, 1900. Macklem was a graduate of Upper Canada College and of St. John's College, Cambridge. He accepted the provostship on condition that he should be free to advocate the federation of Trinity and the University of Toronto and to enter into immediate negotiations with the Provincial government and the University of Toronto.

[16]Sissons, *Victoria University*, 250.

The negotiations which culminated in the entry of Trinity into the University of Toronto covered the period between 1900 and 1903.[17] After Macklem's appointment in 1900, negotiations were opened with the Hon. George Ross, premier of Ontario and minister of education. An act passed in 1901 removed some of the impediments to the entry of Trinity. The principle of representation in the university Senate of graduates of the federated colleges was accepted.

Although the Act of 1901 was not entirely acceptable to Trinity, it provided for the continuance of negotiations. A year later they were resumed between a commission representing Trinity and the Trustees of the University of Toronto. By 1903 the Trinity commission reported that, except for small details, agreement had been reached. The report was adopted on June 25, 1903. The definitive agreement was concluded on August 25, 1903, and proclaimed by the Lieutenant-Governor on November 18, 1903. The statutory provisions for the carrying out of the act consisted in the Act of 1887, the relevant sections of the Act of 1901, and a short amending Act of 1904. The agreement went into effect on October 1, 1904.

One may ask why Trinity, after resisting federation for some fifty years, finally came to accept it. A letter from Bishop Sweatman to Provost Macklem on July 8, 1903, suggests that the reason was the insufficiency of Anglican support to Trinity. Sweatman, after describing federation for Trinity as a "calamitous necessity," asserted that the College had been weakened by "the party attacks upon the teaching of the College" which had led to the establishment of Huron and Wycliffe. He continued:

> I am convinced too that the divisions in the Church, during the period when these two rival institutions were brought into being, are largely responsible for that lack of support, financial and otherwise, accorded to Trinity University which has reduced it to the position which has made federation with the Provincial University a practically vital necessity.[18]

In spite of Bishop Sweatman's regrets, the entry of Trinity to the University of Toronto had an important bearing upon the whole position of church colleges within the University.

The terms of Trinity's entry were similar to those of Victoria's entry fourteen years earlier. The agreement with Trinity was based upon the same distinction between college subjects and university subjects. This distinction was stated in the Act of 1901 and repeated in the

[17]T. A. Reed, *A History of the University of Trinity College, Toronto* (Toronto, 1952).
[18]Quoted in *Ibid.*, 128–9.

Agreement of 1903. College subjects were to include: theology, Greek, Latin, ancient history, English, French, German, oriental languages, and ethics. The university subjects were to be: mathematics, physics, astronomy, geology, mineralogy, chemistry, biology, physiology, history, ethnology, philology, Italian, Spanish, philosophy, logic, metaphysics, education, political science, jurisprudence, constitutional law, and constitutional history.

However, the agreement with Trinity clarified and strengthened the position of the church colleges in a pluralistic university. Unlike Victoria, Trinity was insistent on safeguarding its right to teach religious knowledge to all its students. This right was safeguarded by a clause in the Act of 1901. After making a provision against religious tests at the University of Toronto the act went on to state:

Nothing herein contained shall be considered as interfering with the rights of any federated University or federated College to make such provision in regard to religious instruction and worship for its own students as it may deem proper.[19]

In accordance with this statement, the Agreement of 1903 gave Trinity the right to provide for its students religious instruction and religious influences in accordance with the teachings of the Church of England. Provision was made for the inclusion of religious knowledge subjects as a regular part of the arts curriculum of the University of Toronto. This curriculum was to include the subjects of Biblical Greek, Biblical literature, Christian ethics, apologetics, the evidences of natural and revealed religion, and church history, distributed as evenly as possible over the four years of the arts course. Instruction and examination in these subjects was to be entirely in the hands of the colleges as heretofore. Optional subjects were to be provided in the arts curriculum for any of the above-named courses; but under the agreement, Trinity, like other church colleges, could make religious knowledge compulsory for students taking their arts course there.

Trinity made provision for the distribution of theological options evenly over the four years of the pass course and, as far as possible, over each year of the honours courses. In making religious knowledge compulsory for all its undergraduates, Trinity made effective what Professor Sissons later described as "a right which Victoria had never sought, or indeed desired."[20]

Under Macklem's long provostship (1900–21), the process of Trinity's

[19]Quoted in *Ibid.*, 126.
[20]Sissons, *Victoria University*, 223.

integration with the University was carried on. Macklem was anxious to move Trinity from its old Queen Street site to a position in close juxtaposition to the rest of the University. By 1912 he had sold the Queen Street site and buildings to the city of Toronto and had had plans prepared for the new buildings in Queen's Park.

During the Macklem regime a number of significant appointments were made to the staff of Trinity. A great teacher of classics, Eric Trevor Owen, was appointed to the staff in 1903. A graduate of Trinity, Owen had a long career, first at Trinity and later at University College. Owen's gifts as a teacher were appreciated by all who sat under him. A contemporary has written of him, "His lectures, especially perhaps in the Greek epic and in Greek drama, were a constant source of inspiration; as a teacher, as a literary critic, and as a man of genuine dignity and sound judgment, his influence was deep and lasting."[21]

Francis Herbert Cosgrave was appointed to the Faculty of Divinity in 1906. A man who is remembered for the charm of his mannerisms, Cosgrave served with distinction for many years, and eventually became vicar of a church in Toronto. He returned to Trinity as its sixth provost in 1926.

Another important figure in the history of the University of Toronto, George Sidney Brett, was appointed to the staff of Trinity in 1908 as lecturer in classics and as librarian. Brett became one of Canada's great teachers of philosophy and held various posts at the University of Toronto: he was head of the Department of Philosophy and dean of the Graduate School. He had a great influence in the determination of the university curriculum. Throughout his long career at the University (1908–44) he kept in close touch with Trinity and strengthened the liaison between the College and the University.

Brett's greatest contribution to Canadian thought lay in his insistence that the history of philosophy must be thoroughly mastered before critical or speculative activities can be profitably undertaken.[22] He gave influential leadership in this direction and also pioneered the introduction of realism into the study of philosophy in Canada. Although a realist, Brett was fascinated by the great British idealists, Green, Bradley, and Bosanquet. He was suspicious of the special and limited interests of the Canadian idealists. His most outstanding and

[21]From notes supplied to the National Conference of Canadian Universities and Colleges by the University of Trinity College.
[22]John A. Irving, "Philosophical Trends in Canada between 1850 and 1950," *Philosophy and Phenomenological Research*, XII (2), Dec. 1951, 233–8.

permanent contributions were concerned with intellectual history, including the history of psychology, rather than systematic epistemology or metaphysics. He insisted that all through history creative achievements in literature and art have been the result not of accident or fancy but of great ideas critically maintained. To Brett, the history of philosophy was itself a living body of thought. Professor John A. Irving writes:

In the history of philosophy he [Brett] sought, rather, the meaning of existence for humanity. His unceasing use of the historical method must have been inspired also by a belief in the essential unity of civilization: he did much to establish that unity by exhibiting the logical and historical relationships between philosophical ideas and other great systems of ideas in science, literature, politics, and religion. In his dynamic mind the whole intellectual past of mankind seemed to live again.[23]

Brett's ideas had an important spokesman at Trinity, George Frederick Kingston, who was appointed to the staff in the Department of Ethics in 1922. Under Kingston, the Department of Ethics showed the influence of Brett to whose conception of education he adhered. Kingston later became dean of residence. In his work with students he showed a temperate wisdom combined with sound standards, a quality which later distinguished him as Bishop and Metropolitan.

Two years after the entry of Trinity, the position of the federated colleges in the University of Toronto was further strengthened by the passage of the University of Toronto Act of 1906. The act followed the presentation of the report of a royal commission which the Whitney government had appointed to consider the organization of the University. The commission was under the chairmanship of J. W. Flavelle and included Goldwin Smith, W. R. Meredith, B. E. Walker, H. J. Cody, D. Bruce Macdonald, and A. H. V. Colquhoun.[24]

The Act of 1906 was chiefly concerned with the transfer of direct authority from the government to the Board of Governors of the University over all but the purely academic interests of the University. The latter were left to the Senate. The feature of the act of especial importance to the federated colleges was the creation of a council of the Faculty of Arts to provide a forum for the discussion of arts work. In addition to the staff in university subjects, all members of the teaching staffs of the colleges above the rank of lecturer were voting members. Even lecturers on the permanent staff were non-voting members of the council.

[23]*Ibid.*, 238.
[24]Sissons, *Victoria University*, 225–8.

At McMaster the period between 1890 and 1920 was one of steady growth. Registration increased from forty in 1890–91, to two hundred and seven in 1899–1900, and three hundred and four in 1909–10.[25] In 1892 the Arts and Theology Faculties were merged into one university faculty. By 1894 the four year course in arts was in full operation. The *McMaster University Monthly*, a combined learned journal and undergraduate record, was founded in 1895 and the first beginnings of science studies were made. In the decade after 1900 the Chapel and the Science Building were constructed.

In 1908–10 a controversy began in regard to McMaster between the conservative and more liberal wings of the Baptist Church. The immediate issue was the question of the soundness of Professor I. G. Matthews' opinions in regard to the Old Testament. The Baptist Convention of Ontario and Quebec in 1910 considered the question and ended by merely stressing the need of a common ground on which both sections of disputants could unite.[26] According to the historians of McMaster, who had contemporary knowledge, "The right of the university to pursue investigation was vindicated, but there were wounds that were difficult to heal."[27] Dr. A. C. McKay who had been chancellor since 1905 was succeeded in 1911 by Dr. A. L. McCrimmon who met the task of "steering the institution through very troubled waters," the result of the Matthews controversy and of the dislocation occasioned by World War I. By 1920 the University appeared well on the way to recovery.

During the period 1895–1908 Western University had a further period of Anglican control and financial difficulty. Huron College which had severed its connection with the University in 1885, was itself in financial difficulties in 1895 and suggested reaffiliation with the University. This was arranged by a joint committee representing the two institutions. In 1895 too, the Senate re-established the Faculty of Arts on a denominational basis but altered the constitution to make it possible to engage professors and lecturers who were not members of the Church of England. During the next ten years the proposal to throw open the Senate to members of all religious denominations came up repeatedly but was not accomplished.

During the period from 1895 to 1905, Western tried to raise the quality of instruction in English, history, modern languages, and

[25]W. S. W. McLay, C. W. New, and G. P. Gilmour, *McMaster University, 1890–1940* (Hamilton, 1940).

[26]W. G. Carder, "Controversy in the Baptist Convention of Ontario and Quebec, 1908–1929," unpublished B.D. thesis, McMaster University.

[27]McLay, New, and Gilmour, *McMaster University*, 13.

classics, but gave only elementary courses in science.[28] A number of important appointments to the faculty were made in this period. In 1896, Dr. N. C. James, a graduate of the University of Toronto and a Ph.D. of Halle University, Germany, was appointed professor of modern languages. James served as provost of the University from 1902 to 1908. By his loyalty and devotion to the interests of Western he tided it over a period of grave difficulties.[29] Dr. W. F. Tamblyn was appointed to the Chair of English and History in 1901. In 1902 the Rev. C. C. Waller was appointed principal of Huron College. Waller, a strong Evangelical, played an active part in the affairs of the University and served as professor of Hebrew.

The movement toward secularization of the University came to a head in the years between 1905 and 1908. In 1905 the University was still in grave financial trouble. It was neither under direct control of the Church of England nor under any form of public supervision and failed to secure adequate support from either denominational or public sources. The Senate was divided over the question of a solution to the problem, some favouring complete secularization and others more control by the church. Progress toward a solution began in 1905 with the appointment of a joint committee representing the Diocese of Huron and the Senate. The committee decided to explore the possibilities of secularization. A large public meeting in London on February 24, 1906, debated the future of the University and appointed another committee. In 1906 an act of the Ontario legislature increased the influence of the Huron Synod in the University but abolished all religious tests for membership in the Senate. On October 21, 1907, a deputation from the Senate with other interested citizens appeared before the London City Council with a request for assistance. Subsequently H. A. Beattie, chairman of the finance committee of the city council, agreed to attempt to secure the passage of an act authorizing the city to give financial aid to the University on condition that the Bishop of Huron agreed that the university should be completely non-denominational. The Bishop of Huron, David Williams, gave his reluctant consent. Beattie and the city council were successful in obtaining the necessary legislation. The act (8 Edward VII., cap 145) authorized the city to make an annual grant for a period not exceeding five years, for the maintenance of the University, now to be

[28]Talman, and Talman, *Western, 1878–1953*, 43–54.
[29]Dr. A. C. Hill, a nephew of Dr. James, has told the author that Dr. James used to spend his summer vacations touring South-Western Ontario in order to solicit financial support from Anglican churches.

called The Western University of London, Ontario. In return, the Church of England surrendered control of the University. The act declared:

> The government of the University shall be undenominational and under public, municipal, or provincial control, or any or all of these . . . no religious test shall be required of any professor, lecturer, teacher, officer or servant, or of any student.

The Church of England, having given up control of the University, retained control of Huron College which continued as a theological seminary in affiliation with the University.

Huron continued its career under Principal C. C. Waller, a scholarly and devoted man, who piloted the College through many difficulties during his long period in office (1902–41). Waller, an Englishman, had been educated at St. John's College, Cambridge and Ridley Hall, Cambridge and had served on the staff of Montreal Diocesan (1890–97) and St. John's Hall, Highbury, England (1897–1900).

At Huron, Principal Waller was a vigorous administrator and an able teacher. J. J. Talman, in his history of Huron College, has described Waller's heavy teaching load.

> The Principal did not spare himself. He lectured for two hours on the Bible, the Greek Testament, and the Articles, and one hour in Latin, the Prayer Book, and the Book of Genesis. He lectured to the graduates for two hours each week in Greek Testament and one hour on Greek Patristics. When practicable, he also had an hour of reading. On four days each week he devoted fifteen minutes before Chapel to Greek Testament Exposition. He reviewed two sermons by students. Finally, he taught Greek in the University. This teaching load made his lightest possible week one of seventeen hours of lecturing. In addition, he spoke in Chapel and visited most of the places being supplied by his students: Sombra, Teeswater, Charing Cross, and Westminster. After he retired he wrote that there were few missions which he had not visited.[30]

It has been shown in Chapter IV that the connection between Queen's University and the Presbyterian Church was slight after the negotiation of Presbyterian Church Union in 1875, except that the church continued to give support to the Theological Faculty. The Faculty of Theology and the University were closely connected during the years from 1875 to 1911. From 1877 to 1902, Principal Grant also acted as primarius professor of divinity. D. M. Gordon, who succeeded Grant in 1903, carried on in the same dual capacity.

[30]James J. Talman, *Huron College 1863–1963* (London, 1963), 68.

T. R. Glover and D. D. Calvin have provided a glimpse of the life of a Queen's theological student during the Grant period.

Dean Inge once made a caustic criticism of Anglican seminaries for training clergy in small cathedral towns; what could be hoped when the gardeners were kept in greenhouses and the plants grew in the open? At Queen's everybody grew in the open, not least the Divinity students. Picture the training. Summer by summer the future parson might be working on a lake steamer, one year waiting at table, another lifting baggage, and later on he might be purser. . . . When he entered Divinity Hall, he would be pitchforked summer by summer into a prairie parish in the North West, where he must buy buggy and horse to cover his four hundred square miles of parish and see for himself how his Gospel affected the solitary farmhouses. Or it might be a mining camp with its peculiar types of men, and the women who went to mining camps. In the fall he came back to College, to study Theology with Grant and his colleagues, and perhaps Honour Philosophy with John Watson. Three or four winters in Arts, three winters in Theology, and the summers just described—they made the man or found him out; and the Presbyterians of Canada in those years had the strongest type of clergy to be met anywhere.[31]

After 1875, the staff of the Theological Faculty was gradually expanded. New chairs were established—Apologetics and New Testament Criticism in 1883, Church History and the History of Dogma in 1900, and Practical Theology in 1909.

Under Principal Gordon, an important change in the status of the Theological Faculty occurred. After deliberation extending over a number of years, the General Assembly of the Presbyterian Church in 1911 resolved that the Faculty should no longer be an organic part of Queen's University and obtained an act from the Dominion Parliament incorporating it under the title "Queen's Theological College." The act received the royal assent in April 1, 1912. The Rev. Donald Ross became interim principal of the Theological College in 1912 and principal in 1913.

At Bishop's University teaching in the Faculty of Arts was still dominantly humanistic although there was somewhat more emphasis upon science than in the previous period. Science was established in two rooms on the third floor of the building occupied by Bishop's College School. Here the King Science Laboratory was established since a donor from Sherbrooke, Colonel King, had donated a thousand dollars in 1891 for equipment but the laboratory received no further donations for many years.

The system at Bishop's was opposed to specialization in any par-

[31]T. R. Glover, and D. D. Calvin, *A Corner of Empire: The Old Ontario Strand* (Cambridge, 1937), 153–4.

ticular subject. Bishop's was very much in the English tradition of higher education. The whole object of the faculty was to give a general education, rather than a highly specialized training in any one field. The function of Bishop's was to provide a general arts course for students who then proceeded into theology, law, medicine, or teaching. Bishop's had not yet been much affected by the German and American idea that the university should be a centre of research and original scholarship.

The Faculties of Law and Medicine gave Bishop's a means of providing professional training for its arts graduates. Unfortunately the University failed to maintain these professional schools. Teaching in the Faculty of Law was suspended in the eighteen-nineties.

The Faculty of Medicine had a longer career. The calendar of the Faculty for 1895–96 indicated the nature and scope of the work of the institution. It was announced that "The Faculty of Medicine of Bishop's College aims at imparting a thoroughly practical medical education and its facilities for doing so are in many respects unequalled in Canada." Western Hospital was closely associated with Bishop's as most of its staff of fourteen were members of the Bishop's Faculty. Sixty students were registered in the Faculty in 1894–5.

Despite this appearance of stability in the eighteen-nineties the Medical Faculty suspended operations in 1905 and was merged with the Medical Faculty of McGill University. There were several reasons for this step. Despite its apparent prosperity, the Bishop's Faculty felt the lack of adequate endowment. It seemed doubtful whether the English-speaking community in Montreal would support two medical schools. Moreover, Bishop's had just suffered a grievous loss in the death of the Dean of the Medical Faculty, Dr. Francis Wayland Campbell, whose energy had been largely responsible for the continuance of the Faculty for so long.

By the agreement negotiated between the two universities Bishop's agreed to suspend teaching or conferring degrees in medicine. In return, Bishop's was given certain concessions; students in attendance in the Medical Faculty were to be received *ad eundem statum* in the McGill Medical Faculty. Members of the Bishop's Faculty were to be given the McGill degree of M. D. C. M. should they so desire. McGill undertook to add some of the Bishop's Faculty to the McGill Faculty "as opportunity offers."

The Medical Faculty of Bishop's University had taught for thirty-four years and had rendered valuable service to Quebec and to Canada. Its graduates numbered two hundred and forty-six. Its disappearance, like that of the Law Faculty, was an example of the difficulties of small, struggling church colleges in broadening and diversifying their programme of teaching.

At the turn of the century the University made a tentative, but short-lived, attempt to establish training in another field of professional training—education. In 1898 the Quebec Protestant Committee of the Council of Public Instruction proposed that diplomas for teaching be granted only to those with some professional training. The University accordingly inaugurated a course of lectures on the art of teaching to qualify graduates of the University for Academy diplomas. A course of fifty-two lectures was outlined in the calendar for 1899-1900. In the first year seven students took the course which was given concurrently with the last year in arts. Apparently the course gradually petered out. Subsequent calendars gave a brief announcement of it, but warned that it would be given only if a sufficient number of candidates applied.

Within the field of the humanities there was some broadening out of the course of study. A new Chair of English was established in 1899 with L. R. Holme as the professor of English. E. E. Boothroyd came to the University in 1906 as lecturer in English and history. F. O. Call was appointed professor of modern languages in 1912.

The scope and character of the work at Bishop's is shown by the faculty list for the year 1913-14.

Dean of the Faculty of Arts, Principal, and Hamilton Professor of Classics	R. O. Parrock
Dean of the Faculty of Divinity, Vice Principal, Harrold Professor of Divinity	The Rev. Canon F. J. Allnatt
Professor of History	E. E. Boothroyd
J. J. S. Mountain Professor of Pastoral Theology	The Rev. F. G. Vial
Professor of Philosophy and Economics and Lecturer in Church History	The Rev. H. C. Burt
Professor of Modern Languages . .	F. O. Call
Lecturer in Mathematics and Natural Sciences	A. V. Richardson
Lecturer in Preparatory Arts . . .	C. P. Gwyn

The teaching of science was still only a part-time occupation for some members of the school or university staffs. Between 1908 and 1911 C. F. Gummer, the professor of mathematics, taught some science as well as mathematics. From 1911 to 1914 A. V. Richardson was lecturer in both mathematics and science. Despite a heavy load placed on Gummer and Richardson, science became established as a regular part of the curriculum. Completion of a library wing to the orginal university building in 1909 provided space for a more satisfactory science laboratory. It was established in the face of some opposition from more humanistic members of the staff.

Science secured formal recognition from the university authorities in June, 1914, when for the first time a full-time lecturer in science, Norman C. Qua of the University of Toronto, was appointed. The decision to make this appointment had been made by the corporation "in view of the large amount of work in Mathematics and Science which it is impossible for one lecturer to cover." Qua remained at Bishop's only a short time, but his appointment as a full-time lecturer in science was an important precedent.

Perhaps the most influential personality at Bishop's in the 1890-1920 period was Francis Allnatt who came to Bishop's as professor of pastoral theology in 1887. In 1891 he succeeded Henry Roe as dean of divinity. Allnatt had been born in England, but in 1864 came to Canada where he was ordained to the Anglican ministry. As dean of divinity, Allnatt exercised a great influence over many students at Bishop's, clerical and lay. A fine scholar, and a man of rather shy charm, Allnatt was essentially a teacher. He has been vividly described by a former student, Canon C. E. S. Bown:

Dr. Allnatt was almost more than a Dean of Divinity, he was an institution. A man of rather halting speech, who devoted his full time to his divinity classes. . . . He was a man of very fair mind, non partisan, kept up to date in his reading. Passed on the results to his classes. . . . He created a unity among his students that for many years did much to solidify the far flung Diocese of Quebec. He was a very devout man, and [one] who strengthened the faith I believe of every student whom he taught.[32]

E. E. Boothroyd, the professor of history, was one of the great personalities of Bishop's and one who soon endeared himself to the students. Boothroyd, a Cambridge graduate, was the old English type of don who never wrote anything but who read widely and carefully and passed on the results to his students. An interesting teacher, Boothroyd made his lectures the means of exciting an interest in his

[32]Masters, *Bishop's University: The First Hundred Years* (Toronto, 1950), 84.

subject. Ralph Gustafson, an old student of Boothroyd's has given a picture of him as a lecturer:

"Boots" always held a roll-call to start off with—the dash of discipline and, as he would say, "benevolent despotism," and then we were launched— almost anywhere in the stretch of a lecture, from the Holy Roman Empire to the latest press despatch on world affairs, to the state of Cleopatra's morals. They all seemed to have something to do with one another and gather significance because of it. I don't know how Boots did it, but I early came to the conclusion that his special brand of informed wry humour was seven-tenths of it.[33]

In the years after 1890 the character of Montreal Diocesan College gradually altered. It became less dominantly Evangelical and less conservative in its attitude to Biblical criticism. The ideas of F. J. Steen and G. Abbot-Smith in regard to Biblical criticism have been referred to at the beginning of this chapter. Abbott-Smith taught at Montreal Diocesan for forty-two years (1897–1939), during the latter part (1928–39) as principal. His comments written at the close of his career indicate the manner in which the position of the College had been broadened. He wrote in 1947:

What is really fundamental and essential in that which is known as the Evangelical position is, if I understand aright, an emphasis upon the mediatorial work of Christ coupled with the personal relationship which should exist between the believer and his Lord. We have, indeed, learned much in the years since this College was founded. We have learned something of a dignity and beauty of worship increasingly revived during those years. And we have learned that the historic schools of thought within the Church are not really incompatible with, but rather complementary to one another; that laying the foundation of faith is not enough alone, but that for the full development of the spiritual life there is needed the doctrine, discipline and, above all, the complete sacramental teaching of the Church and that in this last especially we owe much to movements within the Church which had hardly touched these shores seventy-five years ago. While faithful to the best of its old tradition, the Montreal Diocesan Theological College is today, more than in its early years, representative of the fuller life and thought of the Church of England.[34]

In 1912–13 Montreal Diocesan College, Presbyterian College, Wesleyan Theological College, and the Congregational theological college participated in a significant scheme of co-operation. "The Co-operative Scheme," as it was usualy called, took the form of organizing co-operative courses in general theological subjects, the various colleges pooling their instructors. Denominational theology was given by the individual colleges. To administer the scheme a Board was incor-

[33]*Ibid.*, 134.   [34]G. Abbott-Smith, *I Call to Mind*, (Toronto, 1947), 71.

porated with six representatives and the Principal *ex officio* from each college. The autonomy of the individual colleges was guaranteed.

Co-operative courses were given in Old Testament, New Testament, apologetics, and some parts of church history. Later on some parts of systematic theology were added. Montreal Diocesan gave separate courses to its own students on the church, the ministry, the sacraments, liturgics, and pastoral theology. During the first two years of co-operation, lectures were given in the several colleges, each professor, as a rule, delivering his lectures in his own and in one other college. In 1914 a temporary building was secured on University Street for the presentation of lectures in the co-operative scheme. The inauguration of the scheme was a significant step in inter-denominational and inter-college co-operation, the forerunner of the establishment of the Faculty of Divinity at McGill in 1948.[35]

In 1896 Thomas Trotter succeeded Artemas Sawyer as president of Acadia. Trotter had been educated at the University of Toronto and McMaster University. After holding pastoral charges in Woodstock and Toronto, he had been appointed professor of homiletics and pastoral theology at McMaster in 1890. Under Trotter, Acadia experienced a decade of expansion and development. The trend toward a greater stress on science and such practical studies as engineering, household economics, and education continued. New emphasis was placed on the function of the humanities and science as a background for the study of law and medicine.

The increased emphasis on science was marked by the appointment of Ernest Haycock, an Acadia graduate, as professor of geology and chemistry in 1898. Haycock was assisted in the Department of Science by Professors F. R. Haley and C. C. Jones. In 1910 H. G. Perry was appointed as the first professor of biology.

The history of Presbyterian College, Halifax in the period covered by this chapter was notable for the appointment of a number of men who went on to distinguished careers in other Canadian universities. The Rev. Robert Falconer, appointed professor of New Testament in 1892, became principal in 1904 and in 1907 president of the University of Toronto. Dr. D. B. Gordon, appointed professor of systematic theology in 1894, became principal of Queen's University in 1902. The Rev. A. S. Morton, appointed lecturer in church history in 1904, was

---

[35]John Irwin Cooper, *The Blessed Communion, The Origins and History of the Diocese of Montreal 1760–1960* (Montreal, 1960), 166–7; Abbott-Smith, *I Call to Mind*, 163–7; John Cragg Farthing, *Recollections of the Right Rev. John Cragg Farthing, Bishop of Montreal 1909–1939* (n.d.), 119.

subsequently (1914–40) head of the Department of History at the University of Saskatchewan. The Rev. H. A. Kent, lecturer in Old Testament exegesis (1908), became principal of Queen's Theological College in 1926. By these appointments the influence of Maritime Presbyterianism was carried into various areas of Canadian university life.

Queen's College, Newfoundland continued to function, still heavily dependent on the mother country. The College was closed for two years, 1892–94, and reopened under a new Principal, the Rev. Charles Knapp. Grants from various sources including two hundred and fifty pounds from the S.P.C.K., a thousand pounds from the S.P.G., and a legacy of two hundred pounds made it possible to enlarge the buildings and to increase the endowment.[36]

During the years between 1889 and 1917 the University of Manitoba was in the process of reconsidering the nature of its organization. The church colleges were vitally concerned with this discussion. It will be recalled that when the University was set up in 1877, it was a purely examining body and all the teaching was carried on by the colleges: St. John's, Manitoba, St. Boniface and, from 1888, Wesley. In the late eighteen-eighties this arrangement came to be questioned, chiefly because some Manitoba and St. John's men believed that certain subjects, particularly in natural science, should be taught by the University. The issue was accordingly raised as to whether the University should enter the teaching field. The extended debate which followed involved a lengthy and, at times, acrimonius discussion of the whole question of the University's organization. Central in this discussion was the question of the role of the church colleges within the University. Three principal viewpoints were expounded: (1) that the existing system should be maintained, with teaching in the hands of the church colleges except for natural science; (2) that a secular, state-controlled university be set up, teaching a wide variety of subjects, and completely divorced from the church colleges; (3) that the University should teach all subjects but should maintain its previous connection with the colleges. Through a welter of talk and controversy the University moved slowly toward the third solution. This was adopted with the passage of an amendment of the University Act in 1892.[37]

[36]J. J. Curling, and Charles Knapp, *Historical Notes Concerning Queen's College, St. John's, Diocese of Newfoundland 1842–1897* (London, 1898), 31–2; J. A. Meaden, *Queen's College Newfoundland* (St. John's, 1947), 11–12.

[37]W. L. Morton, *One University: A History of the University of Manitoba 1877–1952* (Toronto, 1957), 47.

The attitude of Wesley College indicated a desire to co-operate with the policy of the University while preserving the autonomy of the College. In 1889 the University Council recorded its approval of the establishment of a teaching faculty other than that of the affiliated colleges. In the following year the Board of Wesley unanimously endorsed this action.[38] Since funds were not immediately available to establish a university Faculty of Science, Wesley, St. John's, and Manitoba College came to the rescue of the University. Dr. G. J. Laird of Wesley, Dr. George Bryce of Manitoba, and E. B. Kenrick of St. John's set up a co-operative scheme for the teaching of natural science. This scheme of inter-college co-operation was begun in 1890 and carried on for some fourteen years.

In the eighteen-nineties those anxious to make the University a teaching body urged the government of Manitoba to make provision for higher education commensurate with the needs of the time. Wesley was in sympathy with this request. In a report to the Methodist Conference in 1897, the College stated:

This course will be hailed as a movement in the right direction and it may be anticipated that the University Building proposed to be erected will ultimately give accommodation for instruction in other branches of the University course to all Colleges.[39]

At the same time Wesley enunciated the principle which successive Wesley Boards held, "the federation of the Colleges into the University of Manitoba will be upon a similar basis to that which has been found to work so successfully in the case of the University of Toronto."[40] In 1904 the University was finally able to begin teaching in natural science with the appointment of professors of botany, physics, chemistry, mathematics, and physiology.

There were limits to the lengths Wesley was prepared to go in its support of the proposal that the University should become a teaching body. After the appointment of a royal commission in 1907 to consider the future of the University, the Wesley Board, in a statement to the commission, argued that if the Provincial government established an organization to teach subjects long covered by the colleges there would be needless duplication. The Wesley Board also asserted that the principle upon which the University had been founded was that of a federation and that this principle should be preserved.

[38]A. S. Cummings, "A History of Wesley College, Winnipeg," unpublished manuscript, 2.
[39]*Ibid.*, 3.
[40]*Ibid.*, 3.

In spite of these protests, the University in 1909 took another significant step into the field of teaching. Previous university appointments had been in the field of science, but the University now entered the liberal arts with the appointment of professors of English, history, and political economy.

Faced with the prospect of competition from the University in the teaching of the liberal arts, the Wesley Board made a significant proposal in November, 1910. The Board indicated its willingness to accept provision by the Province of instruction even in the subjects taught by the colleges, provided this instruction was given in a college "under its own separate management and sustaining precisely the same relation to the University as that sustained by the Colleges already in existence."[41] In short, the Board suggested the establishment of a university college similar to the University College which was an integral part of the Toronto system. The Methodist Conference of 1911 supported this proposal. It recommended that the University should give instruction in all subjects and recommended that such instruction should be given in a college with separate buildings, faculty, and name.

In 1912 a committee of the University Council suggested a means of implementing the Wesley proposal. The committee reported to the Council in February, 1912, that its members had agreed on the establishment of a university college, to be known as King's College, to be supported by the University and controlled by the Board of Governors. King's College was to have its own Principal and its own building and was to teach specified subjects, classics, modern languages, philosophy, history, and junior mathematics. The old colleges were to be colleges of the University with no more rights and no fewer rights than in the past, and members of the colleges teaching any of the subjects assigned to King's College were to be members of the "University Faculty of Arts." King's was to have its own faculty council, but a joint faculty council of the professors and lecturers of all colleges was to have power to recommend changes in the curriculum of King's to the Senate of the University. W. L. Morton, the historian of the University of Manitoba, has written of the King's College proposal, "It seems in retrospect to have been the best calculated attempt to take account at once of the university's historical development and of the needs of its future growth."[42] According to Morton the plan was

[41]*Ibid.*, 7.
[42]Morton, *One University*, 89. Eventually (in 1964), the University of Manitoba established a University College with Professor Morton as its first principal.

doomed to failure by an unfortunate divulgence in the press before it could be further developed and the committee did not recommend its adoption.

While the relation between the colleges and the University was under consideration, Wesley and Manitoba College undertook an experiment in amalgamation. Contacts between the two institutions had been fairly frequent since 1889-90 when three students from Manitoba studied mathematics in Wesley and two students from Wesley studied classics and "mental and moral science" in Manitoba. In 1912-13 the two institutions formulated a Bachelor of Divinity course which was to be common to both. Early in 1913, a joint committee on closer co-operation between the two colleges was appointed. Further discussion culminated in a plan of amalgamation. The two institutions were to have one principal and a common Board of Governors composed of representatives from the Boards of the two colleges. The session of 1913-14 was carried on under this plan, but it proved unacceptable to the Wesley constituency and was abandoned in 1914.

Meanwhile, the discussion about university organization proceeded and the colleges were subjected to strong pressure to forego teaching in arts. In 1914, the new President of the University, Dr. J. A. MacLean, urged the colleges to abandon the teaching of arts. He gave assurances that the colleges would still have representation on the University Council, that the University would occupy rooms in the college buildings, and that the colleges would retain the right to resume teaching in arts at any time if they considered it desirable.

In July, 1914, the Boards of Wesley and of Manitoba College agreed to accept President MacLean's proposal. In the autumn of 1914 the two colleges discontinued arts classes in all subjects which the University was prepared to teach. The University rented space at Wesley for which the College was reimbursed to the extent of two thousand dollars. Wesley professors continued to teach their courses at Wesley but as members of the Arts Faculty of the University. Philosophy was still taught at the University.

The scheme was not popular at Wesley. The administration was alarmed at the resultant decline in registration. Incoming students, when they found that Wesley was not teaching arts, registered instead at the University. Wesley claimed to have been given assurances that students previously registered at the College would still be connected with its student body but it could not control the decision of individuals to register with the University.

The students at Wesley were not keen on co-operation with the University, nor with Manitoba College. A significant article appeared in the college magazine, *Vox Wesleyana*,[43] arguing the case for the maintenance of church colleges within the University. This article was probably a fair indication of the attitude of the Wesley community toward the future of the College. The article argued that there would be a growing demand for instruction in the arts course at Manitoba, that the University would eventually be swamped with students and that the College would be needed to cope with the surplus. The article went on to point out that Wesley as a small church college had special advantages to fulfil its function as an arts college. The College could provide a more intimate contact between professor and students. Students who would be obscured in the larger university community, would have more opportunity to enter into the social life of the group at Wesley. There were advantages in the mingling of arts and theological students in one institution. "The Arts student produces a more virile and robust life and thought, while the Theological student contributes a steadying influence and a moral stimulus."[44] Some arts students who entered Wesley undecided as to their future or proposing to follow a secular profession, would be influenced to enter the ministry.

The article insisted on the practical reasons for maintaining the arts course at Wesley. A purely theological college would have a very small registration and would not command much support from the community. An institution with a wider clientele would bring a corresponding response. The article concluded by insisting that there were positive intellectual reasons why a student should register in a church college. In a large institution the student was subjected to a welter of conflicting ideals and approaches to life. These conflicting forces might well produce bewilderment leading to a life with but little sense of direction. The church college was better equipped to prepare its students for the problems of life. The article asserted:

An institution which stands definitely for a sympathetic relation between the religious life and culture brings to that young mind a steadying influence and a moral power which not only assists him to find his own way in life but also enables him to bring strength to others.

The *Vox* article helped to provide the basis for the decision of the Methodist constituency not to continue the Arrangement of 1914 with

[43]A. J. Irwin, The Future of Wesley College, *Vox Wesleyana*, XVIII, No. 1, November, 1914, 10–13. The author was Professor of New Testament exegesis at Wesley College, 1913–17.   [44]*Ibid*.

the University. In November, 1914, the Methodist Board of Education and the Annual Conference Special Committee released Wesley from any obligations that might have been implied in the Arrangement of July, 1914. They released Wesley on the ground that the University had not fulfilled certain material conditions.

Resumption of teaching in arts at Wesley was anticipated by a conference between the college Board and the Methodist Board of Education on November 26, 1914. A committee was appointed to survey the curriculum and report concerning the subjects and the extent to which the College should provide instruction. It was finally agreed that Wesley should undertake a course of instruction which charted its future. The curriculum was to include: (1) in the first two years of the arts course, the compulsory subjects and French, German, New Testament Greek, physics, Icelandic, and Hebrew; (2) in the third and fourth years, English, history, philosophy, and political economy. Teaching in arts was resumed at Wesley, but not at Manitoba College, in September, 1915.

Discussion about the university question continued in Winnipeg. Finally the long process of re-appraising the organization of the University of Manitoba came to a conclusion with the passage of the University Act of 1917. This measure changed the university system from a federation to a system in which there existed a monolithic, non-sectarian, university structure. The relation of the colleges to this nucleus was radically changed: they were left in affiliation to the University but they ceased to be integral parts of a university federation. Morton has described the position of the colleges as one of "now true affiliation rather than federation."[45]

By the Act of 1917 the University was given a Board of Governors on which the affiliated colleges were not represented. Control of finances and administration of the University was vested in the Board. The colleges were represented on the new council which controlled academic matters, subject to the overruling power of the Board of Governors.

Thus emerged a system in which the position of the colleges was much more peripheral than was the case with the church colleges in the University of Toronto. In retrospect it is clear that the failure to establish a university college in Manitoba helped to create an atmosphere of mutual suspicion between "the university" and "the colleges." Failure to divide the university administration from its Arts Faculty meant that the University was in a sense the superior of the colleges

[45]Morton, *One University*, 109.

and at the same time a rival in the competition for students. At Toronto, where the university college occupied a position similar to that of Victoria, Trinity, and St. Michael's, the relationship between these church colleges and the University was much less fraught with suspicion. In fact, the author, a Toronto graduate who taught at Manitoba, was at first puzzled by the Manitoban habit of considering "the University" and "the colleges" as mutually exclusive terms. At Toronto, members of all the colleges regard themselves as integral parts of "the University."

There were some important advantages in the position of the affiliated church colleges at Manitoba. They were able to teach a wider range of subjects than was the case with the federated colleges at Toronto. The latter were restricted to the so-called "college subjects," while the colleges in Manitoba could teach the full arts programme. The Manitoba church colleges were able to expand their programmes to keep pace with new developments in the liberal arts and science subjects. New fields of study at Toronto such as political science, sociology, anthropology were controlled by the University and taught in centralized, monolithic departments; the federated colleges for the most part, were restricted to the subjects given to them in the 1887–1904 period.

During the years after 1889, when the University of Manitoba was moving toward the Settlement of 1917, St. John's continued to function as a sort of northern outpost of the university federation. St. John's was perplexed by the indecisive character of the discussions in regard to the permanent site of the University of Manitoba. At one point, assured that the University would remain on the Broadway site in the centre of the city of Winnipeg, St. John's purchased nearby land on Osborne Street only to have the University shift its ideas in favour of the Tuxedo site in 1910. In 1913 the Manitoba government forced the abandonment of the Tuxedo project by setting aside a large tract of land adjacent to the new Agricultural College property on the Fort Garry site and by offering to erect certain buildings for the University. In the meantime St. John's College and its affiliate, St. John's College School, were under considerable pressure to expand their accommodation. In 1912 the College and School erected a new temporary building, long known as "the Annex," and extended the main building.[46]

As already indicated, St. John's co-operated with the other colleges during the period 1890–1904 to provide some instruction in science

[46]Boon, *The Anglican Church*, 271–2.

but abandoned the scheme when science was taken over by the University. On the whole, the College was less antagonistic than Wesley to the University Settlement of 1917. St. John's was a less formidable rival of the university Arts Faculty than was Wesley and did not have the Methodist tradition of nonconformity.

St. John's continued to be embarrassed by the inadequacy of its financial resources in the period covered by this chapter. The College never seemed to command the whole-hearted support of the church.[47] The fact that it had endowments gave the impression that it was wealthy. The clerical members of its faculty, as part of the mission staff of the Cathedral, were so busy fostering the work of the church in new parishes in Winnipeg as well as in rural areas, that they had no time to make appeals for the College and its work, "a characteristic annual feature of other colleges affiliated with the University."[48] There was no one at St. John's with the special talents of Principal Sparling of Wesley. The financial perplexities of St. John's were increased by another development. In 1902, Archbishop Machray announced to the Synod of the Province of Rupert's Land that the C. M. S. was preparing for a reduction of its grants, including presumably that to St. John's, and that they would cease in twelve and a half years. This abandonment of C. M. S. support had important implications other than the financial one. The influence of the C. M. S. had always been strongly low church and Evangelical. Its curtailment probably facilitated the transition of St. John's to a more moderate, middle-of-the-road Anglican position.[49]

Despite its problems, St. John's enjoyed high prestige as a liberal arts and theological college in this period. It was more literally a church college than was the case with many such institutions described in this volume. The close association between the College, the Diocese of Rupert's Land and the Cathedral meant that most of its staff continued to be Anglican clergy. A number of important appointments were made in this period. They have been described in some detail by T. C. B. Boon in his standard work *The Anglican Church from the Bay to the Rockies*.[50] Prior to his death in 1904, Archbishop Machray appointed the Rev. J. O. Murray as professor of systematic theology and the Rev. E. E. M. Phair as professor of pastoral theology.

[47]*Ibid.*, 270–1.
[48]*Ibid.*, 271.
[49]The C. M. S. continued to hold the right to appoint the professor of exegetical theology and made two appointments in the nineteen-twenties.
[50]Boon, *The Anglican Church*, 270. The quotations in this paragraph are all from Boon.

Boon has described Murray as "a doughty fighter on behalf of any principle he felt should be upheld," and referred to "his agile mind, sound scholarship and warm-hearted interest in people." Phair, a St. John's graduate, had studied at Ridley Hall, Cambridge, an indication of the continuing low church connections of St. John's. In 1905, the Rev. John William Matheson, who had been an outstanding scholar at St. John's, was appointed lecturer in exegetical theology. He became a professor in 1912 and dean in 1922. "Regarded as one of the best scholars in the church in western Canada, a man of forceful personality, Matheson left an impression on his students and associates that will not be forgotten." Canon E. A. W. Gill, after twenty years in parochial work became lecturer in moderns in 1910 and in 1918 professor of pastoral theology, a position which he held for some twenty-five years. "His wide reading was shared with his students rather than imparted to them." The Rev. J. F. Cross became Machray Fellow in Mathematics in 1899 and dean of the College in 1916.

In 1899 the Baptists organized an arts college in Manitoba—Brandon College. The new institution absorbed an older secondary school, called Brandon Academy, which had been founded at Rapid City, Manitoba, by Dr. S. J. McKee and moved to Brandon in 1890.[51]

Brandon College began under the presidency of Dr. A. P. McDiarmid, with Dr. McKee as vice-president and registrar. McDiarmid, a graduate of Toronto, McMaster, and Newton Theological Seminary, has been described as a dignified and austere man with an occasional twinkle in his eye. His great achievements were the early organization of the College and the establishment of a good scholastic standard. He remained president until 1914. McKee was an effective assistant to McDiarmid. He gave the impression of absent-minded amiability but was assiduous in securing students for the College. The reminiscences of Mrs. H. L. MacNeill (née Vera Leech), an early student at Brandon, give evidence of the care with which McKee cultivated the Brandon constituency.

Born into a pioneer Methodist family in Brandon it was taken for granted that after high school I would enter Wesley College in Winnipeg for university work. However, staunch as they were in the Wesleyan tradition, my parents were unable to resist the urgings of Dr. McKee who came several times to the house persuading them to enroll me in Brandon

---

[51]At Rapid City, Dr. John Crawford, later joined by Dr. McKee established a school called Prairie College about 1880. Later Dr. McKee started Rapid City Academy which he moved to Brandon as Brandon Academy. Dr. Crawford returned to the Baptist Ministry and went to the United States. See Statement by H. L. McNeill in *History of Brandon College, Inc.* (Brandon, 1962), 9–11.

(Baptist) College. At the age of fifteen I had no choice in the matter, but I well remember the calm insistent voice that later became very well known. Looking back now I can believe it was this personal seeking of a wanted student and the watchful interest that continued through the course that established the unique Brandon College tradition.[52]

Brandon was chiefly an arts college but it began a Theological Department in 1907. In that year, in addition to arts and theology, the College maintained a secondary school or "academy" and Departments of Music and Business. In spite of the precariousness of Brandon's position and the lowness of its salaries, the faculty was characterized by a high level of ability. D. A. MacGibbon, who was professor of political economy from 1908 to 1917, recalled that most of the faculty members were "keen on their subjects and looking forward to academic careers." They included Dr. W. Sherwood Fox, later president of the University of Western Ontario, Dr. W. A. Mackintosh, later principal of Queen's University, Dr. D. C. McIntosh, later dean of theology at Yale, W. Burton Hurd, later professor of economics at McMaster, and D. A. MacGibbon, later a commissioner on the Board of Grain Commissioners for Canada.

The students at Brandon in MacGibbon's time numbered between three hundred and four hundred. Coming from a frontier community, the students were hard-working and self-reliant. McGibbon recalled:

> The college attracted to its classes a number of students who were to make their mark in later life. Characteristically these students were coming up the hard way, relying upon themselves for the means that would enable them to go to college. These men and women formed the backbone of the student body and gave it an undercurrent of seriousness not always noticeable in university life today.[53]

Dr. Charles G. Stone, who was a student at Brandon in MacGibbon's time, confirms MacGibbon's impression that a considerable number of the students were quite mature. A number of them were already serving as pastors of churches in adjacent communities, while making a creditable record in their classes. Others had chosen law, medicine, teaching, or other professions as their life work.

> They were people of definite purpose: they were concerned that life should be of a high quality in the College halls and on the playing fields; they accepted their full share of responsibility for committee work in the different student activities; and in the course of a student generation, they influenced many a younger person to make the right choices. They certainly had a large part in making Brandon College what it has become.[54]

[52]*Ibid.*, 13.   [53]*Ibid.*, 15–16.
[54]*Ibid.*, 18.

Of course not all the students at Brandon showed the same high seriousness. Under the heading "Fun and Escapades in College Life," Dr. Stone recalled some famous student pranks during his undergraduate days.

So far as the student body in general was concerned, the Baptist influence at Brandon did not appear to be very great. Mrs. MacNeill, coming from a Methodist background, recalled:

> I do not think that the Baptist connection weighed greatly in the minds of the non-Baptist students. Most of us had no knowledge of or interest in special Baptist beliefs or controversies. But we did come to know and revere the devoted Baptist professors and to realize that they were contributing their brilliant talents to this western Baptist outpost of education with a zeal as great as that of any missionary, and under conditions similar in primitiveness and stringency.[55]

Since the administration and the faculty did not stress the denominational character of the College, Brandon secured a considerable number of non-Baptist students. In 1907 the religious composition of the student body was: Baptist, 160; Presbyterian, 68; Methodist, 43; Church of England, 13; Congregational, 2; Roman Catholic, 1; Lutheran, 1; Brethren, 1.

The Faculty of Theology was less conservative in its position than some of the constituents of the College would have liked. The Department of Theology was subjected to vigorous attack in the period from 1912 to 1923. As a result the Western Baptist Union set up a committee to make a thorough review of the Department. The report of the committee in 1921 upheld the Department of Theology and censored its conservative critics.

The early history of Brandon was characterized by continuous financial difficulties and regular annual deficits. The exceptionally large deficit of 1914 spurred an effort to raise an endowment of one hundred thousand dollars, an effort which was only partially successful. In 1922 a special commission of the Western Baptist Union commented, "The financial burden of maintaining a University is enormous. This is not always appreciated by a denomination when it undertakes this work."[56]

During the period 1899–1911, the relations of Brandon College with the University of Manitoba were perplexing to both institutions. Brandon's difficulties in regard to this problem were partly a result of its Baptist character and partly a result of the policy of the Manitoba

[55]*Ibid.*, 14.
[56]*Ibid.*, 10.

government in reference to higher education.[57] As a Baptist institution, Brandon was prevented by the principles of its church from seeking affiliation with a provincial university which received financial aid from the state. Yet it was unable to develop as an independent institution because it could not secure the power to grant degrees. The University of Manitoba, supported by the Manitoba government, determined to maintain the principle of "only one university in the province" and successfully blocked the efforts of Brandon to achieve the degree-granting power.

Between 1899 and 1911, Brandon developed a relationship of what might be called quasi-affiliation with the University of Manitoba. Brandon taught some courses which were prescribed by the University and its students wrote some university examinations. The system was always unsatisfactory from the Brandon point of view.

This relationship between the University of Manitoba and Brandon College had begun before the organization of the College. In 1896 the Council of the University, in response to a petition from the old Brandon Academy, had agreed to hold matriculation examinations in Brandon, but the Council had refused to extend the practice to senior examinations. After the establishment of the new Brandon College in 1899, the University still refused to hold examinations at Brandon other than those for matriculation. In 1902, the city of Brandon protested against this refusal on the part of the University Council. The Council replied that Brandon College might seek affiliation with the University, but insisted that a common examination centre was necessary to ensure uniformity in examinations.

The citizens of Brandon, unsatisfied, began to lay plans for a regional university in western Manitoba. They were not appeased by an extension, in 1905–6, of the holding of university examinations at Brandon in natural science for matriculation and the first year, and in a special third and fourth year philosophy.

In 1906 Brandon secured the introduction into the legislature of a bill to grant degree-conferring powers to the College. In 1907, Dr. McDiarmid, accompanied by a large delegation, presented the case for the College before the Private Bills Committee of the legislature. The application was opposed by the representatives of the Council of the University of Manitoba. According to Dr. McKee's subsequent account given in the college chapel, Dr. McDiarmid "stood like the Rock of Gibraltar." However, the delegation failed in its purpose. After three or four hours of discussion, the Brandon authorities

[57]Morton, *One University*, 60–1, 68, 83.

thought it best to withdraw the application for a time.[58] The University was given assurances by Premier Rodmond Roblin that the matter would not be revived in the future. Early in 1911, Brandon made another unsuccessful attempt to secure the degree-granting power.[59] In 1911, Brandon solved the problem of its immediate future by securing affiliation with McMaster University.

During the 1890-1920 period, the Methodist Church established in the west, three institutions which offered some courses at the university level, as well as instruction in the high school work.

Regina College was established in 1909-11, after the Educational Committee of the Saskatchewan Methodist Conference had made a statement to the effect that while the effort on the part of the Saskatchewan government to establish a provincial university was to be applauded, there were areas in education not covered by the provincial work, especially in the field of secondary education. The College began as a purely secondary institution. Its objectives, as indicated in the report of the Board of Governors in 1912, were "to build up a strong, independent educational institution, which would meet the needs of this western land, that the educational department of the Government is not prepared to meet, and at the same time throw around the student life a moral influence that would make for character and higher citizenship." Later in its history the College taught courses in the first two years of university work, in connection with the University of Saskatchewan. This enabled students in the southern part of Saskatchewan to do some of their degree work in Regina.

Alberta College, Edmonton developed as a combination of secondary school, junior college, and theological seminary. The establishment of the College was undertaken by a local group associated with the Rev. T. C. Buchanan, a Methodist minister in Edmonton. Alberta College had close ties with Wesley College, Winnipeg. Principal J. W. Sparling of Wesley was chairman of the committee which recommended the establishment of the new college to the Manitoba and the Northwest Conference of the Methodist Church. The advisory committee which was appointed by the Conference in connection with Alberta College included Principal Sparling, J. A. M. Aikins, the chairman of the Wesley Board, J. H. Riddell, a member of the Wesley staff, and J. H. Ashdown, a prominent member of the Wesley Board. The College opened in 1903 under the principalship of J. H. Riddell. In the following year its first permanent building was completed on the north bank of the Saskatchewan River. The work was organized

[58]McNeill, in *History of Brandon College*, 24, 31.   [59]Morton, 68; McNeill, 31.

so as to include Departments of Arts, Business, Music, Physical Culture, and Elocution. The arts curriculum of the University of Manitoba to the end of the second year was adopted by the College.

The establishment of the University of Alberta in 1907 stimulated the College to adopt a more diversified programme. In 1907 the Faculty of Theology was established and courses in the first year of the theology programme were commenced. In 1909–11, Alberta College began construction of buildings on the University of Alberta campus on the south side of the Saskatchewan River. The way was prepared for the development of two colleges called "The South Side" and "The North Side" respectively. In 1913 the two institutions were given separate boards. In the South Side the Faculty of Theology gave courses in theology, arts, and matriculation subjects. The North Side concentrated on "preparatory work, Commercial, Musical, and Art Branches." Soon the South Side came to be called Alberta College South while the other institution became Alberta College North. In 1914–15 Alberta College South co-operated with the Presbyterian theological institution, Robertson College, in conducting classes.

The early success of Alberta College was largely a result of the efforts of its first Principal, J. H. Riddell, who was described by one of the founders, as "capable of successfully building from the foundation up an institution of a type suited to this new and rapidly growing west, and at the same time worthy of the Methodist Church."[60] After fourteen years of service, Dr. Riddell left Alberta in 1917 to become principal of Wesley College, Winnipeg.

Columbian College, New Westminster, British Columbia, was established as a secondary school by the Methodist Church in 1892–93. Subsequently it also taught theology and some arts subjects. After the establishment of the University of British Columbia, the theological work of Columbia College was taken over by a new Methodist institution, Ryerson College, and the theological college of the British Columbia Conference was opened at Point Grey, on the outskirts of Vancouver, in affiliation with the provincial University. Columbian College discontinued its courses in arts in 1914–15.[61]

In the boom period which followed the turn of the century, the Presbyterians established three theological colleges in Saskatchewan, Alberta, and British Columbia respectively.[62]

---

[60]T. C. Buchanan, *Historical Sketch of Alberta College* (1924).
[61]I am indebted to the United church Archives for information in regard to Regina College, Alberta College, and Columbian College.
[62]Westminster Hall, Vancouver, was established in 1908.

The Presbyterian Theological College, Saskatoon (later St. Andrew's College) was incorporated by act of the Saskatchewan legislature. In 1913 the General Assembly of the Presbyterian Church appointed E. H. Oliver, the professor of history and economics at the University of Saskatchewan, as principal. The College encountered serious financial difficulties at the outset of its career owing to the collapse of the real estate boom in Western Canada. The plan to erect a building on land provided by the University of Saskatchewan had to be abandoned and the College opened in 1914 in a rented house at 209 Albert Avenue. The institution managed to carry on during World War I, although Principal Oliver and a number of the students went overseas. The first students to complete their training, four in number, graduated in 1916.

Robertson College, named after Dr. James Robertson, the superintendent of Presbyterian Missions in Western Canada, was founded by the Presbyterian Church in 1910 and opened in temporary quarters in Edmonton South, in the following year. Its Principal was the Rev. S. W. Dyde, who had been professor of mental philosophy at Queen's University. The work of the College was carried on in close co-operation with Albert College and most of the subjects were taught by professors in the Methodist college.

Emmanuel College, Prince Albert, which had reverted to the status of an Indian school after the death of Bishop McLean in 1886, was revived as a theological college in 1906–7.[63] At this time the Diocese of Saskatchewan was in great need of clergy to serve the Barr colonists in the Lloydminster area. Bishop J. A. Newnham made Emmanuel into a theological college and revived the charter of the old Anglican "University of Saskatchewan." By this time the Saskatchewan government was planning to establish a provincial university with exclusive right to the name and powers claimed by the Anglican university which had been created by the Dominion Parliament. In 1909, Bishop Newnham and his Synod decided to affiliate their theological college with the provincial University of Saskatchewan. Emmanuel was moved to Saskatoon where the provincial university had been located. The Anglican university retained its charter rights; but in 1914, by act of the Dominion Parliament, it secured a new title, the University of Emmanuel College.

In 1907 another Anglican theological college, St. Chad's, was established by the Synod of the Diocese of Qu'Appelle in Saskatche-

[63]Jean E. Murray, "The Early History of Emmanuel College," *Saskatchewan History*, IX (13), autumn, 1956, 98–101.

wan and was affiliated with the University of Saskatchewan. In 1964 St. Chad's was removed to Saskatoon and combined with Emmanuel.

In the decade prior to World War I, the desire for an Anglican theological college in British Columbia produced two institutions, reflecting the division of opinion within the Church of England.[64]

The movement to establish St. Mark's Hall was begun in 1907 by the Ven. E. W. S. Pentreath, the Archdeacon of Columbia, with strong support from Bishop J. C. Dart, the bishop of New Westminster. After encountering various obstacles, St. Mark's was finally opened in Vancouver in 1912 under the principalship of the Rev. C. A. Seager. The College was incorporated in 1913.

The position of St. Mark's might be described as moderately high church. Seager was a graduate of Trinity College, Toronto. In the first issue of the *St. Mark's Hall Bulletin* he assured his readers that the College was not to be an extreme high church institution and that ". . . it was not designed to turn out men of a certain 'stripe,' but men who, sound in knowledge and with a basis of broad but definite Churchmanship, should learn to think for themselves."[65] Seager remained as principal until 1917. During this period he gave the College strong leadership. One of his students later recalled:

> Dr. Seager had two ideals for his College. First, there was to be only one rule, and that was a moral sense of responsibility. This was the students' guide to attendance at Chapel, lectures, and whatever event took place in connection with the life of the Hall. We were expected to be there, and that was that. The other ideal was for each one of us to give the first five years of our Priesthood to the Church as celibates; if we did, the Bishops could send us wherever the need was greatest.[66]

In spite of the grave financial difficulties Seager launched St. Mark's on its somewhat tenuous career.

Bishop Latimer College was established in Vancouver by a group of Anglican Evangelicals of whom the moving spirit was the Rev. C. C. Owen, the rector of Christ Church, Vancouver. Owen has been described as "a dominating personality of strong Evangelical convictions, beloved by all who shared his views, admired and revered by those who differed from him."[67] Discussion among the British Columbia Evangelicals began in 1909 and plans were developed for opening the College. They were pushed forward in the face of opposition from

[64]Frank A. Peake, *The Anglican Church in British Columbia* (Vancouver, 1959), 149–166; "Jubilee Year 1960–1961," in *Via Media* (Year Book of the Anglican Theological Seminary of British Columbia.).
[65]*St. Mark's Hall Bulletin*, I, Nov., 1919; quoted in Peake, 158.
[66]See "Jubilee Year 1960–1961," in *Via Media*, 17.   [67]Peake, 152.

Bishop Dart and Bishop Perrin [the Bishop of British Columbia]. As the movement to establish St. Mark's was already under way the Bishops were unwilling to have its prospects of support weakened by the establishment of a second college. Probably too they regarded an Evangelical institution as "divisive." Early in 1909 the two Bishops wrote to the Colonial and Continental Church Society "strongly deprecating the action of the committee in supporting Bishop Latimer College."[68] In June, 1909, Bishop Dart wrote a firm letter to Owen concluding, "Of course, I could not recognize in any way your proposed rival Theological College in my diocese."[69] In spite of this opposition, the College was opened in October, 1910, and in 1911 was incorporated by act of the British Columbia legislature.

Bishop Latimer College was in large measure an off-shoot of Wycliffe College, Toronto. The committee which selected the first Principal of Latimer included the Principal and the President of Wycliffe and the Rev. H. J. Cody, of St. Paul's Church, Toronto, a distinguished Wycliffe graduate. They selected as Principal, the Rev. William Harry Vance, a graduate of Toronto and Wycliffe. In 1911, Vance was joined by another Wycliffe graduate, the Rev. Harry Ralph Trumpour.

The establishment and development of Latimer was largely the work of Vance and Trumpour. Vance was a man of drive and determination. The character of his relations with the students is indicated by the reminiscences of a Latimer alumnus, describing his experiences as a freshman:

> Dr. Vance, the Principal, rarely failed to visit students during evening study, and spent a few moments with each. At first, he appeared as a cold, stern disciplinarian; but after a few months, the students learned to regard him with deep respect and to look forward to his visits.[70]

Trumpour was a New Testament scholar in the field of New Testament Greek and exegesis. A fine lecturer, Trumpour made a lasting impression on his students. He appears to have been a liberal Evangelical. The character of his influence was indicated by some of the reminiscences in *Via Media*:

> He was a great man. He shattered many of my ideas for me, and I must admit he shook me. Now I realize how much he did for me, and how much I owed to him. His exposition of the New Testament was thoughtful and scholarly, so frequently bringing out the expressive differences in English and Greek thought.

---

[68]*Ibid.*, 156.
[69]*Ibid.*, 154.
[70]"Jubilee Year, 1960–1961," in *Via Media*, 22.

Professor H. R. Trumpour took most of the subjects, and my personal debt to him increases as the years pass by. I kept full notes of the lectures, and find that after forty-eight years, these are still comprehensive and still in advance of much modern thinking.[71]

St. Mark's and Latimer continued their separate existence for the first few years, each struggling to make ends meet financially; but eventually they were united. The first step was taken in 1915. After presentation of a memorandum by the Bishops of the Province, an act of the provincial legislature (March 6, 1915) established the Anglican Theological College with which Latimer and St. Mark's were affiliated. The College was to be under a board responsible for lecture rooms, the library, and the appointment of professors in subjects to be taken in common by all students, such as Old Testament and apologetics. Each of the component colleges was to be governed by an independent council, to maintain residences and a chapel and to employ its teaching staff.

The process of unification was completed after the passage of a resolution of the provincial Synod on January 6, 1920 calling for closer integration of the two colleges. The two institutions were now fused under a single head. The St. Mark's building was sold and the entire College was located in the old Latimer building. The staffs of Latimer and St. Mark's were combined.

The formation of Anglican Theological College was of significance in that it was effected by the representatives of two traditions of Anglican churchmanship. Vance, who became principal, and his colleague Trumpour were both Wycliffe men. The Rev. C. H. (Dad) Shortt, the former St. Mark's principal, who became warden of the new college, was a Trinity graduate. It was perhaps indicative of the mingling of two traditions that Shortt loved his pipe of tobacco whereas Vance rather frowned on smoking except in the Common Room. Both sides made concessions in the interests of unity. This was indicated in a letter from Vance in May, 1920:

I have agreed to place the cross on the table. The lights are to be done away with; also wafer bread. They had both of these. The Eastward position is to be optional. Vestments are not allowed. This will give a general idea of the spirit of the new plan.[72]

Vance piloted the Anglican Theological College through the early period of amalgamation and got on well with the graduates of St. Mark's as well as with those of Latimer.

[71]K. B. Frampton, E. Moss, and F. G. Shepherd, "Jubilee Year, 1960–1961," in *Via Media*, 15, 16, 18.
[72]Quoted in Peake, *The Anglican Church in British Columbia*, 160–1.

The developments which have been described in the various church colleges occurred in an atmosphere of vigorous theological controversy. From about 1890 two conflicting views of the Hebrew-Christian tradition were being proclaimed in Canadian church colleges.

The one view might be termed old and conservative. According to this view God had revealed himself directly to man and had left the testimony to Himself in his law and in the written word. In Old Testament times the Hebrew people had strayed from the worship of God to polytheism and had been called back to the worship and revelation of God by the Prophets. Divine revelation was the ultimate test of human thought and conduct. All doctrine and action must be judged against the norm revealed by God concerning Himself and His Son.

The second view might be termed new and liberal. It was based upon a fundamentally different view of Scripture. The Bible, instead of being God's revelation of Himself to man, became the product of man's gropings after God from animism through polytheism to monotheism. This view left room for a very evolutionary concept of religion. In its extreme form it left the way open for the departure from old doctrines and even creeds as the search of man after God continued. The old norm became only a stage in a process of upward development which had no place for the concept of "absolute truth."

The conflict between the conservative and liberal viewpoints had not of course been resolved in 1920; it led directly into the ideological controversies in the post-1920 period.

6. The Modern Adjustment

(1920 and after)

THE MODERN POSITION of church colleges and former church colleges must be considered against the background of current schools of thought in regard to religion and philosophy.

A consideration of religious periodicals in the period after 1920 indicates the continuance of a liberal attitude toward the Scriptures and a growing concern for the social implications of Christianity. These attitudes were widely proclaimed in such church papers of the period as the *Presbyterian Witness*, the Methodist *Christian Guardian*, and the *Canadian Journal of Religious Thought*. A few examples may be cited. The *Christian Guardian* of January 19, 1921, published an article by Salem Bland, a former member of the staff of Wesley College reviewing Stephen Leacock's volume, *The Unsolved Riddle of Social Justice*, and an older volume by W. G. Sumner, *What Social Classes Owe to Each Other*, which had just been republished. Bland, a famous liberal, disliked Sumner's volume which was a thoroughgoing exposition of laissez-faire principles. He much preferred Leacock who advocated policies of social amelioration while declining to accept socialism. Bland concluded:

The immensely significant thing that a comparison between these two books discloses is a profound and general change of heart in the last thirty years. He would be a rash prophet who would venture to fix a limit to the social changes which that change of heart will effect in the next thirty years—or less. The socialistic feeling which throbs in Professor Leacock's book is the divinest thing in the world, and no one can tell what miracles it is destined to effect.[1]

In an article entitled "The Church Militant," published in October, 1921, the *Christian Guardian* insisted that the church should proclaim the message of social amelioration strongly and clearly. The *Guardian* concluded:

If there are abuses in city or state, in business or social life, the Church of God has a right to make these things clear . . . even if the Church knew

[1] Salem G. Bland, "The Christianization of Political Economy," *Christian Guardian*, Jan. 19, 1921.

that by outspoken criticism it were sealing its own doom, it would have no choice; for the church in which dwells the Spirit of God can never be silent when humanity and patriotism and conscience bid it speak. Many of us tremble for the ark of God when the Church draws upon it the fire of the enemy's guns, but the church which is fighting the battles of her Lord is never in danger; only she must be sure the battle she fights is really the Lord's battle.[2]

Representative of many articles in the *Guardian* critical of people with a conservative attitude toward the Bible was one entitled "No Real Literalists" which appeared on October 26, 1921. The *Guardian* asserted that literalists who claimed that the Bible means "just what it says," did not always interpret it literally. The paper argued:

> The truth is no one takes the Bible just as it reads, and it was never meant to be so taken. . . . And our friends, the so-called literalists, in their interpretation of prophecy have not the slightest hesitation in fastening upon certain passages a meaning for which there is absolutely no warrant in the context.

In the *Presbyterian Witness* of January 18, 1923, J. E. McFadyen wrote on "The Moral Difficulties of the Old Testament." He pointed out that in the Old Testament good men like Abraham and David occasionally committed serious offences "and God Himself is represented as making demands or inflicting penalties which seem to our modern sense capricious or cruel." The author thought that some of the views attributed to God in the Old Testament were a result of the fact that man was at a preliminary stage of moral and spiritual development. Man's gradual evolution toward a more mature moral outlook could be traced even in the Old Testament.

> The savage law which demanded the extermination of the enemy was dictated by the unenlightened conscience of ancient Israel. . . . Some of the later books of the Old Testament itself rise immeasurably above those early barbarities, and display not only tolerance but a noble generosity towards foreign peoples.[3]

In the *Presbyterian Witness* of February 12, 1925, E. D. Freeman, a Presbyterian theologian and later the dean of theology at United College, expounded the same argument in regard to Old Testament prophecy which George Workman had set forth in the eighteen-eighties. Like Workman, Freeman attacked the idea of prophecy as prediction. He insisted that the prophecies of the Old Testament must be understood as meaning only what the writer consciously intended

---

[2]"The Church Militant," *Christian Guardian*, Oct. 19, 1921.
[3]J. E. McFadyen, "The Moral Difficulties of the Old Testament," *Presbyterian Witness*, Jan. 18, 1923.

to convey to his readers. Writing in reference to a passage in Isaiah he asserted:

> The prophet did not speak the words in reference to Jesus but about himself. He did not predict the ministry of Jesus and the blessings that would flow from it. He predicted the return of the exiled Jews. It is very easy for us to say that the prophet predicted the work of Jesus just because his words do describe it, and yet to make prophecy in its essence prediction, and prediction of events scores of years or hundreds of years before the event, is to create and to perpetuate a view of scripture that is responsible for some of the most fantastic interpretations of the Bible that are being presented by earnest but deluded people today as the plain word of God.[4]

The preoccupation of liberal theologians with evolution was indicated by an article entitled "Evolution and God" published in the Victoria College periodical, *Acta Victoriana* in 1925–26. *Acta* was a student publication with faculty assistance. As a reflector of student thought, always sensitive to trends in faculty thinking, it had a special significance. The author of the article asserted that evolution or development "and that in a certain ascending direction" appears to be the law of the universe. Even the idea of God had evolved, he asserted. The concept of a personal God was the product of evolution. Man had projected the idea of human personality into his idea of cosmic powers. God had always been endowed with the ideal of the community. In Old Testament times he was thought of as a tribal God; but modern ideas of God were more mature.

The author went on to assert that the idea of God had evolved even since the time of Jesus. Our idea of God would have to be modified as a result of our acceptance of evolutionary theories. The new concept of God would comprehend the latest scientific discoveries. It would include an awareness of the importance of religious tolerance and of the idea that knowledge is relative and partial. The article concluded with a final assertion of emancipation:

> The supernatural will be gone, and it will be possible to construct "a single general view of the universe for civilization." Irrational fear will gradually disappear. We will be able to analyze our mental processes in such a manner that we will be better able to use our faculties, and all will be able to build up rich treasures of spiritual experience. God will mean more to more people than was ever possible before.[5]

In the same volume of *Acta Victoriana* appeared an article by W. T. Brown on "The Religious Problems of the Last Fifty Years."

[4]*Presbyterian Witness*, February 12, 1925. Isaiah 61: 1–4 begins "The Spirit of the Lord God is upon me; because the Lord hath anointed me to preach good tidings unto the meek; he hath sent me to bind up the broken hearted, to proclaim liberty to the captives, and the opening of the prison to them that are bound. . . ."
[5]"Evolution and God," *Acta Victoriana*, L, 1925–26.

The author described the conflict between science and religion, the growth of disbelief in the inerrancy of the Scriptures, and the increased interest in the study of psychology. He also described the growing social consciousness of the church and its attempt to transform the social order. He asserted:

With the realization of a common membership in a social order there came the consciousness that the present economic order did not offer to all the fullest development of their capabilities. This fact burned into the Christian consciousness and the church set herself to the Herculean task of transforming the social order that it would more fully embody the teachings of Christ. This along with the foreign missionary programme of the church meant that the Christian energies were being directed neither to theology nor to the deepening of spiritual life, but primarily to religious activities.[6]

A significant indication of the trend toward liberal theology was the *Canadian Journal of Religious Thought*, an ably written periodical which was published in Toronto between 1924 and 1932. The *Journal* was an inter-denominational periodical, but the United Church was particularly prominent in its Board of Directors and in its Editorial Board. The Board of Directors, eighteen in number, included eleven members of the United Church and four Anglicans. The Educational Committee, twenty-two in number, included twelve members of the United Church, two Anglicans and two Presbyterians. G. B. King, later the dean of theology at United College, was business and editorial manager. The *Journal* was closely connected with the church colleges. Its Board of Directors included members of the staffs of Victoria College, United Theological College, Montreal, Pine Hill, Wesley, Ryerson College, Vancouver, Robertson College, Edmonton, and the Anglican theological college, Saskatoon. Its Editorial Committee included three members of the faculty of Victoria, three from United Theological College, Montreal, one from Regina College, one from Trinity, one from Montreal Diocesan, and two from Knox. The contributors included many of the leading Canadian Protestant theologians. One of its most frequent contributors was the Rev. Richard Roberts, the minister of Sherbourne St. United Church, a great preacher and liberal theologian. Others were H. A. Kent, principal of Queen's Theological College, James Smyth, principal of United Theological College, Montreal, L. H. Marshall, the professor of Homiletics in McMaster University, and James W. Falconer, professor of New Testament at Pine Hill Divinity Hall.

[6]W. T. Brown, "The Religious Problems of the Last Fifty Years," *Acta Victoriana*, L, 1925–26, 10–15.

The tone of the *Journal* was critical in regard to the Bible and it laid considerable emphasis upon the Social Gospel. Typical of the attitude of the *Journal* to the Bible was the article by H. A. Kent on "The Final Authority in Religion."[7] The Bible, he asserted, was a teacher of God's way, "but it is a teacher, nevertheless: the authority lies in God, not in the book." Principal Kent found his authority in the Methodist idea of the Inner Light. Although admitting its testimony to be vague, he insisted that the final auhority was "the inward witness of the Holy Spirit." Similar in viewpoint was Edward E. Braithwaite, a Congregational minister and former president of the University of Western Ontario, who denied that the Bible could be regarded as a coherent whole. He wrote, "One point of view, characterizing every period and represented by all the Biblical writers, cannot possibly be maintained."[8] One should not apply universally a precept which was intended for a particular emergency, he insisted. He gave as examples of precepts which had little meaning except in the original context "Believe on the Lord Jesus and though shalt be saved" (Acts 16: 31), and "Whosoever believeth that Jesus is the Christ is begotten of God" (I John 5: 1).

Typical of the social emphasis of the *Journal* was F. Herbert Stead's article on "Social Christianity." Mr. Stead was impressed by the social genius of Christianity. "Few, if any, social structures can compare with that of the church." He continued:

From the earliest monasteries down to the latest social settlements in our great cities and the missionary colonies in heathen lands, Christianity has created social cells whence could be disseminated a better order of life, civic and religious, in the community. These have been centres of many-sided culture, in the tillage of land, the breeding of cattle, the storing and origination of literature, the higher arts of civilization, the influencing of governments, the initiation of movements of reform, and of much that tends to the amenity of life.[9]

Other practical exponents of Christian liberalism included such men as Arthur L. Phelps, professor of English at United College and later at McGill, Henry Marshall Tory (1864–1947), the founder of Carleton University, and R. C. Wallace, the principal of Queen's University.

Phelps' article "In the Winter of Our Discontent," published in

[7]H. A. Kent, "The Final Authority in Religion," *Canadian Journal of Religious Thought*, March-April, 1927, 101–11.
[8]Braithwaite, "Sound Biblical Interpretation," *Canadian Journal of Religious Thought*, January-February, 1928, 38–43.
[9]F. Herbert Stead, "Social Christianity," *Canadian Journal of Religious Thought*, II, Nov.–Dec., 1925, 402–9.

1950, was a striking example of Christian liberalism. Originally a radio address, the article had the subtitle, "On Re-reading the New Testament." Phelps asserted that for the reasonably intelligent but unprepared reader the New Testament was "a fashionable hodge-podge"; but he felt that it challenged people to a campaign of social action. He pointed out that John Boyd Orr had given the money for his Nobel Peace Prize to help feed the people of the world. Phelps made this item of news his point of departure for the exposition of a programme of social amelioration. He asserted that Boyd Orr's idea that all people could be fed,

> assumes not only the desirability but the possibility of shelter, educational and cultural opportunity for all humans—else why feed them?—irrespective of colour, race or creed. It's a bill of rights for humanity with incalculable local and personal explosiveness.

Phelps advocated fair wages for the worker and invoked "the grand phrase, the brotherhood of man."[10]

E. A. Corbett's life of Henry Marshall Tory[11] is a case study in Christian liberalism. Beginning his life in an Evangelical family in Nova Scotia, Tory eventually progressed to an essentially liberal position. He remained a devout Christian, but he largely discarded the traditional Christian concept of human sinfulness. He came to believe in the essential goodness of man and his panacea for man's problems was the accumulation and dissemination of knowledge. An article in *The Carleton*, published after his death, caught the essence of his thinking. "With fist clenched and robes whirling he challenged us to participate actively in his great adventure of seeking knowledge and of seeking to use knowledge for the common good."[12]

R. C. Wallace's article, "As I Look Back," published shortly before his death, was another significant example of Christian liberalism.[13] Wallace was a firm believer in human progress which he stated in terms reminiscent of the turn of the century. Until his death, Wallace remained an idealist, a firm believer in an ethic derived from Christianity and in the capacity of man for continuous improvement through its practice.

The Christian liberals exercised a tremendous influence upon Protestant thinking in Canada, both inside and outside the churches. Their ideas constituted the new orthodoxy of the generation which

---

[10]A. L. Phelps, "In the Winter of Our Discontent: On Re-Reading the New Testament," *United Church Observer*, Mar. 1, 1950.
[11]E. A. Corbett, *Henry Marshall Tory, Beloved Canadian* (Toronto, 1954).
[12]*Ibid.*, 196.   [13]*Queen's Quarterly*, LXI (4), winter, 1955, 490–7.

went to College in the nineteen-twenties. Their distinguishing characteristics was faith in the goodness and perfectability of man. They did not believe in the sinfulness of man and consequently there was no need of redemption in their scheme of things. They did not believe in the Atonement, the New Birth, or Justification by Faith, all concepts which had meant much to the founders of church colleges in the nineteenth century. Practically they were concerned with such good works as the redistribution of the material comforts of life, the abandonment of racial prejudice, and the extension of political liberty.

The Christian liberals pushed to greater lengths the view expounded in 1877 by Principal Grant that action and not thought, is the principal object of man.[14] For them Christianity was a code of action rather than a system of beliefs. If a person's actions appeared to be consistent with the Christian ethic, they regarded him as a "Christian" whether he was a believer in Christ or not.

The Student Christian Movement (S.C.M.), an international organization which entered Canada in 1920, provided an important mouthpiece among university students for the opinions of Christian liberalism. The S.C.M. was organized at a nationwide conference at Guelph, Ontario, on December 31, 1920. Prior to 1920, student Christian work had centred in the college programmes of the student Y.M.C.A. and Y.W.C.A. and in the Student Volunteer Movement (for missions). Those three streams of student activity came together and formed the Student Christian Movement of Canada. From 1921, the movement functioned in almost every English-speaking university and college.

The S.C.M. emphasized the study of the Christian faith and of the relevance of that faith to personal and social problems. It has been described by the *Encyclopedia Canadiana* as having been theologically liberal in the twenties, socially liberal in the thirties, and later emphasizing a recovered orthodoxy.

That the movement was becoming socially liberal in the twenties in Canada is suggested by contemporary articles. In December, 1920, *Acta Victoriana* published an article entitled "Internationalism and the Student Christian Movement." It suggests that the emphasis on international goodwill, which was characteristic of the international movement, was also characteristic of the Canadian movement from its outset. The article declared:

Already the student movement is proving a channel of international goodwill. The first meeting in amity between Briton and German after the

---

[14]See p. 91 of this volume.

war, took place between English and German student members of the S.C.M. at Doorn in Holland. The representative of the Chinese Republic at the League of Nations Congress was Mr. Wang, a student trained at an English missionary college in China, familiar to many of us as a Chinese student representative at the summer camp at Swanswick, and who has served for several years as Secretary of the Chinese Student Christian Movement. There is no greater service that the student body can render to the cause of true Christian internationalism than the endeavour to understand the national point of view of other nations.[15]

A further indication of the liberalism of the S.C.M. was provided in an editorial published by the *Presbyterian Witness* on January 11, 1923, after a national conference of the S.C.M. in Toronto. The *Witness* predicted that the movement was destined to become "one of the most potent agencies for the reconstruction of our social and national life on Christian ideals." The description of the subjects discussed at the conference provided a further indication of liberalism.

The range of subjects covered by the Conference was very wide, embracing rural, social, industrial and moral conditions, and the problems arising out of our international relationships and our obligations to the non-Christian world. The members of the Student Christian Movement are supposed to approach these questions with unprejudiced minds, unfettered by the creeds or dogmas of any church, but only convinced that Jesus is the supreme revelation of God to man and that it is through the infusion of His spirit into all our national and international relations that a solution is to be found for the perplexing problems arising out of these relationships.[16]

The establishment of the S.C.M. was followed by the organization of the Inter-Varsity Christian Fellowship (I.V.C.F.), a conservative and Evangelical student association. In 1928, Howard Guinness, a young British physician, came to Canada in order to organize Evangelical student groups in Canadian universities. In 1928-29, Guinness visited Toronto, London, Winnipeg, Saskatoon, and Vancouver where he formed Christian groups among students, some of whom had found the S.C.M. too liberal. In August, 1929, representatives of a number of these groups met at Queen's University where they founded the I.V.C.F. Among its leaders in the early period were Arnold Hart Davies, a Wycliffe student, and two medical students from the University of Western Ontario, A. C. Hill and W. J. Klinck. A. C. Hill was national secretary in 1933-34. He was succeeded by Stacey Woods, an Australian, who became the dominant personality in the movement in Canada and later in the United States. The I.V.C.F.

[15]"Internationalism and the Student Christian Movement," *Acta Victoriana*, Dec., 1920.
[16]"The Student Christian Movement," *Presbyterian Witness*, Jan. 11, 1923.

eventually established branches in most of the Protestant universities in Canada and maintained a head office in Toronto.

Within the churches the rise of neo-orthodoxy after 1920, inspired by Karl Barth and Emil Brunner, in some measure checked the inroads made by liberalism. Neo-orthodox theology rejected speculative metaphysics in favour of revelation as the *locus* for the knowledge of God. It was sometimes called *kerygmatic* theology, since it drew attention to the content of theology as a *kerygma* or proclamation of the revelatory and saving acts of God. Another descriptive term "theology of crisis" implied the theology which emerged after the crisis of World War I and also the crisis or judgment of the divine Word upon the world. Neo-orthodox theology did not mean assent to orthodox propositions, nor literal assent to the words of the Bible. The Word was conceived as the living incarnate Word, Jesus Christ, to whom the words of the Bible bear witness without being able to express the fulness of the Divine Word. John Macquarrie suggests that theologians "of the word" were neo-orthodox in the sense that they tried to recapture the spirit of Reformation theology.[17] Neo-orthodoxy was characterized by a more orthodox estimate of human nature than that of the Christian liberals, but as a dynamic force in the churches, it lacked the power of the older type of Protestantism.

A significant paper written by the Rev. Thomas Saunders, a young United Church clergyman, gives a picture of the cross-currents of thought in *avant garde* United Church circles at the time when liberalism was being challenged by neo-orthodoxy. The author, a graduate of United College in the nineteen-thirties, had entered the ministry as a professed liberal. He had then encountered the thinking of Karl Barth. Having been a chaplain in the Canadian army during World War II he returned to Manitoba, dissatisfied with the position of theological liberalism. In reference to former Canadian Protestant army chaplains, he wrote:[18]

> I do not say that most of us had become Barthians. Most of the men, I gathered, were much like myself. We could not embrace Barthianism, but neither could we go back to the old liberalism that we had known. Liberalism had taught us a method, and that method, we felt, still was good. But liberalism didn't tell the whole story. It was man-centred, not only in its approach, but in its findings; and the war had taught us to look for a

[17]John Macquarrie, *Twentieth Century Religious Thought* (London, 1963), 317–20.

[18]I am indebted to the Rev. Thomas Saunders of Winnipeg for permission to quote from his unpublished paper on doctrine.

theology that was God-centred. The war and Karl Barth had taught us the need of that.

In the years since the war, as far as I can see, that attitude in Canadian Protestant theology hasn't changed very much. We admit a debt both to liberalism and to Barth. God is much more real, much more personal, to most of us than he was, and God's judgment and grace are more real. Whereas in liberalism and humanism man tended to be the measure of all things, we have come to the place, I think, where we realize that man, of himself, doesn't amount to very much. The great words of the faith have come back into their own: sin, judgment, grace, salvation, forgiveness ... we hear much more about these things today than we used to. And the United Church, through these things, has become much more a doctrinal Church than it was. Not only our ministers but our people are coming to realize that "just the art of being kind" *isn't* all that the world needs. Doing good, of itself, isn't enough. We are coming to realize anew the old biblical truth that there is none good, save one, God. We are coming to realize that a church without doctrine is in danger of being no church at all. We can be the greatest do-gooders on the face of the earth, and yet be far from His Kingdom. We can preach the social gospel and try to live the social gospel, and yet have no theology worthy of the name. At the same time, I think we are also realizing that we must beware of the danger of pietism. We can't afford to sit back and leave everything to God, which is one of the real dangers of Barthianism.

In the forties and fifties the so-called existentialist theologians, notably Bultmann, Niebuhr, Tillich, and Bonhoeffer, began to exercise a considerable influence upon the *avante garde* in the Canadian churches. According to John Irving, writing in 1951, "the slogans of Kierkegaard's Existentialism have replaced the slogans of Watson's Idealism in the enthusiasm of neo-orthodox theologians."[19]

No one in Canadian church colleges used the ideas of the existentialists as the main basis of theological teaching, but a number of Canadian university theologians were attracted by the existentialists to a greater or lesser extent. Many continued to be influenced by the ideas of Barthian neo-orthodoxy. The files of the *Canadian Journal of Theology*, which commenced publication in 1955, indicate the preoccupation of many Canadian university theologians with the thought of Barth and the existentialists. In this connection the writings of W. O. Fennell, D. R. G. Owen, Kenneth Hamilton, Donald Mathers, Pieter de Jong, E. R. Fairweather, and J. S. Thomson should be noted.[20] Other more conservative Canadian theologians, such as R. C.

[19]John A. Irving, "Philosophical Trends in Canada Between 1850 and 1950," *Philosophy and Phenomenological Research*, XII (2), December, 1951.

[20]See the files of the Canadian Journal of Theology 1955–1964, particularly the following: I, April, 1955, W. O. Fennell, review of Paul Tillich, *Love, Power and Justice* (New York, 1954); II, Oct., 1956, D. R. G. Owen, review of Paul Tillich,

Chalmers and John B. Corston were at variance with the existentialists. They reacted particularly against Bultmann's demythologizing theories, especially his conception of the biblical passages on the Resurrection and the Second Coming.[21]

In the world of new ideas the older Evangelical attitudes still had their adherents. There were still Evangelicals who espoused the same basic ideas which had been expounded by Evangelicals in the nineteenth century. They insisted that man was a sinner saved by grace, that man's salvation was effected by a sovereign God through the Son "in whom dwelleth all the fulness of the Godhead bodily," that man was justified by faith in the crucified and risen Saviour, that man was strengthened and upheld by the Holy Spirit, and that God's plan of salvation was communicated to man by the Scriptures, God's written word.

There were few advocates of the older Evangelical position in the independent or affiliated church colleges. With the possible exception of Waterloo College (Waterloo Lutheran University), most of the church colleges, in so far as they were concerned with religion at all, were liberal, neo-orthodox, or existentialist in tone.

Detailed ideas on Christian doctrine were largely confined to the theologians in the church colleges. To a large extent the liberal arts faculties in these institutions were secular and rationalist. The author made an analysis of religious attitudes in the arts faculties of two small church colleges in the modern period and found them prevailingly liberal and humanist.

Some mention should be made of the influence of the new trends of thought upon the curricula in Canadian theological schools and

---

Biblical Religion and the Search for Ultimate Reality (Chicago, 1955); IV, Jan., 1958, W. O. Fennell, "The Essential Oneness of Christ's Body"; IV, April, 1958, D. R. G. Owen, review of David E. Roberts, *Existentialism and Religious Belief* (New York, 1957); V, Jan., 1959, D. M. Mathers, "Biblical and Systematic Theology"; V, April, 1959, K. Hamilton, "Tillich's 'Method of Correlation'"; VII, Oct., 1961, Pieter de Jong, "Camus and Bonhoeffer on the Fall"; VIII, July, 1962, W. O. Fennell, "Dietrich Bonhoeffer: The Man of Faith in a World Come of Age"; IX, Jan., 1963, E. R. Fairweather, "Christianity and the Supernatural, I"; IX, April, 1963, Fairweather, "Christianity and the Supernatural, II"; IX, July, 1963, Kenneth Hamilton, "Revelation's Supernatural Dimension"; See also *Cap and Gown* (Wycliffe College), D. R. G. Owen, "Myth and Truth." J. S. Thomson, "The Challenge of Existentialism," in R. C. Chalmers, and John A. Irving, *Challenge and Response* (Toronto, 1959), 73–90.

[21]See R. C. Chalmers, "Eschatology and Its Cultural Relevance," in Chalmers and Irving, *Challenge and Response*; John B. Corston, "St. Paul," *United Church Observer*, Mar. 15, 1953; John B. Corston, "'Demythologizing' the New Testament," *United Church Observer*, April 15, 1953.

faculties. While the liberal, neo-orthodox, and existentialist effected important changes in the content of courses, the framework of the curricula remained comparatively unchanged. It still consisted mainly of Old Testament and New Testament studies, church history, systematic theology, philosophy of religion, homiletics, liturgics, and pastoral theology. There were some additions reflecting the increased interest in the social implications of Christianity. Courses were added to provide the candidate for the ministry with some knowledge of mental health and sociology. I shall cite a few examples culled from recent or current calendars.

Queen's Theological College offered a course entitled the "Minister as Counsellor," which described the techniques of Christian counselling, "bringing the gospel to bear on such matters as guilt, fear, worry, domestic troubles, alcoholism, etc." This course in counselling was supported by two courses in pastoral psychiatry. The first year course provided a basic orientation to the field of psychiatry. It consisted of "lectures on the mental mechanisms and the functioning of the normal mind with its deviations as expressed in the psychoses, neuroses, and personality disorders." Emphasis was placed on "descriptions of the different clinical entities and on the understanding of pathological mental processes as the results of logical causes and as illnesses which can be treated." The second year course gave the students an introduction to the practical psychological aspects of their pastoral relationships. It consisted of "a series of twelve lectures dealing with the neurotic psychopathic and psychotic problems arising in pastoral work." In addition, marital maladjustments and related problems were discussed.

Similar courses were offered in other church colleges. King's College, Halifax, offered "Pastoralia 10, Relevant Insights of Depth Psychology." The School of Theology at Acadia offered a number of courses in clinical pastoral education, including "510, Clinical Pastoral Training; 622, Clinical Pastoral Training with the Mentally Ill; 741, Seminar in Delinquency and the Church; 751, Seminar in Alcoholism and the Church." A striking indication of the concern of the church colleges for mental health was provided by the incorporation of The Institute of Pastoral Training by the Nova Scotia legislature in 1958. The Institute was a co-operative effort in which Acadia University, Pine Hill Divinity Hall, the University of King's College and the Faculty of Medicine of Dalhousie University combined to produce clinical training courses for pastors and theological students under expert guidance. Courses were given at the Nova Scotia Sanatorium,

Kentville, Nova Scotia, and the Nova Scotia Hospital, Dartmouth, Nova Scotia.

A similar co-operative scheme in mental health was maintained in Toronto. Courses in clinical pastoral education at the Ontario Hospital, New Toronto, and the Toronto General Hospital were offered to a limited number of qualified students from the four theological colleges in the University of Toronto, Emmanuel, Knox, Trinity, and Wycliffe. These courses provided psychiatric seminars, supervised visitation of patients, and group discussion of the pastoral visits under the direction of the chaplains.

The Faculty of Divinity at Bishop's University stressed the importance of clinical training in hospitals for divinity students. Its programme in pastoral theology, included, along with other features:

> A Clinical Pastoral Training course designed to equip the ordinand for his ministry to the sick, aged and troubled. It occupies the greater part of a day in each of ten weeks, and consists of lectures and discussions led by members of the medical staff of Sherbrooke Hospital and other visiting lecturers; and hospital visitation with the writing of reports, under the supervision of the Medical Consultant for Clinical Pastoral Training and the Professor of Pastoral Theology.

Some theological faculties offered courses designed to illustrate the relationships between the church and society. St. John's College, Winnipeg offered a course on "The Church in Society" which was described as "A study of the institutional structure of the local church related to the community. Some analysis of recent sociological surveys of the churches. The local church as a divine society. . . ." Acadia University offered a course entitled "In-Parish Training in the Rural Church" which undertook to apply the methodology of clinical pastoral training to the situation in the depressed rural community. Particular emphasis was placed on the social structure of the community as it affected the life of the parish. Emmanuel College, Toronto gave a course in sociology, entitled "Church and Society."

A number of theological colleges and faculties offered courses in Christian education, reflecting the philosophy and techniques of secular faculties of education. Among those offering such courses were Emmanuel College, Toronto, Knox, Queen's Theological College, and the Department of Theology at Acadia.

So much for the intellectual climate in the church colleges. Details of the histories of individual colleges in the modern period must now be described.

The accomplishment of church union between the Methodist

Church and a part of the Presbyterian Church and the Congregational Church in 1925 necessitated a division of church-related colleges between the United Church and the continuing Presbyterian Church. The continuing Presbyterians were given Presbyterian College, Montreal and, after a preliminary period of joint occupation, Knox College, Toronto. The other Methodist and Presbyterian colleges all became associated with the United Church. In 1926, the faculties of the Wesleyan and Congregational Colleges and part of the faculty of Presbyterian College were united into a single faculty under the name, The United Theological College, Montreal.

After Church union in 1925, Victoria University became a university of the United Church of Canada, while continuing its previous position in the University of Toronto. The nature of its relationship with the United Church was indicated by the fact that United Church clergy composed a majority of its Board of Regents. In 1964-5 the Board consisted of forty-two members of whom twenty-two were representatives of the General Council of the United Church and five were elected by the alumni of Emmanuel College, the theological part of the University. The Senate of the university, its supreme academic body, with a total membership of twenty-six in number, included three clerical members of the Board of Regents and six representatives of the alumni in Theology.

Victoria University included Victoria College and Emmanuel College, while Albert College, which had been a secondary institution since 1884, was in affiliation with the University.

Victoria College, the Faculty of Arts of Victoria University, continued its relationship with the University of Toronto and gave instruction in the same subjects as were taught in the other arts colleges. In 1964-5 these "college subjects" consisted of Latin, Greek, Greek and Roman history, English, French, German, philosophy, religious knowledge, Near Eastern history. All other subjects, the so-called "university subjects," were taught by the departments of the University of Toronto Faculty of Arts and Science to the combined students of all the colleges.

Emmanuel College was organized in 1928 out of the former Theological Faculty of Victoria. Emmanuel gave professional training to candidates for the ministry of the United Church of Canada as well as academic instruction to other qualified students, a number of whom proceeded to the higher degrees in theology offered by Victoria University.

Trinity College continued to maintain its previous relationship with the University of Toronto, giving instruction in the college subjects: English, French, German, classics, Hebrew, and ethics, while all other subjects were taken in the University. One departure was reported in the calendar of 1964-65. Trinity offered courses in the three most frequently chosen options in the first year honours courses, economics, history, and political science, in order that the students in these courses might have the advantage of the smaller classes associated with instruction in the College.

One feature of the Trinity system, comparatively rare even in church colleges, was that all students, except those in commerce and finance, were required to take college courses in religion as a regular part of their programme. The courses were non-denominational and were attended by students of different faiths and denominations. The character of the courses was indicated by the description in the college calendar:

They are based upon a broad concept of the fundamental significance of religion in human nature and human society, and particularly of Christianity throughout the development of Western Civilization. The intention is to provide the student with the opportunity to deepen his understanding of man and his institutions and to find a basis for integrating the many facets of human activity within an ultimate frame of reference.

In the decade 1920-30 an important change was effected in the history of McMaster University—the transfer to Hamilton. The change was rendered necessary by the fact that limitations of space and resources in Toronto prevented McMaster from keeping pace with the University of Toronto which was making tremendous strides in buildings, equipment, and in the development of highly specialized courses. Various alternative solutions were considered by McMaster which finally decided on the move to Hamilton. Adhering to its early principles, McMaster refused to consider a suggestion made in Hamilton that the city council give a grant of a million dollars to the University. The university authorities made it clear that most of its denominational supporters would feel that McMaster could not accept any money from a city council, financed, as it must necessarily be, by the taxes of the whole community. The Friends of the University in Hamilton respected the principle of the separation of church and state and organized a committee to raise half a million dollars by voluntary subscription. The financial campaign was completed successfully in the boom year of 1928. New buildings were erected and formally opened in 1929. Dr. Howard P. Whidden, who had succeeded Dr. McCrimmon as chancellor in 1923, was the moving spirit in the task of removal. Transfer of the University to Hamilton was completed in 1930.[22]

While McMaster was dealing with the problem of removal to Hamilton, it also faced another problem. It will be recalled that in the 1908–1910 period, McMaster was under fire from the conservative wing of the Baptist Church. In the nineteen-twenties it continued to be under heavy attack by Dr. T. T. Shields, the leader of the conservatives, in his periodical, the *Gospel Witness*.[23] In 1925–26 Dr. Shields made an unsuccessful attempt to secure the expulsion of Professor L. H. Marshall, the newly-appointed professor of practical theology at McMaster, on the grounds of modernism. As a result of this controversy Dr. Shields and his associates organized "The Toronto Baptist Seminary" in 1926–27 and the "Regular Baptist Missionary and Educational Society" in 1927. In 1927 the Baptist Convention expelled the delegates of the Jarvis Street Baptist Church, Dr. Shield's church, and in 1928, the delegates of twelve other Baptist churches. The conservative minority proceeded to form the Convention of Regular Baptists in 1927. Within a year this new convention included seventy-seven churches and eight thousand five hundred members. With the organization of the Toronto Baptist Seminary and the Convention of Regular Baptists, the separation between McMaster and a considerable body of conservative Baptist opinion was completed.

The transfer of McMaster to Hamilton placed the University in an advantageous position in a rich urban environment. It was able to develop as, in effect, the university of Hamilton. In the years after World War II, the University, which had remained in close constitutional connection with the Baptist Church, was secularized. The first step toward secularization was taken in 1948 when a substantial part of the University's work was committed to the non-denominational Board of Hamilton College. This affiliated College assumed responsibility for the science departments and science research. Until 1957 the Governors of the University were elected by the Baptist Convention of Ontario and Quebec. In 1957, McMaster became a non-denominational private institution. At the time of this reorganization, the two former corporations of the University which had been divided in 1948, were united. The historic Baptist connection was

[22]McLay, New, and Gilmour, *McMaster University 1890–1940*.
[23]W. G. Carder, *Controversy in the Baptist Convention of Ontario and Quebec, 1908–1929*, unpublished B.D. thesis, McMaster University.

continued through the separate incorporation and affiliation of a theological college, McMaster Divinity College, under the control of a board of trustees representing the Baptist Convention of Ontario and Quebec and the university's graduates in theology.

With the coming of church union in 1925, control of Queen's Theological College passed to the United Church of Canada whose General Council now appoints the Board of Management and gives approval to the Board's appointments to the faculty. In 1926, the Rev. H. A. Kent of Pine Hill Divinity Hall, Halifax, was appointed principal and professor of Semitic languages and Old Testament criticism. In 1952, Kent was succeeded as principal by the Rev. Samuel Maclean Gilmour. The Rev. Elias Andrews became principal in 1955. The Theological Faculty looked back on a notable career of service. Between 1841 and 1964 it had trained in whole or in part, eight hundred and twenty-four candidates for the Christian ministry.

Action by the Lutherans at Waterloo led to the establishment of a university which was more conservative in its theological background than most of the other church colleges in Canada.

Waterloo College had its origin in the establishment of the Evangelical Lutheran Seminary, a training school for Lutheran clergy, at Waterloo in 1911. Like other theological seminaries in Canada, the Lutheran seminary felt the need of providing some general educational background for candidates for the Lutheran ministry. In 1914, the seminary established facilities for pre-theological education. In 1923-24 the seminary took formal action in establishing a liberal arts institution, the Waterloo College of Arts. The College of Arts offered a four year arts course. In 1925, it was affiliated with the University of Western Ontario.

The primary function of the Seminary was to provide facilities of higher education for the Lutheran Church and for the community of German descent in the Kitchener-Waterloo area. Like other church colleges Waterloo employed no religious tests for the Arts College: it was open to Lutherans and non-Lutherans alike.

Until 1956, the Seminary and the College functioned together as a small, compact, church college. Waterloo was able to preserve its Evangelical character in a period when most Canadian church colleges were moving theologically in a liberal direction. It was also able to preserve its distinctive character, partly because of its relative isolation from the rest of the university world. This was a result of its identification with a rather self-conscious ethnic group. The first language of a number of the faculty members was German. A former member of the faculty has recalled that when the discussion at faculty meetings was exciting, members would sometimes lapse into German. This is not to say that Waterloo was quite uninfluenced by the religious currents of thought which had been sweeping the Anglo-Saxon academic world in Canada since about 1860. There was a good deal of controversy on the faculty between "fundamentalists" identified with the Missouri Synod and "modernists." That members of the faculty were self-conscious about their theological identifications was indicated by an incident as late as 1960. In the tense negotiations of that year, a member of the faculty at the conclusion of a speech asserted, "I'm only Missouri synod and you don't think much of me." While there was this division of opinion at Waterloo, the conservative, Evangelical viewpoint was more strongly represented than was the case in this late period in most other Canadian church universities.

Waterloo College suffered from the same financial disabilities as other church colleges in Ontario since provincial grants were not available for denominational institutions. McMaster had achieved a partial solution of this problem by incorporating a separate, non-denominational institution for the teaching of science, Hamilton College. Waterloo College attempted a similar solution in 1956, when it established Waterloo College Associate Faculties as an administratively independent, non-denominational institution devoted to the teaching of engineering and science. While Waterloo College continued to be affiliated with the University of Western Ontario, the affiliation did not extend to the engineering course.

The establishment of Waterloo College Associate Faculties set going an important train of developments which led to the establishment of not one, but two, universities. In 1959 a plan was developed to establish in Kitchener and Waterloo a university federation modelled on that of the University of Toronto. The Governors of the Waterloo College Associate Faculties decided to seek incorporation as the University of Waterloo. The new institution was to be a central, degree-granting, non-denominational university with which would be federated church-related universities, holding their degree-conferring powers in abeyance, and a number of church-related affiliated colleges. The nucleus around which the University was to be built was to consist of the Waterloo College Associate Faculties (in effect an engineering school), Waterloo College, and St. Jerome's College, a Roman Catholic (Resurrectionist) college in Kitchener which for many years had been an affiliate of the University of Ottawa. There was one significant difference between the Waterloo plan and that developed at Toronto. The University of Toronto had been built around a central, non-denominational arts college, University college. The Waterloo proposal, as originally conceived, would have established Waterloo College, a Lutheran institution, as the arts college of the university. This was the most controversial feature of the plan and the one on which the original scheme foundered.

In order to establish the university complex, degree-conferring powers were granted to the Evangelical Lutheran Seminary in the name of Waterloo Lutheran University. According to the act, Waterloo Lutheran Seminary was to give theological training, and Waterloo University College, studies in arts and science. Also as a part of the master plan, a degree-conferring charter was given to St. Jerome's College, which became the University of St. Jerome's College.

It was expected that both Waterloo University College and St. Jerome's College would become federated with the University of Waterloo in the same way as Trinity College, Victoria, and St. Michael's are federated with the University of Toronto. This federation arrangement was worked out between St. Jerome's and the University of Waterloo in 1960. St. Jerome's dropped its affiliation with the University of Ottawa in June of that year.

The other central feature of the original plan failed to be completed. Waterloo University College failed to come into the University of Waterloo. From the beginning, many Lutherans in the College and in the Lutheran Church were dubious about the proposal to have their college federated with a non-denominational and largely sectarian university. Some argued too that the proposal to make a Lutheran college the arts section of the university would never work satisfactorily. At first the Board of Waterloo Lutheran University decided to federate with the University of Waterloo; but after sharp criticism of the scheme in the Canada Synod of the Lutheran Church, the Board reversed its decision. Waterloo Lutheran University dropped the affiliation of Waterloo College with the University of Western Ontario at the end of 1960 and decided to proceed as a separate and independent university.

The outcome of the negotiations of 1959–60 was thus to produce two universities: the University of Waterloo and Waterloo Lutheran University. The University of Waterloo began its career with problems which would have been staggering in any period but one of rapid expansion in the field of higher education. Initially, the University had little but an engineering school, a board of governors, and one federated college, St. Jerome's. However, it soon established an arts faculty and began an extensive building programme on the campus around its engineering school. By the spring of 1961 the institution had every appearance of prosperity and rapid expansion.

While the Lutherans had declined to enter the University of Waterloo, the plan of developing a pluralistic university was nevertheless retained. In 1959 the Anglicans formed a residential college known as Renison College which became affiliated with the University of Waterloo. In 1960 the United Church achieved incorporation of St. Paul's United College which bore the same relationship to Waterloo as Renison. In 1964 another residential college, Conrad Grebel College, a Mennonite institution, was incorporated as part of the University.[24]

Waterloo Lutheran University was less affected than the University of Waterloo by the rejection of the scheme of university integration. Waterloo Lutheran remained in possession of its original campus and buildings. It entered on a period of expansion as a comparatively small, church-related university. To some extent the University was rendered more homogeneous in the thinking of its faculty in regard to religion by the departure of some of its more liberal faculty members to the University of Waterloo.

The University of Waterloo represented an example of the Canadian practice of federating church-related colleges with pluralistic, non-denominational universities. There were two other examples of this practice in the period since 1959, the Laurentian University of Sudbury and the University of Windsor.

The Laurentian University of Sudbury, a bilingual university, was formed in 1960 by the federation of l'Université de Sudbury, an older established Roman Catholic institution, and Huntington University (United Church). It was proposed that Huntington College should teach a few subjects. All other instruction was to be given in Laurentian's University College. In 1961 Thornloe College, an Anglican institution, was chartered and federated with Laurentian. Thornloe offered courses in religious knowledge and philosophy, leaving instruction in other subjects to the University College.

In 1963 Assumption University, a Roman Catholic institution, was reorganized as the non-denominational University of Windsor. The University of Windsor assumed control of the arts and science part

---

[24] The College was named after a young Swiss University scholar of the sixteenth century who was founder of the Swiss-South German Anabaptists, the name given to the early Mennonites.

of Assumption. Assumption became a theological seminary in federation with the University of Windsor. Canterbury College, an Anglican institution which had previously been affiliated with Assumption University, signed an affiliation agreement with the University of Windsor in December, 1963.

In the post-1959 period, other small church-related institutions affiliated with larger, non-denominational universities. In 1960 Camrose Lutheran Junior College, at Camrose, Alberta, began operation in affiliation with the University of Alberta. In 1964 the Methodist Church's Aldersgate College in Moose Jaw sought affiliation with the University of Saskatchewan. In one case, a church-related college was affiliated with another church-related institution. In 1961, Mennonite Bible College, Winnipeg became a junior college of arts and science, changed its name to Mennonite Brethren College, and was affiliated to Waterloo Lutheran University.

The structure of church-related colleges established by the Anglican and United Churches since 1957 has been different from the older church-related colleges. The new church college is affiliated with a pluralistic university and consists of a residence, a chaplain and chapel, and a small staff offering a very few arts subjects. The students take most of their courses in a university arts college or in some other parts of the university. In some cases, the church-related college has established a student centre as a rallying point for university students of the faith represented by the college. Of this type are the Anglican Colleges, Canterbury (Windsor), Renison (University of Waterloo), Thornloe (Laurentian), and the United Church institutions, Huntington (Laurentian), and St. Paul's (University of Waterloo). Of the same type is the United Church College, Westminster (founded in 1960), at the University of Western Ontario. St. Andrew's College, a United Church institution at the University of Saskatchewan, is primarily a theological college, but maintains a student centre.

Co-operation between the affiliated theological colleges at McGill, which had begun in 1912, was continued without interruption.[25] When the United Church was formed in 1925, Presbyterian College remained with the continuing Presbyterian Church and ceased to be one of the co-operating colleges. In 1926, Wesleyan College, the Congregational College and some Presbyterian personnel were merged to form the United Theological College. Montreal Diocesan and the United

[25]Oswald Howard, *The Montreal Diocesan Theological College: A History from 1873 to 1963* (Montreal, 1963), chapters 12 and 15.

Theological College carried on the system of co-operation. To house the co-operative project, the Divinity Hall on University Street, Montreal, was completed and opened in 1931.

In 1948 a significant development occurred in the setting up of the Faculty of Divinity at McGill.[26] Since its inauguration in 1912-13, the co-operative system had been presided over by a Joint Board of Governors. The new plan was initiated by members of the Joint Board, especially Mr. W. M. Birks. After careful study the Joint Board and McGill University agreed to constitute the Faculty of Divinity of McGill University. The faculty was to be given a five-year trial from September, 1948, and thereafter, if satisfactory, was to become permanent. The Joint Board of Governors transferred to McGill all its endowments and the Divinity Hall. United Theological College and Diocesan College both agreed to make annual contributions to McGill ($10,500 and $6,500 respectively) for the support of the Faculty. McGill agreed not to charge any tuition fees in divinity to students registered in the Faculty who were regular candidates for ordination and who were registered at Diocesan College or United Theological College. Final approval was given to the scheme by the Joint Board of Governors on March 10, 1953.

The initial Faculty of Divinity included six chairs: Old Testament, New Testament, History of the Christian church, theology, philosophy of religion, and comparative religion. The Faculty offered a three-year course leading to the degree of Bachelor of Divinity (B. D.) general, or with honours. Additional courses in practical and pastoral theology and in subjects for which a distinctive form of training was required by a particular communion, were provided by the participating colleges. The colleges also granted their own diplomas on completion of the course for ordination.

The period after 1920 at Bishop's University was distinguished by the long principalship of A. H. McGreer (1922-47). It was a time of expansion and reorganization at Bishop's. McGreer was a man of tremendous vitality. He was also genial, dynamic and somewhat autocratic towards his staff. Although a clergyman, he was important as the great secularizer of the University. Convinced that Bishop's could not prosper under the old clerical régime, he displaced the clergy from the corporation and instead brought in a group of business men, mainly from Montreal.

This policy was implemented by the passage of two acts of the Quebec legislature, in 1927 and 1947 respectively. The first act (17

[26]*Ibid.*, chapter 15.

George V, cap. 44, 1927) changed the method of appointing members of the corporation. The old complicated system of choosing the corporation had meant that it was exclusively Anglican and dominantly clerical. The new act abolished this system of choice and provided that all present members of the corporation should cease to hold office on July 1, 1927. The Bishops of Montreal and Quebec then appointed the new corporation. From that time on, appointments were made by the Bishops after recommendation by a committee of the corporation. This act made possible the appointment of many prominent Canadians, some of them non-Anglicans, whose appointment would not have been possible under the previous legislation.

While the Act of 1927 increased the number of non-Anglican laymen on the corporation, it left the senior Anglican Bishop in Quebec as president of the corporation with very wide powers, including the right to veto the resolutions of the corporation. This important residuum of clerical control was removed by the Act of 1947 (11 George VI, cap. 130) giving the corporation the right to elect its president and vice-president and to nominate its new members. It also repealed the provision that the Bishops must sanction all rules, orders, and regulations passed by the corporation. The act meant that the president of the corporation could now be a layman. The first president so elected was John Molson of Montreal.

The McGreer régime was marked by a great expansion of the teaching of science at Bishop's. The real beginning of science as a major field of study came with the appointment of A. L. Kuehner as lecturer in science in 1925. Kuehner, a fine chemistry teacher and a great organizer, was mainly responsible for the development of the Science Faculty.

Science occupied a very minor place in the life of the University in 1925 but progress was steady from the time of Kuehner's appointment. In 1925–26 there were no third-year students in science, but Kuehner had a full programme, teaching chemistry, physics, and biology to the first and second years. In 1926, he was joined by M. Home, a graduate of the University of British Columbia, as lecturer in physics. Increased laboratory and lecture room space was placed at the disposal of the Department of Science. These developments were accompanied, in fact made necessary, by a considerable increase in the number of science students. By the year 1928, the Principal was reporting to the corporation "great congestion" in the chemistry laboratory. An important step was taken in 1936 when the University offered a new degree, Bachelor of Science. Biology achieved formal recognition in 1937 with the appointment of A. N. Langford, a graduate of Queen's and a Ph. D. of Toronto, as lecturer in biology. In 1946 A. W. McCubbin, a graduate of Queen's and a Ph. D. of McGill in chemistry, was appointed to the Department of Science. In 1948 the Department of Science was divided into three Departments: Chemistry, Physics, and Biology. Kuehner became in effect dean of science although he was not formally appointed until 1962.

Professional training in education, which had lapsed after tentative beginnings around 1900, was now revived and put on an established basis. At first students took courses in education concurrently with their courses in arts. W. O. Rothney, an inspector of schools for the Province of Quebec, was in 1922–23 appointed lecturer in charge of courses leading to the high school diploma. At first he lectured on Saturday mornings only; but in 1928–29 the Department of Education became a full-time department when Rothney was appointed professor of education. His appointment was made possible by a considerable annual grant to the University by the Quebec government. The course in education was now made to fill a whole year subsequent to the granting of a degree.

The success of the Department of Education was largely due to Professor Rothney. Although quiet and unassuming, he was a man of strong character and determined views. He was highly respected by his students and, a great teacher himself, he was able to produce many fine teachers from the ranks of Bishop's graduates. He was succeeded in 1944 by J. D. Jefferis, a graduate of Bishop's and a Ph.D. of Toronto. Jefferis, a man of unique personality, was a forthright and able teacher. Like Rothney he exerted a strong influence on successive classes in education.

Progress in the arts was less striking under McGreer than under the two succeeding Principals of Bishop's; but there were a number of significant appointments. W. O. Raymond was appointed professor of English in 1928. In 1944 E. H. Yarrill, who had joined the staff at Bishop's in 1938, succeeded F. O. Call as professor of modern languages. In the same year, 1944, the Rev. S. Childs succeeded the Rev. H. C. Burt as professor of philosophy, and D. C. Masters succeeded E. E. Boothroyd as professor of history.

Under the principalships of A. R. Jewitt (1948–60) and C. L. O. Glass (1960–) Bishop's, like other Canadian universities conducted an extensive building campaign which radically changed the appearance of the University.

Expansion in registration was accompanied by the establishment of new Departments: Economics (1948); Business Administration (1958); Psychology (1960), and Political Science and Geography (both in 1961).

Mount Allison had begun its career as a liberal arts college. In 1875, the Faculty of Theology had been added and in 1904, the McClelan School of Applied Science had been established. By 1921, the university was giving full courses in arts, divinity, science, music, and the first two years of the engineering course. Honour courses were provided in Latin, Greek, mathematics, chemistry, physics, philosophy, and in English language and literature. Some lectures were also delivered in law.

In 1921, a Methodist commission on church schools and colleges, headed by the Hon. Vincent Massey, commented on some of the difficulties experienced by the staff at Mount Allison. They were typical of those found in many struggling church colleges. The commission reported:

> It is evident that in endeavouring to cover all the subjects in these courses with a comparatively small number of professors (as well as to provide for honour courses) some of the members of the staff will be overburdened, with the usual consequence to professors and students. We found, for instance, that one professor teaches philosophy of religion, systematic theology, economics and history of doctrine. The Faculty expressed the opinion that the staff should be enlarged so as to make possible extension of work in economics and in modern history, as well as a division of the large freshman classes in English and in Mathematics.[27]

After 1921, Mount Allison expanded its work, concentrating mainly upon arts and science. As indicated in the section on Pine Hill Divinity School, Mount Allison gave up most of its instruction in theology in 1925. The development of the University's work in science was indicated by the construction of new buildings: Biology (1925), the New Science Building (1931), Animal Pathology (1955), and Physics and Engineering (1958). In 1937, the University established full control over the Departments of Fine and Applied Arts, Home Economics, and Music which previously had been under the control of the Ladies College, an affiliated institution. In 1951 the Commerce Building was opened and in 1953 the Bachelor of Commerce degree was introduced.

Mount Allison continued to be a church-related institution. As late as 1963, the General Council of the United Church of Canada had the right to appoint twenty-two of the forty-four members of the

[27]*Report of the Massey Foundation Commission on the Secondary Schools and Colleges of the Methodist Church of Canada 1921* (Toronto, 1921), 63–4.

Board of Regents; but the internal work of Mount Allison continued to be conducted on strictly non-sectarian principles.

Acadia, like Bishop's, McMaster, and Mount Allison, avoided affiliation with any other university and developed as an independent institution, gradually proliferating many of the functions of a university. Expansion in the work of the University was indicated by the construction of its later buildings, including Carnegie Hall (1909), providing accommodation for physics; Rhodes Hall (1912), engineering; Patterson Hall (1928), biology and geology; and Elliott Hall (1960), chemistry. In 1923 the Department of Theology was formed, offering courses leading to the degrees of Bachelor of Theology, Bachelor of Arts in Theology, and Bachelor of Divinity. By 1964–5, the University offered courses in seven faculties or schools: the Faculty of Arts and Science, the Schools of Theology, Home Economics, Music, Applied Science, Education, and Secretarial Science.

King's College, Nova Scotia, after resisting amalgamation with Dalhousie University for over a hundred years, finally decided to amalgamate in the nineteen-twenties. The immediate cause was a disastrous fire which destroyed the main building of King's at Windsor. Efforts to raise money to rebuild at Windsor failed. The Carnegie Corporation offered King's substantial assistance on condition that it move to Halifax and become associated with Dalhousie. Negotiations were opened with Dalhousie. According to F. W. Vroom, an important factor in the negotiations was the fact that four of the nine King's negotiators were graduates of Trinity College, Toronto and had in mind the terms under which Trinity had come into the University of Toronto.[28]

The negotiations culminated in agreement. King's moved to Halifax and constructed buildings on the Dalhousie campus. The terms of the association, prescribing the conditions of the amalgamation, came into effect on September 1, 1923. King's maintained its Faculty of Arts and Science, but it was more completely fused with that of the secular body than was the case with the federated church colleges of Toronto and Manitoba. King's students in arts and science attended classes jointly with Dalhousie students. Their classes were given by Dalhousie professors or by professors on the King's foundation, depending on the course taken.[29] The students of both institutions followed the

[28]F. W. Vroom, *King's College: A Chronicle 1789–1939*, 149–50.
[29]This was a more thorough-going fusion than at Toronto where students took the "university courses" jointly, but where the individual colleges taught the "college subjects" separately. At Manitoba, the affiliated colleges taught all the arts courses and, in some cases, some science courses, separately.

same curriculum and took the same examinations. King's continued to control its own Divinity School and to confer degrees in theology. Its degree-granting powers in arts and science were held in abeyance.

King's remained in close association with the Anglican Church of Canada. The church was strongly represented on the Board of Governors, the supreme governing body of the University of King's College. In 1964–65 the Board consisted of the Bishops of Nova Scotia and Fredericton, the President, Vice-President and Treasurer of King's, six members each from the Synods of the Dioceses of Nova Scotia and Fredericton, eight elected members of the Alumni Association and not more than eight co-opted members.

One result of church union was the establishment of Pine Hill Divinity Hall in Halifax as the one United Church theological college in the Maritime Provinces. Pine Hill was formed after the decision of Presbyterian College, Halifax and Mount Allison University to pool their resources for the training of candidates for the United Church ministry. The terms of the union of the theological faculties became effective in October, 1926. Pine Hill occupied the buildings of Presbyterian College. Mount Allison theological students were to take classes in the first year of the theological course at Sackville, presumably after completing the arts course at Mount Allison, and were to finish at Pine Hill. Dr. Clarence MacKinnon, the principal of Presbyterian College, continued in office as the principal of Pine Hill. Two professors from the Theological Faculty of Mount Allison joined the staff of Pine Hill.

Pine Hill continued in the tradition of Presbyterian College by recruiting staff members who eventually had distinguished careers in other Canadian universities. The Rev. James S. Thomson, who became professor of systematic theology in 1930, was later president of the University of Saskatchewan and afterwards dean of divinity at McGill University. The Rev. Elias Andrews, appointed lecturer in the philosophy of religion in 1937, was later principal of Queen's Theological College. The Rev. Alexander Kerr became principal of Pine Hill in 1938. In 1945 he was appointed president of Dalhousie University.

Queen's College, Newfoundland continued to maintain its connections with England.[30] Dr. N. S. Facey, the principal in the 1919–37 period, made several visits to England where he raised considerable sums for the maintenance of the College. He also persuaded a number of young Englishmen to enter the College for their training and to

[30]Meaden, *Queen's College, Newfoundland*, 13–18.

serve in the diocese. Through the efforts of the Rev. E. J. Simpson, the principal from 1938-46, Queen's was affiliated with Memorial University College, later Memorial University of Newfoundland, and all its students were required to take the first year in arts before beginning their theological studies. By 1947, Memorial University College was giving the students of Queen's two years work in English, history, Latin and Greek before the commencement of their theological studies.

One important result of the United Church union in 1925 was to bring together Manitoba and Wesley Colleges. It will be recalled that in 1914 the scheme of union between the two colleges had broken down; but they had continued to maintain some co-operation. From year to year arrangements had been made between the two colleges in regard to the theological courses to be taught in each college. Students of each college had continued to take some theology courses in the other. These measures of co-operation had been partially abandoned in 1920.

Church union in 1925 resulted in a series of discussions in regard to the union of the two colleges; but it took thirteen years for the process of unification to be completed. In the discussions of 1925-26, Wesley, led by its President, J. H. Riddell, favoured fusion of the two colleges into one institution, with one Principal and one course in arts and theology. Manitoba, under its Principal, the Rev. John Mackay, insisted upon a course which would preserve Manitoba College as an entity. Lengthy negotiations resulted in the "United Agreement" of 1926 which Wesley accepted with reluctance.[31]

The Agreement of 1926 was a compromise between the fusionist ideas of Wesley and the separatist ideas of Manitoba. The two colleges were loosely connected as "The United Colleges." In the phraseology of Little Black Sambo, they were united, but not very. Each college was to retain its separate identity. Both were to teach arts and theological subjects. Mackay was head of the work in theology and principal of Manitoba College. Riddell was head of the work in arts, including the preparatory department, and president of Wesley.

The chief cause of difficulty in the discussions preceding the Agreement lay in the question of the control of theology. Manitoba refused to accept any plan calling for joint control of the Department of Theology, but Wesley was unwilling to give up its connection with theology. The problem was partially solved by a division of the

---

[31]The Agreement of 1926 was published in the *Calendar of the United Colleges*, 1929-1930, 6-7.

teaching of courses in religious knowledge. Students taking religious knowledge for arts credit were under the supervision of the Arts Faculty, and professors teaching these subjects were recognized as members of the Arts Faculty under Dr. Riddell. Similarly religious knowledge options for theological credit were under the Theological Faculty and Dr. Mackay. The delicate nature of this arrangement was indicated by the provision in Section 4b of the Agreement:

In the stages leading to recommendations for appointments to the theological staff, or adjustments in the theological staff, which would involve the question of the teaching of religious knowledge options for Arts credit, the Head of the Arts Department shall be consulted in ample time by the Head of the Theological Department as to any proposed recommendations before such are presented to any committee or board, and in the event of an agreement not being reached by the respective Heads, the Head of the Arts Department has a right to present his recommendation to the Committee or Board concerned.

The whole nature of the Agreement of 1926 was calculated to preserve the dichotomy in the organization of the "United Colleges." An Executive Board had general supervision over the two colleges; but the Executive Board was composed of two executive committees representing the two colleges and appointed by their respective Boards.

A number of significant appointments were made to the staff of Wesley in the nineteen-twenties and thirties. They included A. L. Phelps and Watson Kirkconnell (English), and Louis Moffitt (economics) in 1921; A. R. M. Lower and J. W. Pickersgill (history) in 1929; Victor Leathers (French) in 1931; and David Owen (philosophy) in 1932.

Discussions in reference to the possibility of closer union between the two colleges continued after 1926. In 1928 the Executive Board, which had been considering the finances of the two colleges, submitted a report looking toward closer union, particularly in respect to current finances. In 1931 Manitoba College sold its building to the Roman Catholic Archiepiscopal Corporation of Winnipeg and began teaching in the Wesley College building. The financial difficulties of the two colleges continued in the early thirties; but attempts to launch a financial campaign were blocked by criticisms of a system which was allegedly too expensive because it maintained two colleges.

The final movement toward union began in the summer of 1936 when President Riddell of Wesley drew up a proposed plan of union. This was followed by discussions in the counsels of the two college

Boards and consideration by the General Council of the United Church. Dr. Riddell, always a strong adherent of fusion, took the lead in the movement toward union. Since personalities had become involved in the relations between the two colleges, he resigned in order to facilitate the process of union. The lengthy deliberations culminated in the passage of the United College Act in March, 1938.

The Act of 1938 established United College in affiliation with the University of Manitoba. The Act accomplished the complete unification of the two institutions under one Board and one administrative head, having one purse and a complete amalgamation of the assets and liabilities of the two colleges. At the request of the University of Manitoba the governing body of United was named the Board of Regents and the title of the administrative head was the Principal, not the President. The former acts respecting Wesley and Manitoba were repealed except the preamble of the first acts and the first section of the Wesley College Act of 1877. The latter was retained in order that incorporation of United College might date from 1877.

Under the principalship of W. C. Graham, a graduate of Victoria and a former professor of divinity at Chicago, United commenced a period of development and expansion. During the early part of the Graham administration, the prevailing tone of the Arts Faculty was nationalist, a reflection of the influence of A. R. M. Lower and Arthur L. Phelps. Graham himself, a liberal in theology and a great believer in the Ecumenical Movement, presided over the affairs of the College with geniality and tact. The process of expansion was accelerated under Dr. W. C. Lockhart who succeeded Graham as principal in 1955.

After a partial curtailment of its work during World War I, St. John's College, Winnipeg, experienced a recovery in the nineteen-twenties. Teaching of the full arts course was resumed. The Rev. G. A. Wells, who had become warden in 1921, secured considerable funds for training men in theology. Registration increased partly as a result of the re-admission of women to the college in 1929.[32]

After 1930, St. John's passed through a period of severe stress. Like other colleges it felt the impact of the Great Depression. Along with the University of Manitoba and the Anglican Church, St. John's also suffered heavily from the defalcations by John A. Machray, which were exposed in 1932-33. Machray, a member of a respected Winnipeg family, had been chancellor of the Diocese of Rupert's Land, Chairman of the university Board of Governors, and bursar of the

[32]Boon, *The Anglican Church*, 272-3.

University and of St. John's College. His defalcations, practised over a long period, cost the University and the Anglican Church approximately eight hundred thousand dollars each. St. John's lost about one hundred and twenty thousand.[33]

Despite this heavy loss, St. John's emerged from the setback. Partly because of the transference of the University's senior years to the Fort Garry Campus in 1929, St. John's was able to build up a fairly large enrolment in the nineteen-thirties, not only from the children of churchmen but also from among university students in the north end of Winnipeg.[34]

In 1937 Warden W. F. Barfoot went to England to attempt to re-establish the connection between the College and the great missionary societies. He remained there for the first six months of 1938 and achieved some success in getting new support. At the same time efforts were made in Western Canada to resuscitate interest in the College.[35]

The outbreak of war in 1939 caused the collapse of both these efforts. In 1940 the College temporarily abandoned instruction in all subjects in the junior division in arts and continued only such senior work in arts as could be taught by the theological staff.

Recovery after World War II was effected, partly by successive changes in the location of St. John's. In 1945 "the Annex" of 1912 was sold and the College moved into premises at the corner of Broadway and Hargrave. The College benefited from an increased grant from the diocese and from the generosity of private subscribers. Under the Rev. J. Pierce, warden from 1943 to 1950, St. John's further emphasized theological studies, and general arts work began to recover from the effects of the war.

After removal of the College to the Fort Garry site in 1958, St. John's continued its characteristic functions of a theological and liberal arts college, but was more completely integrated with the University. Students were able to take in the College, professional training in theology, the full programme in arts leading to the Bachelor of Arts degree, Bachelor of Science work in certain areas, and courses leading to admission to the Faculties of Law, Medicine, Education, and Social Work. The connection with the Anglican Church of Canada remained close. In 1964–5, the Archbishop of Rupert's Land was the Chancellor of St. John's; the Bishop of Red River was

[33]*Ibid.*, 275–7; Morton, *One University*, 166.
[34]Morton, *One University*, 166.
[35]Boon, *The Anglican Church*, 166.

the visitor. The corporation, which had a variegated membership, included all the Bishops of the Province of Rupert's Land, and representatives of the Dioceses of Athabasca, Saskatchewan, Qu'Appelle, Calgary, Saskatoon, and Edmonton. Out of eighty-two members on the corporation, thirty-one were Anglican clergy.

As a result of the Great Depression, Brandon College, which had become affiliated with McMaster in 1911–12, found it more and more difficult to survive. In 1938, when collapse seemed imminent, the College was saved by the energy of the Principal, Dr. J. R. C. Evans, a graduate of the College and "an academic leader of an ability which far transcended the sphere in which he had elected to work."[36] Evans was strongly supported by A. E. Mackenzie, the chairman of the Board of Directors, and by other citizens of Brandon. In 1938 Mackenzie negotiated an endowment agreement by which he was pledged to contribute five hundred thousand dollars as an endowment for the College during a twenty-year period. The College also secured a grant from the city of Brandon and sought the assistance of the provincial government. The Bracken administration promised aid on condition that the College should affiliate with the University of Manitoba. Under an act of the Manitoba legislature, passed in April, 1939, Brandon College became undenominational. A revision of the University of Manitoba Act effected the affiliation of the College with the University in 1940. In 1945, the financial position of Brandon was further strengthened by the action of A. E. Mackenzie in establishing the Mackenzie Foundation to replace his Endowment Agreement of 1938 with the College. By the Settlement of 1945, a large part of the shares in the A. E. Mackenzie Co. Ltd., a seed company, were transferred to the Foundation.

Supported by civic, provincial, and, from 1951, federal grants, and by the Mackenzie Foundation, Brandon entered a new career as a regional college of the University of Manitoba, maintaining the sound academic reputation it had built up when affiliated with McMaster.

By 1934, the Great Depression had brought Regina College into serious difficulties. The College decided to abandon teaching in the lower grades but to keep up work in the second, third and fourth years of the Bachelor of Arts Course. While the Board was making plans to put this decision into effect, the University of Saskatchewan offered to take over the College and maintain it as a constituent junior college of the University. Many members of the Board expressed regret that the College would lose its connection with the United

[36]Morton, *One University*, 167

Church of Canada; but in view of the financial difficulties the Board accepted the offer.

After World War I the Presbyterian Theological College, Saskatoon, took on a new lease of life. When the Principal, E. H. Oliver, returned from active service the College was given a share of the Presbyterian Peace Thank Offering and opened its new building in 1923. In 1924 the name of the institution was changed to St. Andrew's College. From its inception the College had accepted Congregational and Methodist students to residence and to theological classes. The College also established contact with New Canadian groups, especially Hungarians, Ukrainians, and Bohemians, and trained several candidates for the ministry from among these groups.[37] In 1925, as a result of church union, St. Andrew's went to the United Church of Canada.

Until 1946 the College was almost entirely dependent on an annual grant from the Board of Colleges and Secondary Schools of the United Church; but the launching of an endowment fund campaign in 1946 provided St. Andrew's with an additional source of income. An extension to the college building was completed in 1961. By 1964, St. Andrew's had contributed three hundred and fourteen graduates to the Christian ministry.

As in other parts of the country, the formation of the United Church resulted in a union of church colleges in Edmonton. In 1925–26, Alberta College South, which had become a purely theological college was combined with Robertson College as the United Theological College of Alberta. In 1927, the institution was incorporated by act of the Alberta legislature as St. Stephen's College.

The distinctive achievement of Anglican Theological College of British Columbia after 1920, lay in the field of closer co-operation with other institutions. In 1922, the College became affiliated with the University of British Columbia. Affiliation was along the lines established at the University of Toronto. Students of the College took their arts course at the University but were allowed to offer religious knowledge options for credit in the arts course. The College moved to the Point Grey campus of the University where it opened its new building in 1927.[38]

In 1922, the College also entered a plan of co-operation with other church colleges in the University of British Columbia. A proposal of Dr. S. D. Scott, chairman of the Board of the Methodist institution,

[37]D. S. Dix, "Some Distinctive Features of the Early Life of the College." Address delivered at St. Andrew's College Convocation, Saskatoon, April 21, 1953.
[38]Peake, *The Anglican Church in British Columbia*, 161–4.

Ryerson College, resulted in the inauguration of the plan of co-operation between Ryerson, Anglican Theological College, and the Presbyterian institution, Westminster. The college curricula were divided into common subjects and reserved subjects. The plan was resisted by some supporters of the old St. Mark's Hall, particularly Bishop A. J. Doull, the bishop of Kootenay and Bishop W. C. Pinkham, the bishop of Calgary. They were apparently suspicious of a scheme which, they feared, would give allies to the Anglican Evangelicals. F. A. Peake explains:

> The fear in the minds of both bishops seemed to run along the same lines and was caused, first of all, by the fact that tensions in Anglicanism were still very recent and painful, and great damage might be done within and without if the Church through co-operation with other religious bodies, appeared uncertain of her own distinctive position.[39]

Eventually this opposition was withdrawn. The scheme of co-operation was revised and continued in 1925, 1926, and 1929.

In 1927 Ryerson College, Westminster College, and a Congregational college were combined to form Union College of British Columbia, affiliated to the University of British Columbia.

[39] *Ibid.*, 162.

7. Conclusion

HIGHER EDUCATION IN CANADA owes a tremendous debt to the Christian churches. With the exception of the universities of Alberta, British Columbia, Carleton, Dalhousie, Memorial, Saskatchewan, and some recent establishments, all the Canadian universities originated as religious foundations. Sir George Williams University, although not, strictly speaking, a church college, was established as a strongly Christian institution by the Montreal Y.M.C.A. The university developed from an evening business school inaugurated by the Y.M.C.A. in Montreal and secured a provincial charter in 1948 as a degree-granting institution of Quebec. It should be noted that Carleton University was initiated by the Y.M.C.A. although the Y.M.C.A. quickly pulled out of the project in order to make sure that it was launched as a community enterprise. In retrospect it will be seen that in the nineteenth century, each of the churches made its own special contribution to the development of higher education. The Anglican colleges concentrated on the development of the classical tradition. The Methodist colleges showed more of a capacity for innovation. Surveying and levelling was taught at Victoria in the early period. The Presbyterians were especially strong in the teaching of moral philosophy. The Baptists had a tradition of independence, of not co-operating with governments or with other church groups; so that at the end of our story one of the four non-Roman Catholic colleges which had remained independent as well as church-related was a Baptist institution, Acadia. McMaster had remained as an independent, church-related Baptist institution until its secularization in 1957.

Something should be said about the future of the church-related colleges. This study has been mainly concerned with institutions of which the characteristic feature was a church-related liberal arts faculty, usually in association with a theological seminary. Some attention has been devoted to theological seminaries which were not connected with a liberal arts college (e.g. Wycliffe, Huron, Pine Hill,

Knox and many others), but we have been chiefly concerned with the nineteen institutions which began with church-related liberal arts colleges.[1]

The ultimate status of these institutions may be tabulated as follows:

Remaining Independent
Acadia, Bishop's, Mount Allison, Waterloo Lutheran

Remaining Independent, but Secularized
King's College, Fredericton (became the University of New Brunswick in 1860)
King's College, Toronto (became the University of Toronto, 1849–50)
McGill (secularized in 1852)
McMaster (secularized in 1957)
Queen's (secularized 1877)
Western (secularized 1908)

Affiliated with Larger Universities
Albert College (affiliated with Victoria and became a secondary school, 1884)
Brandon (affiliated with University of Manitoba 1900–1910, with McMaster 1911–1938, with University of Manitoba 1938–)
King's, Nova Scotia ("associated" with Dalhousie 1923)
Manitoba College (affiliated with University of Manitoba 1877, joined to Wesley College, 1938)
St. John's, Winnipeg (affiliated with University of Manitoba, 1877)
Trinity (federated with University of Toronto, 1904)
United (formed out of Manitoba College and Wesley College, 1938; affiliated with University of Manitoba, 1938)
Victoria (federated with University of Toronto, 1887–1892)
Wesley (affiliated with University of Manitoba 1888; joined with Manitoba College to form United 1938)

In addition, Mount Royal College, Calgary is a junior college of the United Church affiliated with the University of Alberta, and Luther College, Regina is a Lutheran junior college affiliated with the University of Saskatchewan.

While the church colleges continued to render fine service in the field of Canadian higher education, their influence over the university

---

[1]Two institutions, Alberta College and Regina College, taught some arts subjects but their programmes were not full enough to justify their inclusion in a list of liberal arts colleges.

world in Canada gradually diminished after about 1870. One reason for this decline in influence was the immense development of the secular institutions of higher learning: state universities such as Toronto and Manitoba, large "private" universities such as McGill and Queen's, and smaller secular universities like Carleton. The secular institutions exceeded the church-related colleges in influence partly through sheer force of numbers. In large measure, however, the diminution in influence was the result of changes in the character of the church-related colleges themselves. Until about the end of the nineteenth century they stood for certain precise religious doctrines which gave them a vigour and a distinctive view-point. Gradually, in the light of changes in the university climate of opinion, these ideas came to be modified. The partial abandonment of older doctrinal ideas meant that the character of church colleges changed, whether they affiliated with larger universities or remained independent. To a great extent they became, in effect, secularized institutions retaining only a nominal relationship with one or other of the religious denominations. The point may be here reiterated that the development of pluralistic universities which included both denominational and secular colleges was a unique Canadian achievement.

The state of quasi-secularization of Protestant church colleges was reached at the end of a process of gradual change in the doctrinal thought which began in the nineteenth century. In the early and middle part of the century when many of the church colleges were established, the Bible was accepted as the inspired Word of God. Similarly, the prevailing concept of God, Christ, and the Christian scheme of things was essentially supernatural. Gradually this concept was changed. Toward the end of the nineteenth century, the influence of the biologists and the higher critics undermined the authority of Scripture and challenged the supernatural character of Christianity. The idealists (John Watson, George Paxton Young, and Clark Murray) rejected the supernatural but claimed that the Christian ethic and the moral code were absolutes.

Some biologists stressed the importance of the moral code as an aspect of life. A. P. Knight, a Queen's biology professor, writing in 1894, proposed to avoid deviations from the moral code by breeding a people who had a reverence for right action. He maintained that people should beware of marrying into families where there was any deviation from accepted social norms.[2] Another example of the emphasis on morality was provided by a psychologist, Maud A. Merrill,

[2]A. P. Knight, "Species," *Queen's Quarterly*, Jan., 1894, I, 222.

in an article entitled "Feeblemindedness and Crime" which was published in the *Dalhousie Review* in 1921. She asserted that an amoral sense appeared to run in some families and that intermarriage with such families should be avoided.[3]

The Christian liberals of the period since 1890, of whom J. S. Woodsworth was typical, showed the same rejection of the supernatural aspects of Christianity and stressed the Social Gospel. Christ became for them a teacher and a great man preaching brotherhood.

"Catholic" elements in the Protestant college world continued to preserve some belief in the mystical character of Christianity by emphasizing the mystical in the idea of the church. But these elements continued to undermine the supernatural concept of Christ by developing the kenosis theory, the idea of a God who emptied himself of knowledge and power to become an ignorant, although very noble man.

Neo-orthodoxy (Barth, Brunner etc.) in the thirties helped to effect in Canada a return to some elements of the older faith. Neo-orthodoxy stressed the concepts of a sovereign God and sinful man who was in need of conversion but retained the ideas of a kenosis Christ and a fallible Bible. The value of the Scriptures was believed to lie in their ability to evoke a subjective response on the part of readers.

The conservatizing influence of the neo-orthodox school of thought was, in effect, countered by the existentialists (Tillich, Bultmann, *et al.*) who rejected the older idea of an objective God in favour of the concept of God as being. The corrosive effects of this school of thought on more orthodox ideas in regard to Christianity was to some extent modified by the fact that most of their discussion was carried on in technical language which meant little to non-theologians. In the sixties, this isolation of the existentialists was to some extent ended by the development of popularizers such as Bishop John Robinson whose volume, *Honest to God*, expounded the views of some modern theologians in language intelligible to the laity.[4]

The gradual transition in thought from conservative Protestantism to liberalism, neo-orthodoxy, and existentialism had one important effect on the church college. It was one of the factors which tended to weaken the hold of the theological faculty and other exponents of Christianity upon the institution as a whole. The transition in doctrinal thinking was accompanied by an increasing gap between the theo-

[3]Maud A. Merrill, "Feeblemindedness and Crime," *Dalhousie Review*, I (4), 1921, 360.
[4]Robinson published his famous volume, *Honest to God* in 1963.

logical faculty and the rest of the church college. The other part of the church college became increasingly secular while the church college as a whole became increasingly fragmented.

One may observe a striking contrast between the nineteenth century church college and its modern descendant. Jasper Nicolls at Bishop's had been representative of the nineteenth century institution in attempting to formulate a unified philosophy of university education. In his thinking the Christian faith not only inspired members of the university community but it also gave unity to the whole college system. This was strikingly indicated in Nicolls' convocation address of 1860:

When man searches and investigates, argues and proves, pronounces at his study table, that this or that field or rock, produces or does not produce a certain precious metal, or indicates by calculations the existence of some hitherto undiscovered heavenly body, and points out the very spot it occupies at the moment; when the human mind thus strides onwards, let it be the University's privilege to demonstrate that the excellency of all this, is not of man, but of God; that while man discovers, he discovers what God has made, what *God gives* him to understand. Universities let us remember are Christian Institutions.[5]

The concept of a university as an institution to which the Christian faith gave unity was shared by Ryerson, Strachan, and the other founders of early church colleges. In contrast to this basic unity in the nineteenth century was the fragmented character of the modern church college in which theologians, historians, biologists, philosophers, and others expounded diverse opinions. There was no coherence or unity to their position. The church college had ceased to represent a corpus of thought and had become an intellectual *mélange*, an epitome of the university world in Canada as a whole. The large university and the small church college were alike devoid of any unifying philosophy. Both were essentially pluralistic. One writer has described the modern university as a "City of God which is all suburbs." The term might well be applied to the modern Canadian church college.

While the Protestant church colleges have to some extent lost their unique character and have become more like the great secular universities, this author has no desire to deny the importance of their continuing services to higher education in Canada. They still fulfil a role of conspicuous importance, particularly in the field of the liberal arts.

[5] J. H. Nicolls, *An Address delivered before the Convocation of Bishop's College, Lennoxville,* June 27, 1860, 12.

Bibliography

The first volume in this series, *A Bibliography of Higher Education in Canada*, compiled by Robin C. Harris and Arthur Tremblay, was of basic importance in the preparation of this volume on Protestant church colleges. Most of the calendars of the church colleges and universities contain brief historical sketches. They are particularly useful in indicating recent developments.

I. MONOGRAPHS

ABBOTT-SMITH, G. *I Call to Mind* (Toronto, 1947).
ADAMS, F. D. *A History of Christ Church Cathedral, Montreal* (Montreal, 1941).
ALEXANDER, W. J. A., ed. *The University of Toronto and Its Colleges 1827–1906*, (Toronto, 1906).
BAILEY, ALFRED G., ed. *The University of New Brunswick Memorial Volume* (Fredericton, 1950).
BAIRD, A. B. *Notes on Introduction to the Old Testament Printed for the Use of the Students in Manitoba College, Winnipeg* (Toronto, 1898).
BOON, T. C. B. *The Anglican Church from the Bay to the Rockies* (Toronto, 1962).
BURWASH, NATHANAEL. *The History of Victoria College* (Toronto, 1927).
COOPER, JOHN IRWIN. *The Blessed Communion, The Origins and History of the Diocese of Montreal 1760–1960* (Montreal, 1960).
CORBETT, E. A. *Henry Marshall Tory, Beloved Canadian* (Toronto, 1954).
CROWFOOT, A. H. *Benjamin Cronyn, First Bishop of Huron* (London, 1957).
DAWSON, SIR WILLIAM. *Fifty Years of Work in Canada* (London and Edinburgh, 1901).
DOUGLAS, GEORGE. *Discourses and Addresses* (Toronto, 1894).
FARTHING, JOHN CRAGG. *Recollections of the Right Rev. John Cragg Farthing, Bishop of Montreal (1909–1939* n.d.).
GLOVER, T. R., and CALVIN, D. D. *A Corner of Empire: The Old Ontario Strand* (Cambridge, 1937).
GRANT, W. L., and HAMILTON, F. *Principal Grant* (Toronto, 1904).
HIGGINS, T. A. *The Life of John Mockett Cramp* (Montreal, 1887).
HIND, HENRY YOULE. *The University of King's College Windsor, Nova Scotia, 1790–1890* (New York, 1890).
HODGINS, J. GEORGE. *Documentary History of Education in Upper Canada*, 2 vols. (Toronto, 1894).

HOWARD, OSWALD. *The Montreal Diocesan Theological College: A History from 1873 to 1963* (Montreal, 1963).
LONGLEY, R. S. *Acadia University, 1838-1938* (Wolfville, N.S., 1939).
MACVICAR, JOHN H. *Life and Work of Donald Harvey MacVicar* (Toronto, 1904).
MACQUARRIE, JOHN. *Twentieth Century Religious Thought* (London, 1963).
MASTERS, D. C. *Bishop's University: The First Hundred Years* (Toronto, 1950).
MCMILLAN, CYRUS. *McGill and Its Story 1821-1921* (London, and Toronto, 1921).
MORTON, W. L. *One University: A History of the University of Manitoba* (Toronto, 1957).
ONTARIO, DEPARTMENT OF EDUCATION. *The Universities of Canada: Their History and Organization.* Appendix to the Report of the Ontario Minister of Education, 1896 (Toronto, 1896).
OXENDEN, ASHTON. *My First Year in Canada* (London, 1871).
―――― *History of My Life* (London, 1891).
PEAKE, FRANK A. *The Anglican Church in British Columbia* (Vancouver, 1959).
Queen's University, A Centenary Volume 1841-1941 (Toronto, 1941).
REED, T. A. *A History of the University of Trinity College, Toronto* (Toronto, 1952).
Report of the Massey Foundation Commission on the Secondary Schools and Colleges of the Methodist Church of Canada 1921 (Toronto, 1921).
RIDDELL, J. H. *Methodism and the Middle West* (Toronto, 1946).
SIMEON, CHARLES. *Memoirs of the Life of the Rev. Charles Simeon, M.A.* (London, 1847).
SISSONS, C. B. *A History of Victoria University* (Toronto, 1952).
TALMAN, JAMES J., and TALMAN, RUTH DAVIS. *Western, 1878-1953* (London, 1953).
TALMAN, JAMES J. *Huron College 1863-1963* (London, 1963).
VROOM, F. W. *King's College: A Chronicle 1789-1939* (Halifax, 1941).
WALKER, FRANKLIN A. *Catholic Education and Politics in Upper Canada* (Toronto, 1955). Contains material on Egerton Ryerson.
WALLACE, W. S. *A History of the University of Toronto* (Toronto, 1927).
WYCLIFFE COLLEGE. *Jubilee Volume* (Toronto, 1927).
YOUNG, GEORGE PAXTON. *The Ethics of Freedom. Notes Selected, translated and arranged by his pupil, James Gibson Hume* (Toronto, 1911).

II. ARTICLES AND PAMPHLETS

Alumnus of Queen's College. *Presbyterian Union and the College Question* (Kingston, 1871).
BAIRD, A. B. "The Story of Manitoba College." Manuscript of radio broadcast, February 12, 1939.
The Centenary of the Granting of the Charter of Knox College, Toronto, 1858-1958 (Toronto, 1958).

CHALMERS, R. C., and IRVING, JOHN A. *Challenge and Response* (Toronto, 1959).
CURLING, J. J., and KNAPP, CHARLES. *Historical Notes Concerning Queen's College, St. John's, Diocese of Newfoundland 1842–1897* (London, 1898).
DIX, D. S. *Some Distinctive Features of the Early Life of the College.* Address delivered at St. Andrew's College Convocation [Saskatoon], April 21, 1953.
FALCONER, J. W., and WATSON, W. G. *A Brief History of Pine Hill Divinity Hall and the Theological Department of Mount Allison University* (Halifax, 1946).
FIRTH, FRANCIS A. "King's College, Fredericton, 1829–1859," in Alfred G. Bailey, ed., *The University of New Brunswick Memorial Volume* (Fredericton, 1950).
GILMOUR, J. L. "The Baptists in Canada," in Adam Shortt and Arthur G. Doughty, eds., *Canada and Its Provinces* (Toronto, 1914), xi, p. 368.
Historical Sketch of the University of Bishop's College (Montreal, 1857).
History of Brandon College, Inc. (Brandon, 1962).
IRVING, JOHN A. "The Development of Philosophy in Central Canada from 1850 to 1900," *Canadian Historical Review*, xxxi, 1950.
——— "Philosophical Trends in Canada between 1850 and 1950," *Philosophy and Phenomenological Research*, xii (2), December, 1951.
"Jubilee Year 1960–61," in *Via Media*. Year book of the Anglican Theological Seminary of British Columbia.
LEWIS, W. S. R. "One Aspect of Human Character," *The Montreal Diocesan Theological College Magazine*, VII(5), March, 1899.
MACGILL, ROBERT. *Letters on the Condition and Prospects of the Queen's College, Kingston, addressed to the Hon. William Morris, Chairman of the Board of Trustees* (Montreal, 1842).
MACKLEM, T. C. S. "Trinity College" in W. J. Alexander, ed. *The University of Toronto and Its Colleges 1827–1906* (Toronto, 1906).
MCLAY, W. S. W., NEW, C. W., and GILMOUR, G. P. *McMaster University, 1890–1940* (Hamilton, 1940).
MCNEILL, W. E. "Queen's or Victoria, which was First," *Queen's Review*, December, 1943.
——— "The Story of Queen's," in *Queen's University, A Centenary Volume 1841–1941* (Toronto, 1941).
MASTERS, D. C. "G. J. Mountain: Frontier Bishop," *Annual Report, Canadian Historical Association*, 1963.
MEADEN, J. A. *Queen's, College Newfoundland* (St. John's, 1947).
MITCHENER, RALPH D. "On Determining the Seniority of Canadian Universities," *Dalhousie Review*, XLI(2).
MURRAY, JEAN E. "The Early History of Emmanuel College," *Saskatchewan History*, IX(3), autumn, 1956.
NICHOLLS, JASPER H. *An Address delivered before the Convocation of Bishop's College Lennoxville, June 27, 1860* (Sherbrooke, 1860).
——— *The End and Object of Education*, lecture delivered before the Quebec Young Men's Protestant Education Union (Montreal, 1857).
RIDDELL, J. H. *Address delivered at the Semi-Centennial Anniversary of the University of Manitoba, October 6, 1927* (Winnipeg, 1927).

SCAMMELL, HAROLD L. "The Rise and Fall of a College," *The Dalhousie Review*, XXXII, spring, 1952. An account of the career of Pictou College.
SMITH, WALDO E. L. *Albert College 1857–1957*, n.d.
STEAD, F. HERBERT. "Social Christianity," *Canadian Journal of Religious Thought*, II, 1925, 402–409.
THOMAS, L. G. "The Church of England and Higher Education in the Prairie West before 1914," *Journal of the Canadian Church Historical Society*, III(1), January, 1956.
WISE, S. F. "The Origins of Anti-Americanism in Canada," *Fourth Seminar on Canadian-American Relations*, Assumption University, Windsor, Ontario, 1962.

III. MANUSCRIPTS AND PRINTED COLLECTIONS

CARDER, W. G. "Controversy in the Baptist Convention of Ontario and Quebec." Unpublished B. D. thesis, McMaster University.
CUMMINGS, A. S. "A History of Wesley College Winnipeg." Unpublished manuscript.
Elgin-Grey Papers, Toronto, 1937. They contain material in reference to the university question in Toronto during Elgin's tenure of office, 1847–54.
General Council, United Church of Canada, *Record of Proceedings*, 1926. "Reports of Former Methodist Colleges," Wesleyan Theological College, Montreal.
HAMILTON, R. "The Founding of McMaster University." Unpublished B.D. thesis, McMaster University.
Journal of the Second General Conference of the Methodist Church of Canada, 1878.
MACLACHLAN, A. J. "Canadian Baptists and Public Questions before 1850." Unpublished B. D. thesis, McMaster University.
National Conference of Canadian Universities and Colleges, "Biographical Notes" (manuscript).
Nicolls Papers, Bishop's University. The papers of Jasper H. Nicolls and his wife Harriet, covering the period 1820–1877.
Queen's University Domesday Book, 1831–1924. A manuscript chronology of the history of Queen's University, Kingston, in the Douglas Memorial Library, Queen's University. It was compiled by various authors: Dr. James Williamson covered the period 1831–1878. The period between 1878 and 1924 was written by successive authors: Miss Lois Saunders, Dr. Malcolm Macgillivray, Mr. Hall of Cecil, Saskatchewan, the Rev. Mr. Baldwin of Kingston.
SAUNDERS, THOMAS. "Doctrine." Unpublished manuscript, 1954.

IV. PERIODICALS AND NEWSPAPERS

Acta Victoriana, Toronto, 1878. The student magazine at Victoria College, Toronto.

Canada Baptist Magazine and Missionary Register, Montreal, 1838–49.
Canadian Baptist, Toronto, 1859–.
Canadian Journal of Religious Thought, Toronto, 1924–1932. A significant guide to trends of thought among Canadian theologians during a period when Christian liberalism appeared to be in the ascendent.
Canadian Journal of Theology, Toronto, 1955–. The *Journal* contains a number of significant articles and reviews which throw light on contemporary trends of thought among Canadian theologians.
Christian Guardian, Toronto, 1829–1925. Methodist magazine.
Christian Messenger, Brantford, 1854–1859.
Dalhousie Review, Halifax, 1921–.
McMaster University Monthly, Toronto, 1891–1930.
Mercury, Quebec, 1805–1903.
Montreal Diocesan Theological College Magazine, 1893–circa 1930.
New Outlook, Toronto, 1925–1939. United Church newspaper. Title changed in 1939 to *United Church Observer*.
Presbyterian Witness, Toronto, 1848–1925.
Queen's College Journal, Kingston, Ontario, 1873–1893. Queen's University newspaper. Title changed in 1893 to *Queen's University Journal*, and to *Queen's Journal* in 1911.
Queen's Quarterly, Kingston, 1893–.
University Affairs, Ottawa, 1959–. A quarterly bulletin published by the Association of Universities and Colleges of Canada.

Index

ABBOTT-SMITH, G., 124, 129, 136, 152
Acadia University, 3, 10–12, 26, 29, 62, 76–81, 88, 93, 130–32, 153, 184–5, 198, 207, 208. *See also* Horton Academy
Adams, Thomas, 130
Aikins, J.A.M., 166
Alberta College, Edmonton, 166–7
Alberta College, North, 167
Alberta College, South, 167, 205
Alberta, University of, 167, 193, 207–8
Albert College, 4, 6, 12, 16, 29, 59–63, 88, 103–5, 168, 208
Aldersgate College, Moose Jaw, 193
Allison, Charles Frederick, 15, 73–4
Allnatt, F.J.B., 136, 150–1
Alma College, 105
Anderson, David, 87
Andrews, Elias, 189, 199
Anglican Theological College, British Columbia, 171, 205–6; *see also* Bishop Latimer College, St. Mark's Hall
Anson, A. J. R., 100
Ashdown, J. H., 166
Assumption University, 192

BADGLEY, E. I., 103, 107
Bain, A. R., 13, 100–101, 107, 109
Baird, Andrew, 93, 98, 136
Baldwin, M. S., 113
Baldwin, Robert, 42, 49, 53, 88, 106
Baldwin, Robert, 2nd son of the Hon. Robert Baldwin, 111–12
Barfoot, W. F., 203
Barth, Karl, 181
Beattie, H. A., 146
Beatty, John, 35, 101
Beaven, James, 48
Bell, Andrew James, 105
Bell, Robert, 44
Bethune, A. N., 111–12
Bethune, John, 68
Best, George, 70

Bidwell, Marshall Spring, 25
Bill, I. E., 76
Birks, W. M., 194
Bishop Feild College, 85
Bishop Latimer College, 169–71
Bishop's University, 4–6, 9, 12, 15, 29, 57–8, 64–8, 88, 93, 122–5, 128–30, 136, 148–52, 185, 194–8, 208
Black, John, 93–4, 97
Blake, S. H., 111–12
Bland, Salem, 91, 173
Blowers, S. S., 18
Blue, Archibald, 117–18
Body, Charles, 140
Bond, W. B., 125, 135
Boon, T.C.B., 161
Boothroyd, E. E., 150–51, 196
Bown, C.E.S., 151
Boyd, John, 117–18
Boyle, David, 139
Braithwaite, Edward E., 177
Brandon Academy, 162, 165
Brandon College, 162–6, 204, 208
Brett, George Sidney, 143–4
British Columbia, University of, 167, 205, 207. *See also* Anglican Theological College, British Columbia, Ryerson College, Westminster College, Vancouver
Brown, W. T., 175
Brunner, Emil, 181
Bryce, George, 93–4, 155
Buchanan, T. C., 166
Bultmann, R., 182–3, 210
Burns, Robert, 44
Burt, H. C., 150, 196
Burwash, Nathanael, 6, 12, 31, 35–7, 100–103, 107–8, 133

CALL, F. O., 150, 196
Campbell, F. W., 149
Campbell, John, 120, 121
Camrose Lutheran Junior College, 193
Canada Christian Advocate, 59–60

Canadian Journal of Religious Thought, 173, 176–7
Canadian Journal of Theology, 182
Canadian Literary Institute, 64, 114
Canterbury College, Windsor, Ontario, 193
Carleton University, 207, 209
Carman, Albert, 16, 60–62, 103–4, 134
Carman, Philip, 16, 61–2
Castle, J. H., 115–16
Caven, William, 46–7, 138
Chapin, Ashael, 27
Chiniquy, Charles, 121
Chipman, Isaac, 78–80
Christian Guardian, 3–4
Church Missionary Society, 9, 15, 87–8, 161
Cochran, William, 14, 82
Cochrane, R. H., 97
Cochrane, Thomas, 87
Cody, H. J., 135, 144, 170
Colborne, John, 26, 39
Coleman, Arthur Philemon, 105, 109, 133
Columbian College, New Westminster, 105, 167
Connor, Ralph, 119
Conrad Grebel College, 192
Cook, John, 69–70
Cosgrave, Francis Herbert, 143
Cramp, John Mockett, 77–81, 132
Crawley, E. A., 26, 76–8, 80, 132
Croft, Henry Holmes, 48
Croke, Alexander, 18
Crooks, James, 40
Cronyn, Benjamin, 56–8, 110
Cross, J. F., 99, 162

DADSON, E. W., 117
Dalhousie University, 21–2, 28, 76–7, 81–2, 130, 198, 207–8; *see also* King's College, Nova Scotia
Dart, J. C., 169–70
Davidson, L. H., 125
Davies, Arnold Hart, 180
Day, Charles Dewey, 68
Dawson, William, 29, 68, 72, 119, 125
DeMill, James, 81
Denison, G. T., 112
DeWolfe, Charles, 76
Diocesan Theological Institute of Cobourg, 55
Doolittle, Lucius, 65
Doudiet, Charles, 121
Douglas, George, 126–8

Douglas, Howard, 21
Doull, A. J., 206
Draper, W. H., 49–50
Dupuis, N. F., 44
Dyde, S. W., 168

ELDER, WILLIAM, 131
Elgin, James Bruce, eighth Earl, 30, 49, 53, 63, 88, 106
Emmanuel College, Prince Albert, 99–100, 168
Emmanuel College, theological college of Victoria University, 186
Esson, Henry, 44
Evangelical Lutheran Seminary, 189; *see also* Waterloo College
Evans, J. R. C., 204

FACEY, N. S., 199
Falconer, James W., 176
Falconer, Robert, 153
Feild, Edward, 84–5
Ferrier, James, 126
Firth, Francis A., 73
Flavelle, J. W., 144
Fox, W. Sherwood, 163
Freeman, E. D., 174
French-Canadian Missionary Society, Montreal, 121
Fyfe Missionary Society, McMaster University, 137
Fyfe, R. A., 63–4, 114

GEORGE, JAMES, 42–3
Gill, E.A.W., 162
Gilmour, Samuel Maclean, 189
Glass, C. L. O., 196
Gordon, D. B., 153
Gordon, D. M., 147–8
Graham, W. C., 202
Grande Ligne Mission, 137
Grant, George Munro, 90–1, 136, 147–8, 179
Grasett, H. J., 111
Gray, John Hamilton, 72
Guinness, Howard, 180
Gummer, C. F., 151
Gzowski, C. S., 112

HAANEL, EUGENE, 13, 101–2, 109
Haley, Francis R., 132, 153
Hall, Robert Newton, 128
Hamilton College, McMaster University, 188, 190
Harris, Elijah P., 35, 101

INDEX

Harrold, Thomas, 15, 93–4
Haycock, Ernest, 153
Head, Edmund, 72
Hellmuth College, London, 57
Hellmuth, Isaac, 57–8, 110, 113
Hellmuth Ladies' College, London, 57
Henderson, W., 124–6
Hildred, Miss E. L., 139
Hill, A. C., 180
Horning, Lewis Emerson, 109, 133
Horton, Academy, 26–7, 62, 76, 78; *see also* Acadia University
Hough, Henry, 108
Howe, Joseph, 78
Howland, W. H., 112
Hudspeth, R. W., 129
Huntington College, 192–3
Hurd, W. Burton, 163
Hurlburt, J. B., 31
Huron College, 9, 29, 57–8, 112–114, 141, 145, 147, 207; *see also* Western Ontario, University of

INGLIS, CHARLES, 17–18, 20
Inglis, John, 19
Institute of Pastoral Training, Nova Scotia, 184
Inter-Varsity Christian Fellowship, 180
Irving, George Clerk, 55
Irving, John, 46, 48, 182

JACK, WILLIAM BRYDONE, 71
Jackson, Clyo, 134
Jackson, George, 134–5
Jacob, Edwin, 70–71
Jacques, J. R., 104
James, N. C., 146
Jarvis, F. W., 112
Jewitt, A. R., 196
Johnson, J. H., 60–1
Jones, David T., 87

KENNEDY, GEORGE T., 131
Kent, H. A., 154, 176, 189
Kerr, Alexander, 199
Kierstead, Elias Miles, 131–2
King, G. B., 176
King, John Mark, 98
King's College, Fredericton, 12, 17, 19–22, 27, 70–73, 88, 208; *see also* New Brunswick, University of
King's College, University of, Nova Scotia, 9, 14, 17–19, 24, 27–8, 64, 82–4, 88, 184, 198–9, 208; *see also* Dalhousie University

King's College, York (Toronto), 5, 9, 14, 17–18, 21, 23–5, 27, 30, 39, 41–2, 47–51, 58, 62–3, 88, 208; *see also* Toronto, University of
Kingston, George Frederick, 144
Kingston, W., 31, 101
Kirkconnell, Watson, 201
Klinck, W. J., 180
Knapp, Charles, 154
Knight, A. P., 209
Knox College, Toronto, 7, 29, 37, 44–7, 88, 94, 106, 120, 122, 176, 185–6, 208
Kuehner, A. L., 195

LAIRD, G. J., 97, 155
Laurentian University of Sudbury, 192
Leach, W. T., 68
Leathers, Victor, 201
Lewis, Travers, 57
Lewis, W. P. R., 136
Liddell, Thomas, 41
Lobley, J. A., 123–4, 129
Lockhart, W. C., 202
Lower, A.R.M., 201–2
Luther College, Regina, 208

MACDONALD, D. BRUCE, 144
Machar, John, 42
Machray, John A., 202
Machray, Bishop Robert, 5, 88, 94, 98, 100, 161
Machray, Canon Robert, 98
Mackay, John, 200–201
Mackenzie, A. E., 204
MacKerras, John Hugh, 44, 109
MacKinnon, Clarence, 199
Mackintosh, W. A., 163
Macklem, T.C.S., 54, 140–43
Maclay College, 63
Maclean, John, 88, 157
Macnab, Alexander, 34
MacNeill, Mrs. H. L., 162, 164
Macoun, John, 103–4
Macquarrie, John, 181
MacVane, Silas, 12
MacVicar, D. H., 119–20
MacVicar, John H., 120
MacVicar, Malcolm, 115
Maitland, Peregrine, 11, 24
Manitoba College, 93–4, 97–8, 136, 154–9, 200–201, 208; *see also* United College, Winnipeg
Manitoba, University of, 13, 93–5, 97, 99, 154–60, 164–5, 167, 202, 204, 208. *See also* Brandon, Manitoba,

St. John's, United, and Wesley Colleges
Marshall, Joseph, second Baron D'Avray, 71
Mason, J. H., 112
Matheson, John William, 162
Matheson, S. P., 99
Matthews, I. G., 145
McCaul, John, 48
McCawley, G., 71, 84
McClelan School of Applied Science, 197
McCrimmon, A. L., 145, 188
McCulloch, Thomas, 21, 81
McDiarmid, A. P., 162, 165
McFadyen, J. E., 174
McGill, James, 22–3
McGill, Robert, 40
McGill University, 17, 22–3, 27, 29, 68–69, 88, 122, 125–7, 149, 153, 193–4, 208–9. *See also* Montreal Diocesan Theological College, Presbyterian College, Montreal, United Theological College, Montreal, Wesleyan Theological College, Montreal
McGreer, A. H., 194–5
McIlvaine, Charles Petit, 58
McIntosh, D. C., 163
McKay, A. C., 145
McKee, S. J., 162, 165
McLaughlin, John Fletcher, 109, 133–4, 138
McLean, John, 99–100, 168
McMaster Divinity College, 189
McMaster University, 15, 106, 114, 116–9, 132, 137, 140, 145, 166, 188–90, 198, 204, 207–8. *See also* Canadian Literary Institute, Toronto Baptist College, Woodstock College
McMaster University Monthly, 145
McMaster, William, 15, 114, 116, 118
McNaught, W. K., 118
McNeill, W. E., 38
Memorial University, St. John's, Newfoundland, 200, 207
Mennonite Brethren College, Winnipeg, 193
Meredith, W. R., 144
Merrill, Maud A., 209
Metcalfe, Charles, 49, 64
Miles, Henry Hopper, 66
Mills, Lennox, 125
Moffitt, Louis, 201
Molson, John, 195
Montreal Diocesan Theological College, 122–6, 135–6, 152–3, 193–4
Morrin College, Quebec City, 29, 69–70, 88
Morrin, Joseph, 69
Morton, W. L., 156, 159
Morton, A. S., 154
Mott, John R., 138
Mountain, G. J., 5, 8, 15, 23, 29, 57–8, 65–6, 68, 124
Mountain, Jacob, 25
Mount Allison University, 10, 15, 29, 73–6, 197–9, 208; *see also* Pine Hill Divinity Hall
Mount Royal College, Calgary, 208
Mowat, John B., 43
Murray, John Clark, 91–2, 209
Murray, J. O., 161–2

NELLES, SAMUEL SOBIESKI, 34–5, 101–2, 107–8
New Brunswick, University of, 17, 72, 208; *see also* King's College, Fredericton
Newnham, I. A., 168
Nicolls, Jasper Hume, 4–5, 8, 15, 65–6, 211
Niebuhr, R., 182

OLIVER, E. H., 168, 205
O'Meara, J. D., 98
Ontario Ladies College, Whitby, 105
Orr, John Boyd, 178
Owen, C. C., 169
Owen, David, 201
Owen, Eric Trevor, 143
Oxenden, Ashton, 122–5

PARROCK, R. O., 150
Parry, Edward St. John, 55
Payzant, G. P., 132
Pentreath, E. W. S., 169
Perrin, W. W., 170
Perry, Ebenezer, 16
Perry, E. Guthrie, 98
Perry, H. G., 153
Phair, E. E. M., 161–2
Phelps, Arthur L., 177–8, 201–2
Pickard, Humphrey, 74–6
Pictou Academy, 17, 21, 81
Pierce, J., 203
Pigeon, George, 20
Pine Hill Divinity Hall, 176, 189, 197, 199, 207. *See also* Mount Allison University, Presbyterian College, Halifax, Theological Hall, Halifax

INDEX

Pinkham, W. C., 100, 206
Plumptre, E. H., 134
Pollok, Allan, 130
Pople, Gustav, 80
Presbyterian College, Halifax, 130, 153, 199
Presbyterian College, Montreal, 119–22, 127, 152, 186, 193
Presbyterian Theological College, Saskatoon, 168, 205; *see also* St. Andrew's College, Saskatoon
Presbyterian Witness, 173–4, 180
Proudfoot, John, 47
Pryor, John, 76–7

QUA, NORMAN C., 151
Queen's College, Newfoundland, 29, 84–8, 154, 199
Queen's Theological College, 148, 184–5, 189, 199
Queen's University, 10, 12, 15, 29, 37–44, 49–52, 62, 88, 90, 94, 106–7, 109–10, 136–7, 147–8, 208–9

RAINSFORD, W. S., 111
Rand, Theodore M. H., 115, 117
Raymond, W. O., 129, 136, 196
Red River Academy, 87
Regina College, 166, 176, 204
Regiopolis College, Kingston, 49–51
Regular Baptist Missionary and Education Society, 188
Renison College, University of Waterloo, 192–3
Reynar, A. H., 13, 100–101, 103
Riddell, J. H., 97, 134–5, 166, 200–202
Rintoul, William, 45
Robb, James, 71
Roberts, Richard, 176
Robertson College, Edmonton, 167–8, 176, 205
Robertson, James, 93–4, 97, 168
Robinson, John, 210
Robinson, John Beverley, 47, 55
Roblin, Rodmond, 166
Roe, Henry, 129–30
Rolph, John, 25
Romanes, George, 42
Rothney, W. O., 196
Ross, Donald, 137, 148
Ross, George, 117, 141
Ross, James, 81
Royal Institution for the Advancement of Learning, 22, 28, 68

Ryerson College, Vancouver, 167, 176, 206
Ryerson, Egerton, 3, 4, 11, 14–15, 25, 32–4, 46, 50, 72, 96, 211

ST. ANDREW'S COLLEGE, SASKATOON, 168, 193, 205
St. Boniface College, 93–5, 154
St. Chad's College, Regina, 168–9
St. Jerome's College, Kitchener, 190–91
St. John's College, Qu'Appelle Station, 100
St. John's College, Winnipeg, 5, 9, 29, 87–8, 93–5, 98, 154–5, 160–62, 185, 202–4, 208
St. John's Collegiate School, 87, 160
St. Mark's Hall, Vancouver, 169, 171, 206
St. Michael's College, Toronto, 106, 115, 160, 191
St. Paul's College, Waterloo, 192–3
St. Stephen's College, Edmonton, 205
Saskatchewan, University of, 99, 166, 168, 193, 206–8
Sawyer, A. W., 13, 80, 130–32, 153
Scarth, A. C., 129
Schurman, Jacob Gould, 131
Scrimger, John, 120–21
Seager, C. A., 169
Sewell, S. C., 66
Sheraton, James P., 111
Shields, T. T., 188
Shortt, C. H., 171
Simcoe, John Graves, 23
Sir George Williams University, 207
Smith, Waldo, 61
Smyth, James, 176
Snodgrass, William, 44, 109
Society for the Promotion of Christian Knowledge (S.P.C.K.), 15, 83, 86–7, 154
Society for the Propagation of the Gospel (S.P.G.), 15, 26, 83, 86–7, 123, 154
Somerville, James, 20, 70
Sparling, Joseph Walter, 96–7, 135, 161, 166
Speer, Robert E., 139
Spencer, A. G., 84
Stanstead Wesleyan College, 105
Steen, Frederick Julius, 135–6, 152
Stone, Charles G., 163
Strachan, John, 10–11, 14, 24–6, 28, 30, 42, 47, 51–4, 56–8, 211
Stuart, A.P.S., 80

Student Christian Movement, 179–80
Student Volunteer Movement, 138, 140, 179
Sweatman, A., 112, 141
Sudbury, l'Université de, 192
Sumner, W. G., 173
Symonds, Herbert, 140

TALMAN, J. J., 147
Tamblyn, W. F., 146
Theological Hall, Halifax, 81–2, 130; see also Presbyterian College, Halifax, Pine Hill Divinity Hall
Thompson, J. S., 182, 199
Thomson, D. E., 116, 118
Thornloe College, Sudbury, 192–3
Tillich, Paul, 182, 210
Toronto Baptist College, 106, 114–16; see also McMaster University
Toronto Baptist Seminary, 188
Toronto Medical School, 37
Toronto, University of, 13, 51, 62, 106–9, 113–15, 117, 141–4, 159, 185–7, 190–91, 208. See also King's College (Toronto), Knox College, Trinity College, Victoria University and Wycliffe College
Tory, Henry Marshall, 177–8
Townley, Adam, 58
Trinity College, University of, 4, 12, 29, 51–8, 88, 106, 110–12, 115, 140–44, 160, 176, 185, 187, 191, 208
Trotter, Thomas, 118, 153
Trumpour, Harry Ralph, 170–71
Truro College, 81–2
Tufts, John Freeman, 13, 131
Twining, John Thomas, 26

UNION COLLEGE OF BRITISH COLUMBIA, 206
United College, Winnipeg, 201–2, 208; see also Manitoba College, Wesley College
United Theological College, Montreal, 176, 186, 193–4
United Theological College of Alberta, 205
University College, Toronto, 46, 48, 107, 112, 115, 117, 156; see also King's College (Toronto), University of Toronto
Upper Canada Academy, 4, 15, 16, 30, 31, 33, 52; see also Victoria University

Upper Canada School of Medicine, Toronto, 55; see also Trinity College

VANCE, WILLIAM HARRY, 170–71
Van Norman, D. C., 31, 34–5
Vial, F. G., 150
Victoria University: introductory, 3–6, 10–15; origins (1830–1867), 29–37, 49–51, 62, 75, 77, 88; period 1867 to 1890, 96, 100–109, 115, 127; period 1890 to 1920, 133–5, 138–42, 160; since 1920, 176, 186, 191, 207–8. See also Upper Canada Academy

WALLACE, A. R., 139
Wallace, F. H., 5, 105, 133
Wallace, R. C., 177–8
Waller, C. C., 146–7
Waterloo College, 183, 189–91
Waterloo College Associate Faculties, 190
Waterloo Lutheran Seminary, 191
Waterloo Lutheran University, 191–3, 208
Waterloo University College, 191
Waterloo, University of, 189–92
Watson, John, 42, 91–2, 209
Webster, Thomas, 60
Weir, George, 43
Wells, G. A., 202
Welton, Daniel, 131–2
Wesleyan Theological College, Montreal, 126–8, 152, 186, 193
Wesley College, Winnipeg, 96, 154–9, 161, 166–7, 176, 200–2, 208. See also Manitoba College, United College, University of Manitoba
Western Ontario, University of, 9, 57, 112–13, 145–7, 189–91, 193, 208; see also Huron College
Westminster College, London, Ontario, 193
Westminster College, Vancouver, 206
West River Seminary, Nova Scotia, 81
Whidden, Howard P., 188
Whimster, David B., 93
Whitaker, George, 55
Whitlock, G. C., 35, 101
Williams, David, 146
Williams, J. W., 125
Williamson, James, 41–3
Willis, Michael, 45
Wilson, Daniel, 111–12
Wilson, John, 35, 101–2, 105
Windsor, University of, 192–3

Woods, Stacey, 180
Woodstock College, 114, 116–18; *see also* Canadian Literary Institute, McMaster University, Toronto Baptist College
Woodsworth, J. S., 210
Woolcombe, G. B., 129

Workman, George Coulson, 105, 133, 174
Wortman, Luther, E., 131
Wycliffe College, 7, 9, 92, 106, 110–12, 135, 141, 170, 185, 207

YOUNG, GEORGE PAXTON, 45–6, 91–2, 209

www.ingramcontent.com/pod-product-compliance
Lightning Source LLC
Chambersburg PA
CBHW020406080526
44584CB00014B/1200